RACE, CRIME, AND DELINQUENCY

A CRIMINOLOGICAL THEORY APPROACH

George E. Higgins

University of Louisville

Prentice Hall

Boston   Columbus   Indianapolis   New York   San Francisco   Upper Saddle River
Amsterdam   Cape Town   Dubai   London   Madrid   Milan   Munich   Paris
Montreal   Toronto   Delhi   Mexico City   Sao Paulo   Sydney   Hong Kong
Seoul   Singapore   Taipei   Tokyo

Vice President and Executive Publisher:
  Vernon Anthony
Senior Acquisitions Editor: Tim Peyton
Editorial Assistant: Lynda Cramer
Media Project Manager: Karen Bretz
Director of Marketing: David Gesell
Marketing Manager: Adam Kloza

Senior Marketing Coordinator: Alicia Wozniak
Project Manager: Susan Hannahs
Art Director: Jayne Conte
Cover Design: Margaret Kenselaar
Full-Service Project Management/Composition:
  Shiny Rajesh/Integra Software Services Pvt Ltd

Credits and acknowledgments borrowed from other sources and reproduced, with permission, in this textbook appear on appropriate page within text.

Many of the designations by manufacturers and seller to distinguish their products are claimed as trademarks. Where those designations appear in this book, and the publisher was aware of a trademark claim, the designations have been printed in initial caps or all caps.

Library of Congress Cataloging-in-Publication Data

Higgins, George E.
  Race, crime, and delinquency : a criminological theory approach/George E. Higgins.—1st ed.
    p. cm.
  Includes bibliographical references and index.
  ISBN-13: 978-0-13-240948-3
  ISBN-10: 0-13-240948-8
  1. Crime and race. 2. Criminology. 3. Ethnopsychology. I. Title.
HV6191.H54 2009
364.2'56—dc22

                                                                    2009018905

Prentice Hall
is an imprint of

www.pearsonhighered.com

ISBN-10:   0-13-240948-8
ISBN-13: 978-0-13-240948-3

Dedicated to my family

CONTENTS

PREFACE

The role of race in crime and delinquency is an important issue in criminal justice and criminology, and our most important tool for understanding crime and delinquency is criminological theory. However, to date, most treatments of race with respect to crime and delinquency are devoid of inputs from criminological theory.

The goal of this book is to provide students, instructors, and scholars an exposure to criminological theories, with a focus on these theories' assumptions about race, crime, and delinquency. To date, the racial disparity in crime and delinquency continues to persist. Attempts to address the disparity require an understanding of why the disparity exists, and criminological theory is a major tool for understanding this.

Through the readings presented in this book, it is my hope that students, instructors, and scholars can understand the application of criminological theory to race, crime, and delinquency and be able to critically analyze cogent reasons why the disparity exists with race in the context of crime and delinquency. By glancing through the table of contents, it can quickly be seen that understanding race, crime, and delinquency is more than grasping one theory. Upon completing the readings, the reader should be able to critically analyze cogent reasons why the disparity exists with race in the context of crime and delinquency.

Hopefully, the chapters in the following pages will also help readers gain the necessary understanding to think and speak about, as well as research, this issue in more sophisticated ways.

George E. Higgins

ABOUT THE AUTHOR

George E. Higgins is an Associate Professor in the Department of Justice Administration at the University of Louisville. He received his PhD in criminology from Indiana University of Pennsylvania in 2001. His most recent publications appear in *Criminal Justice Studies, Deviant Behavior, Criminal Justice and Behavior,* and *American Journal of Criminal Justice.*

INTRODUCTION

CHAPTER 1: RACE, ETHNICITY, CRIME, AND THEORY

This chapter will examine the scope of crime, delinquency, and race. It also formally defines criminological theory and discusses how criminological theory is used in criminology and criminal justice. A chapter-by-chapter outline of the book is presented next. At the end of the chapter, the reader should have a basic understanding of the racial differences in crime and delinquency.

CHAPTER 2: DETERRENCE AND RATIONAL CHOICE THEORIES

This chapter will examine the central components of deterrence and rational choice theories. These theories are based on the view that crime and delinquency are based on free will and the bounded rational choice to perform the acts. These theories also suggest that racial differences in crime and delinquency could be explained in the rational decision process. The article presented in this chapter is "Crime, Deterrence, and Rational Choice" by Irving Piliavin, Rosemary Gartner, Craig Thornton, and Ross L. Matsueda.

CHAPTER 3: SOCIAL DISORGANIZATION

This chapter will examine the central themes of social disorganization theory. This theory suggests that poverty undermines the core values of a community. The destruction of these values suggests a breakdown in the primary socialization unit—the family. It also suggests that there are racial differences in poverty that are associated with racial differences in socialization in the family. The article presented in this chapter is "Social Anatomy of Racial and Ethnic Disparities in Violence" by Robert J. Sampson, Jeffrey D. Morenoff, and Stephen Raudenbush.

CHAPTER 4: DIFFERENTIAL ASSOCIATION AND SOCIAL LEARNING THEORIES

This chapter will examine the central themes of differential association and social learning theories. Differential association theory suggests that individuals who associate with criminal or delinquent individuals are likely to learn crime and delinquency from these individuals.

Recent versions of social learning theory have subsumed differential association theory, and have extended the view that individuals learn not only through an interaction with peers, but also through reinforcement, modeling, and definitions (i.e., attitudes toward crime). These theories say that the racial differences in crime are due to the racial differences in the above-mentioned factors. The articles presented in this chapter are "Race, Ethnicity, and Deviance: A Study of Asian and Non-Asian Adolescents in America" by Sung Joon Jang; and "Race, Family Structure, and Delinquency: A Test of Differential Association and Social Control Theories" by Ross L. Matsueda and Karen Heimer.

CHAPTER 5: SOCIAL STRAIN THEORY

This chapter will examine the central themes of anomie/strain theory. Strain theories suggest that the inability to achieve certain goals, the removal of certain goals, and/or the presentation of a noxious stimulus is likely to produce stress in an individual's life. These types of stressful events will produce an emotional response. The emotional response may result in delinquency. From a racial perspective, minorities are more likely to experience stress and strain. The article presented in this chapter is "Race, Crime, and the American Dream" by Stephen A. Cernkovich, Peggy C. Giordano, and Jennifer L. Rudolph.

CHAPTER 6: CONFLICT THEORY AND RACIAL THREAT THEORY

This chapter will examine conflict theory. This theory maintains that power and influence are not equally distributed among individuals in a society. Thus, individuals with power will hold key positions that determine the direction of justice administration. The article presented in this chapter is "A Dynamic Model of Racial Competition, Racial Inequality, and Interracial Violence" by Patricia L. McCall and Karen F. Parker.

CHAPTER 7: SOCIAL BONDING AND SELF-CONTROL THEORIES

This chapter will examine the themes in social bonding and self-control theories. These theories maintain that most individuals do not commit crime and focus on the why individuals do not commit crime. Social bonding theory posits that the withering or disconnect of four bonds (i.e., attachment, commitment, involvement, and belief) will result in crime. According to this theory, the fact that minorities have more worn or broken bonds explains the racial differences in crime.

Self-control theory suggests that crime occurs because of the lack of self-control and that the racial differences in crime and delinquency can be explained by the view that minorities have less self-control than whites. The article presented in this chapter is "A Test of Gottfredson and Hirschi's General Theory of Crime in African American Adolescents" by Alexander T. Vazsonyi, and Jennifer M. Crosswhite.

CHAPTER 8: LIFE COURSE PERSPECTIVE

This chapter examines the key themes in the life course perspective. This perspective maintains that an individual may commit crime at different points in their lives or maintain rather consistent and long-term criminal careers. It explains the racial differences in crime by suggesting that there are racial differences in the criminal careers. The article presented in this chapter is "Race, Local Life Circumstances, and Criminal Activity" by Alex R. Piquero, John M. MacDonald, and Karen F. Parker.

CHAPTER 9: FUTURE RESEARCH IN RACE, CRIME, AND DELINQUENCY: A CRIMINOLOGICAL THEORY APPROACH

This chapter provides a brief summary of additional theories that should be considered for studying racial and ethnic group differences in crime. The theories include Tittle's revised control balance theory, Krohn's theory of multiplicity, and Braithwaite's crime and reintegrative shaming.

CHAPTER 10: CONCLUSION

This chapter provides a brief summary of each chapter, and the different views on race, crime, and delinquency presented in them. It closes with a call for future research and publications in the area.

CHAPTER 1

Race, Ethnicity, Crime, and Theory

A great number of excellent individual books on race, crime, and criminological theory already exist. This chapter provides a brief overview of these issues, beginning with an overview of race and ethnicity, followed by a discussion on crime and then on the basics of criminological theory.

RACE AND ETHNICITY

Race and ethnicity are complex subjects in society and criminology. The categories that society uses in these domains are often problematic. Race generally refers to the biological division to which an individual belongs based on color of skin, color and texture of hair, bodily proportions, and other physical features. Three typical racial groups are Caucasian, Negroid, and Mongoloid. These categories may seem simplistic, but are viewed by many as being illogical. This is because intermarriage and evolution over time have made it difficult to definitely place an individual into one of these three groups. Thus, social and behavioral scientists view race differently.

They view race as a social construction. This social construction allows individuals to define themselves and to have labels placed on them. Walker, Spohn, and DeLone (2004) argued that the politically and culturally dominant group defines the labels that are placed on the other groups. There are times when the subordinate group defines the labels that are placed on them. One example is that *Negroid* has undergone change several times to become *African American*.

Another example comes from the Office of Management and Budget (OMB). OMB allows an individual to identify himself or herself in terms of more than just one race. It uses the following categories: (1) American Indian or Alaska Native; (2) Asian; (3) Black or African American; (4) Hispanic or Latino; (5) Native Hawaiian or Other Pacific Islander; (6) White. Here, "Black" is defined as anyone who has origins in any of the black racial groups of Africa. A "White" person is anyone having origins in any of the original people from Europe.

Ethnicity is not the same as race and refers to the group to which an individual belongs based on cultural customs that include language, food habits, religion, family patterns, and other characteristics. Ethnicity allows for the stratification of the categories developed by the OMB. For example, among whites, an individual may be American Italian or American Polish. Ethnicity is important because it allows for further classification while allowing the individual to self-identify into the groups.

In criminology, race and ethnicity are important issues. This is because many official statistics (e.g., Uniform Crime Reports and National Crime Victims Survey) and self-reports seem to show that different races and ethnicities commit crime and delinquency at different rates and severity levels.

CRIME

Crime is an act that society has deemed wrong. This act has been agreed upon by legislators (e.g., city, metro, or borough councils, and those in the state and federal levels) as being wrong, and they codified it as such, with potential penalties for individuals or groups that have been caught performing the act.

Criminologists have a major goal when it comes to crime, but it is not to explain crime in a definitional sense. Criminologists are almost always trying to explain the different patterns in crime. Before these patterns can be explained, criminologists need to understand that there are differences in crime with respect to race. To develop this understanding, several sources of crime data can be used—Uniform Crime Reports (UCR), National Incident-Based Reporting System (NIBRS), and National Crime Victimization Survey (NCVS).

The UCR was developed as a result of a call from the International Association of Chiefs of Police (IACP). It was originally designed to provide a compilation of crime data from across the country. The Federal Bureau of Investigation (FBI) undertakes this task. Police agencies from across the country submit their crime data to a clearinghouse (e.g., state police), which are then submitted to the FBI. The UCR captures both crime data that are reported to the police by individuals and crime data that are not reported to the police (i.e., instances where the police uncovered the crime). The crime data in the UCR include counts, rates, and arrest information. Because the UCR data come from almost all jurisdictions in the country, the UCR is the major source of nationwide crime data. The most important outcome of the UCR data is the annual report "Crime in the United States," with which criminologists are able to compare criminal activities across the country.

Although the UCR is an important tool for understanding the extent of crime, it has some important limitations. First, it does not capture all the information as offenses that are neither reported to nor uncovered by the police will not be accounted for. Second, not all jurisdictions report their crime data. Third, some racial categories are not correctly represented in the UCR. For example, Walker, Spohn, and Delone (2004) reported that Hispanics were not properly represented in the UCR.

The NIBRS was developed to generate more information and rectify the limitations of the UCR. This system collects a substantial amount of data about crimes that are reported to the police. For instance, this system captures the time and location of and victim information about the offense. Further, if an arrest is made, NIBRS captures data about the offenders. This serves as an improvement to the UCR system. NIBRS captures information on 22 categories of offenses rather than on the index crimes that are presented in the UCR. To date, NIBRS has not been fully implemented but it does provide some information pertaining to crime and race.

The NCVS is a data collection mechanism that was designed to capture self-reported victimization data. It was created by the Bureau of the Census and the Bureau of Justice Statistics (BJS). This survey allows for the development of estimates, nationwide or for a sub-population, of individuals who have been victimized either personally or as a member of their household.

To capture data for the NCVS, individuals who are 12 and older are interviewed over the telephone. These individuals are contacted every 6 months for the next 3 years. They respond to questions concerning the demographic makeup of the household and the instances where they or a member of their household had been victimized.

With regard to perpetrators of crime, some differences do exist among the races. Historically, blacks were overrepresented in arrests for murder, robbery, and aggravated assault. Some recent trends showed that whites were more likely to be arrested for assault and aggravated assault. From a victimization perspective, in 2005, per 1,000 individuals more than any other group blacks were likely to be victims of violent crime. However, black and white people were equally likely to be victims of simple assault, rape, and murder. When not compared using the 1,000-person standard, Hispanics were more likely to experience violence than any other group.

An overall difference exists for blacks and whites but the trend remains the same for Hispanics when considering property crimes. For property crimes, blacks had a lower rate of victimization than whites. However, Hispanics had a higher rate than any other group.

Criminologists are charged with the task of understanding criminality and crime rates. Criminality refers to the extent and frequency of criminal activity among a group or for an individual. For example, the indicators of crime show that per capita blacks perform more violent forms of crime. This is a group distinction that refers to the extent of violent criminal behavior among blacks. Crime rate, however, refers to the rate of criminal behavior in a given location. For instance, crime occurs the most in areas that have low socio-economic levels. Although not denoting a specific location, the example in general refers to a location that can be found in almost any city, county, state, or country. Therefore, crime cannot be specifically defined but is often thought of in terms of criminality and crime rate.

Even if crime is viewed in terms of criminality and crime rate, some suggest that the differences among the races in these aspects are consistent with the discrimination faced by them. Discrimination is treating group differently due to some behavior or qualification (Walker, Spohn, & Delone, 2004). Discrimination in this view can take many forms. Because it has different forms, criminologists may not be able to demonstrate that discrimination has taken place in either criminality or crime rate. However, they may be able to demonstrate some disparities in these aspects, which is the main concept of this book. Further, criminologists need specific tools to understand these disparities.

THEORY

One tool that criminologists use is theory. Theory is an important piece of science that provides the means for understanding and explaining societal and individual behavior. In other words, theories explain why or how certain things are connected to each other in order to understand criminal and delinquent acts. For instance, some theories may suggest that poor parenting may have a connection with criminal and delinquent behavior. Other theories may suggest that neighborhood conditions, strain, self-restraint, and racial threat are important in understanding such behavior. In the chapters that follow, several issues that have a link with criminal and delinquent behavior are examined.

In general, theories are comprised of interrelated or correlated concepts. Concepts are typically abstractions from reality. That is, a concept is an abstraction that represents a phenomenon in the world. The key to theory is to explain the interrelationship or correlation among the concepts. For example, is low self-control correlated to crime and delinquency? This interrelationship or correlation among concepts is called a proposition. Propositions are equivalent to hypotheses. That is, propositions provide a testable statement that often has a direction (i.e., positive or negative). For example, as parenting increases, so does the likelihood that an individual will not commit crime or become delinquent. Here a positive direction is predicted among the concepts. Another example is as follows: As strain increases, conformity decreases. This is an example of a negatively directed hypothesis. However, the possibility exists that strain may not have a connection with conformity.

To determine if a theory is scientific, it must be judged based on scientific criteria. The most important of these criteria is that the theory must be verified or refuted with carefully gathered evidence. In addition, theories must meet the following criteria: logical consistency (i.e., the theory must make logical sense), scope (i.e., the theory must use a small number of concepts and propositions to explain a large number of behaviors), parsimony (i.e., the theory must use the smallest number of concepts and propositions possible to explain a behavior), testability (i.e., the theory must be testable and provable), empirically valid (i.e., the theory must be supported by empirical literature), and policy implications (i.e., the theory must provide useful implications for practice).

Further, theories can be divided into three major categories: macrotheories, microtheories, and bridging theories. Macrotheories provide explanations at a societal level. Microtheories provide explanations at an individual level. Bridging theories combine both the macro- and microtheories to explain behavior, and in the case of this text, the behavior is crime or delinquency.

Thus far, several criteria have been presented to examine the scientific relevance of theories—specifically criminological theories. Most of the theories discussed in the following chapters meet many of these criteria, but some do not; they nonetheless provide useful insights into race and crime.

Reference

Walker, S., Spohn, C., & DeLone, M. (2004). *The color of justice: Race, ethnicity and crime in America*. Belmont, CA: Wadsworth/Thomson Learning.

CHAPTER 2

Deterrence and Rational Choice Theories

Deterrence and rational choice theories can be used to examine the differences in crime based on race. This chapter presents an overview of these two theories and their central components.

Deterrence and rational choice theories originate from the classical and neo-classical schools of thought in criminology. Both theories are based on an economic approach to criminal behavior. Specifically, the central premise of these two theories is that individuals are free to choose criminal behavior as one of many other behaviors.

The theories assume that individuals are free and rational decision makers who choose behaviors that satisfy their self-interests. In deciding whether or not to engage in a behavior, the individual weighs the potential benefits of the behavior against the potential costs and engages in the behavior when he or she believes that it will maximize one's benefit at a potentially minimal cost.

According to deterrence and rational choice theorists, individuals need information to make a decision, but in reality individuals make decisions in the absence of adequate information. However, these theorists differ in their views on the use of the information.

Classical deterrence theory has two forms: specific (i.e., deterrence applied to the individual) and general (i.e., deterrence applied to the society as a whole). Specific deterrence theory places the emphasis on the individual's perception of the costs of a behavior and the application of these costs. According to general deterrence theory, punishment is used to provide an example for society. That is, an individual would be punished to show society that the individual would not benefit from a particular criminal behavior. Therefore, society is encouraged to be informed about the punishment of the individual so that the others would be able to learn from the punishment and not perform the crime.

Three components are central to deterrence theory: certainty, severity, and celerity of the costs involved in a crime. Certainty is the degree to which punishment for a crime is made certain. Severity is the amount of pain that would be inflicted upon the individual. Celerity is the speed with which the punishment would be delivered to the individual. Certainty and celerity are more effective components than severity. This is because when a rational individual understood that they would be swiftly punished for their criminal behavior, they were less likely to commit crime. Severity is not as effective because if the punishment was too severe then it would loose its effectiveness.

Neo-classical deterrence theory has begun to identify some specific forms of costs that are significant to deterring individuals. Specifically, some have shown that shame, guilt, embarrassment, parental disappointment, friend disappointment, and official sanction are important in deterring individuals.

Rational choice theory focuses on the motivation to engage in a behavior—including crime. It explains criminal behavior in terms of meeting a need. In this context, rationality is utilized to determine if an opportunity exists to meet one's needs, the potential costs, and the anticipated benefits. The information needed for rationalizing does not have to be complete or accurate, and in a way the individual decides to commit crime using "bounded rationality."

According to the rational choice theory, there are two components to making decisions. The first component is the decision to become involved in a criminal act. The decision to become involved goes beyond initiation and includes the continuance and the desistance of criminal behavior. These types of decisions are influential in performing a cost-benefit analysis of the information. Hypothetically, an individual who is interested in initiating or continuing criminal activity is likely to match the benefits of the crime with his or her needs. However, the individual who is interested in desisting from criminal behavior is likely to pay more attention to the costs of engaging in the crime rather than the benefits.

The second component is the criminal event decision. This component determines the level of difficulty in performing the crime. Individuals who see the crime as being easy and simple to perform make the decision to become involved or continue the criminal behavior if beneficial. If the level of difficulty in performing the crime becomes too high, the individual decides that it is too costly to engage in the criminal behavior.

The criminal event decision emphasizes that each criminal behavior is different. The difference occurs because each crime requires specific decisions to be made. More importantly, the crime-specific event decisions make the rational choices themselves crime-specific.

Rational choice theory places an emphasis on the varying needs and capabilities of individuals. For example, an individual who is computer savvy may not have the same expertise as the individual who is a car mechanic. Therefore, illegally downloading music may be easier for the computer-savvy individual than the mechanic.

Empirically, deterrence theory has enjoyed reasonable success. Two meta-analyses have shown support for some aspects of the theory (Paternoster, 1986; Yu & Liska, 1993). Others have shown support for the more contemporary view of the theory (Nagin & Paternoster, 1991; Paternoster & Simpson, 1996; Pogarsky, 2002). Further, Tibbetts and Gibson (2002) showed that rational choice theory had support in the empirical literature.

These versions of classical deterrence theory would suggest that the differences in the crime rates among the different races are because people of some races do not see or fully comprehend the potential costs of their actions. Specifically, blacks are more likely not to see or care about certainty, severity, or celerity of their actions than whites. Therefore, blacks are less likely to be deterred from criminal behavior than whites. The rational choice theory, however, suggests that the racial differences in criminal behavior are due to differences in the perceptions of motivation. That is, blacks are more likely to associate benefits and needs and increasingly perceive that the criminal behavior is easy or simple to perform than whites.

In the selection presented in this chapter, Piliavin, Gartner, Thornton, and Matsueda examine these propositions.

Crime, Deterrence, and Rational Choice

Irving Piliavin, *University of Wisconsin-Madison*
Rosemary Gartner, *University of Iowa*
Craig Thornton, *Mathematica Policy Research, Inc.*
Ross L. Matsueda, *University of Wisconsin-Madison*

This study examines the deterrent effect of formal sanctions on criminal behavior. While most research on deterrence assumes a rational-choice model of criminal decision-making, few studies consider all of the major elements of the model. In particular, three critical limitations characterize the empirical literature on deterrence: the failure to establish a causal ordering of sanctions and crime consistent with their temporal ordering; the focus on conventional populations and nonserious criminal acts, which are of less interest to the question of how society controls its members; and the inattention to the return or reward component of the decision-making process. To address these issues, we specify, estimate, and test a rational-choice model of crime on data that were collected on individuals, gathered within a longitudinal design, and derived from three distinct populations of persons at high risk of formal sanction. The results support the reward component of the rational-choice model, but fail to support the cost or deterrent component, as measured by perceived risks of formal sanctions.

Traditionally, sociologists have identified two mechanisms by which society elicits conformity in its members: internal control, whereby individuals are inculcated with conventional norms, values, and attitudes; and external control, whereby individuals are coerced, threatened, and sanctioned into conformity. Historically, most research has focused on internal control, leading investigators to examine normative structures, learning processes, subcultural influences, and the like. Recently, however, many social scientists have turned to issues of external control, exploring the process by which illegal behavior is deterred as a significant source of social control. Initially motivated by Wrong's (1961) classic critique of normative sources of control, this work was further stimulated by several theoretical discussions of deterrence (Andenaes, 1974; Zimring and Hawkins, 1973; Gibbs, 1968; 1975), Becker's (1968) seminal paper outlining an economic model of crime and punishment, and finally a subsequent spate of empirical studies.

Unfortunately, despite numerous calls for a general theory of deterrence, nearly all of the empirical research on the issue takes as its framework "a vague congery of ideas with no unifying factor other than their being legacies of two major figures in moral philosophy, Cesare Beccaria and Jeremy Bentham" (Gibbs, 1975:5). This is partly due to the practical concerns of criminologists: since much of the American criminal justice system is based directly or indirectly on ideas of Beccaria and Bentham, the testing of those ideas has immediate implications for public policy. As a consequence, deterrence research has been predominantly concerned with the isolated effects of the severity and certainty of sanctions on illegal behavior. A more fruitful approach to the issue of deterrence would examine the relationship between formal sanctions and crime from within an explicit theoretical framework.

This study examines the deterrence hypothesis from within the rational-choice model, a theoretical perspective proposed by economists that not only provides a general explanation of criminal behavior, but also stipulates a specific mechanism by which formal sanctions deter. Consider the following formal statement of an actor's expected utility under conditions of risk:

$$E(U) = (1 - p) U(y) + p U(y - F)$$

where E(U) = the actor's expected utility from a contemplated activity,

p = the likelihood of being punished for the activity,

y = the anticipated returns (material or psychic) from the activity,

F = the anticipated penalty resulting if the actor is punished for the activity.

According to the statement, if for a given person, the expected utility of an illegal (legal) act is greater than the expected utility of other alternatives, the person will engage in the illegal (legal) act. This behavioral model, which is detailed by Friedman and Savage (1948), Becker (1968), and Block and Heineke (1975) identifies three requisites of a model explaining the decision to engage in crime: it must include the expected rewards from alternative courses of legal or illegal action; it must consider the expected costs of these actions; and it must consider those expectations as subjectively perceived by the actor, not as objectively inhering in the actions.

Empirical research on the importance of deterrence in eliciting conformity has employed one of two strategies. The first, favored by economists, entails macro-level analyses of the relationship between aggregate crime rates and aggregate rates of criminal justice actions such as arrest, conviction, and imprisonment. The second, favored by sociologists and social psychologists, entails micro-level analyses of the relationship between the criminal acts of individuals and their perceptions of the risks of those acts. Such studies, whether micro-level or macro-level, have been hampered by at least four conceptual and methodological shortcomings. First, macro-level analyses have ignored the central role of perceptions in rational-choice models. Second, micro-level analyses have analyzed only restricted populations of conventional persons and nonserious crimes, ignoring more threatening acts that are central to the question of how society controls the behavior of its members. Third, most research has relied on cross-sectional research designs, making causal

inferences questionable. Fourth, the statistical models of most studies have omitted important variables—not only control variables, but also variables representing the reward or return component of rational-choice models.

The research reported here seeks to overcome these problems. Based on a two-wave panel study of three independent samples, it examines how persons' perceptions of the costs and rewards of legal and illegal behavior are related to subsequent criminal activity. It considers the impact of perceived returns from crime, as well as perceived opportunities to commit crime—two crucial elements of the rational-choice model of crime ignored in previous research. The longitudinal design allows us to specify a causal ordering among our variables that coincides with the temporal ordering of their measurement. Our analytical strategy, in addition, allows us to estimate and statistically control for measurement error in our indicators of perceived threat of formal sanctions. Furthermore, the three populations that we sample consist of persons having a high probability of engaging in serious, patterned forms of crime, precisely those persons that previous research concludes will be deterred by threats of sanctions. Finally, the breadth of the dataset allows us to include a variety of exogenous background characteristics in our causal models, thereby reducing the potential bias from specification errors.

The remainder of this article is divided into five sections. In the first, we critically review previous individual-level research on the deterrence hypothesis, highlighting various methodological problems.[1] In the second section we describe our research design, sample, and pertinent variables, and present our structural equation models.

---

[1] A critical review of macro-level studies of deterrence is beyond the scope of this article; moreover, our research is oriented to individual-level processes of rational choice and deterrence. We should mention in passing, however, that such macro-level research has recently received stinging criticisms, to the extent that some conclude the approach is virtually bankrupt for assessing deterrence hypotheses (Brier and Fienberg, 1980; Manski, 1978).

Section three presents our analyses of measurement models of perceived risk, while section four specifies, estimates, and tests our model of rational choice and crime. The final section concludes with a discussion of the theoretical implications of our results.

Previous Individual-Level Studies Of Deterrence

During the past 15 years, a flood of empirical studies has examined the effects of persons' perceptions of the certainty and severity of formal sanctions on their criminal behavior. From this vast and diverse literature, we can draw three conclusions pertinent to the present research. First, prior research has failed to unearth a consistent deterrent influence of perceived severity of formal sanctions (Waldo and Chiricos, 1972; Silberman, 1976; Bailey and Lott, 1976; Meier and Johnson, 1977). Second, while most studies find a consistent but modest effect of perceived certainty of formal sanctions (Jensen, 1969; Waldo and Chiricos, 1972; Grasmick and Milligan, 1976; Kraut, 1976; Silberman, 1976; Erickson et al., 1977; Jensen et al., 1978), others find that this effect is conditional, holding only for persons who are uncommitted to conventional morality (Silberman, 1976) or highly motivated to deviate (Tittle, 1977, 1980). Third, these results may be questionable because of three methodological shortcomings of the studies from which they were generated. We take up these shortcomings in turn.

Inferring Causality From Cross-Sectional Designs

Students of deterrence have long recognized the problem of inferring causality from cross-sectional research designs (Burkett and Jensen, 1975; Logan, 1975; Jensen et al., 1978). This is particularly problematic for individual-level studies of deterrence for two reasons. First, the causal ordering specified among independent and dependent variables contradicts their temporal ordering in the sense that unlawful acts committed prior to an interview are specified

as a function of attitudes measured during the interview. This design cannot rule out the possibility that any observed negative relationship is due to the impact of crime on perceived risks. Second, because data on independent and dependent variables are obtained from respondents in the course of one interview, contamination effects also cannot be ruled out. For example, individuals' *reports* on one set of variables may influence *reports* on another.

Some researchers have justified their cross-sectional designs by assuming that perceptions of risk remain stable over time, which would make the timing of their measurement inconsequential (Silberman, 1976; Anderson et al., 1977). Others have tried to resolve the problem of changing the time frame to which their measures refer. For example, several have used as their dependent variable, respondents' estimates of their future illegal behavior (Tittle, 1977, 1980; Grasmick and Green, 1980; and Jensen and Stitt, 1982). Teevan (1976), on the other hand, used a different independent variable, asking respondents to recall their perceptions of risk prior to engaging in the deviant acts they report. The approach of the first group must be rejected since they assume away what is in fact an empirical problem. The proposed solutions of the other groups are problematic because at minimum they fail to deal with contamination effects.

A more effective way of attacking this issue—but by no means a panacea for the problem (cf. Kessler and Greenberg, 1981)—draws on a longitudinal research design. Indeed, investigators have recently capitalized on such designs with good success (Paternoster et al., 1982, 1983; Saltzman et al., 1982; Minor and Harry, 1982). Finding that (1) persons who reported committing crimes between waves had lower subsequent perceptions of risk than those who did not report committing crimes; (2) persons' earlier perceptions of risk were unrelated to these reports of crimes; and (3) persons' earlier and later perceptions of risk were not stable, these researchers concluded that perceived risk is a consequence of crime, not a cause.[2] Such results underscore the fecundity of longitudinal data for examining issues of deterrence.

Specification Error in the Rational-Choice Model

Many social scientists have correctly noted that to make causal inferences from nonexperimental data, one must have a correctly-specified statistical model. This implies, in particular, that all important nonorthogonal explanatory variables are included in one's model; otherwise, estimates of important parameters may be biased and inconsistent. Viewed in this light, individual-based research on deterrence appears wanting. Most analyses, in fact, are based in large part on bivariate relationships (Waldo and Chiricos, 1972; Teevan, 1976; Kraut, 1976; Erickson et al., 1977; Saltzman et al., 1982; Paternoster et al., 1982; Minor and Harry, 1982). Other analyses include in their models elements of normative controls or informal sanctions, such as deviant associates, moral attachment, criminal motives, and the like (Silberman, 1976; Grasmick and Green, 1980; Meier and Johnson, 1977; Tittle, 1977, 1980; Paternoster et al., 1983). With the possible exception of Tittle (1977, 1980), however, none of these studies include in their models the reward, returns, and opportunity component so crucial to rational-choice models (Heineke, 1978). As we noted earlier, this is the other side of the two-sided rational-choice model, the first being the risks and costs of crime. Because perceptions of risk may be correlated with perceptions of the reward, returns, and opportunity for crime, omitting the reward side may have led to biased estimates

of deterrent effects and consequently to misleading conclusions.[3]

Sampling Criminal Acts and Actors

Students of deterrence are often less interested in the social psychological process by which any sanctions are related to any form of behavior, and more interested in the implications of their research for the general problem of social order—that is, how society controls the behavior of its members (Silberman, 1976; Meier and Johnson, 1977; Tittle, 1977, 1980). However, most individual-level studies of deterrence have either sampled geographically-defined general populations (Meier and Johnson, 1977; Grasmick and Green, 1980; Tittle, 1977, 1980) or sampled students in high schools or colleges (Chiricos and Waldo, 1970; Kraut, 1976; Teevan, 1976; Bailey and Lott, 1976; Silberman, 1976; Erickson et al., 1977; Jensen et al., 1978; Minor and Harry, 1982; Paternoster et al., 1983). Consequently, because serious crimes are a rare event in such populations, researchers have used as dependent variables nonserious forms of deviance, such as petty theft, drunkenness, and marijuana use. These behaviors pose a threat to the values of some groups, but not others; therefore, the results of these studies may be more relevant to the problem of informal controls by specific groups. Of more importance to the larger issues of social control by society in general is the question, "Why do some people refrain from armed robberies, assaults, and burglaries—behaviors that threaten all groups in society—while others do not?" Stated another way, deterrence may be more relevant to serious forms of *mala en se* offenses (crimes prescribed by both law and

---

[2] These researchers argue that the within-wave negative effect of perceived risk on reported crime reflects what they term "experiential effects". That is, by virtue of their accumulated experience of violating the law and avoiding detection, persons who have engaged in more previous crimes will tend to lower their perceptions of risk in the future. This effect, however, could be confounded with a response effect: in the process of admitting their criminal acts, persons may come to perceive—if only momentarily—and report low risks for these acts.

[3] Of course, our research is vulnerable to the same criticism from the standpoint of these earlier multivariate studies: perhaps our estimates of deterrent effects are biased because we fail to consider normative controls, moral attachments, deviant associates and so on. The consideration of such additional variables would take us beyond the scope of the present study. We are attempting to consider deterrence from within an explicit and self-contained model that logically specifies a mechanism by which sanctions should deter. We are not attempting to consider an ad hoc model that includes mechanisms largely inconsistent with the underlying assumptions of deterrence theory.

public mores) and less relevant to trivial forms of *mala prohibita* offenses (crimes proscribed by law but not by public mores) (Gibbs, 1968, 1975; Silberman, 1976).

Potentially serious offenders are of particular interest to the study of deterrence for another substantive reason. Two previous studies of relatively conventional populations find an interaction effect, concluding that persons who are morally uncommitted—that is, potentially serious offenders—are more likely to be deterred by formal sanctions (Silberman, 1976; Tittle, 1977, 1980). The null findings of much of the deterrence literature, then, could be due to the focus on essentially morally-committed persons. Finally, the focus on serious offenders and offenses has obvious implications for public policy within our criminal justice system; these are the crimes and criminals our public fears most.

Supported Work, Samples, And Measures

The data for the present study pertain to both captured serious criminal acts and actors. Collected between 1975 and 1979 in the course of evaluating the National Supported Work Demonstration—a job-creation program for persons with severe employment problems—the data were obtained from three distinct samples: adult offenders who previously had been incarcerated; adults who were known drug users; and adolescents age 17 to 20 who had dropped out of school. Supported Work was evaluated using data from nine different communities throughout the United States.[4] In general, to be eligible for Supported Work, persons had to show they were recently and chronically unemployed. Beyond that, Supported Work required that, in the previous six months, participants in

the offender sample had spent time in jail or prison, those in the addict sample had been enrolled in a drug treatment program, and members of the youth sample had been out of school. In addition, at least half of the youth sample had to have an arrest record.

These criteria notwithstanding, there was no assurance of systematic recruitment into the program across locales. Rather, in large part, enrollment reflected the diverse and unknown referral practices of workers in local social service agencies. Consequently, we do not know the precise relationship of our three samples to larger populations of substantive interest, such as all ex-offenders, addicts, or dropouts in the United States. Therefore, while our samples appear to capture serious offenders, and thus have a decided advantage over those of previous research, they have the drawback of being nonprobability samples, which limits generalizations based on statistical inference.[5]

A total of 5,005 participants in the evaluation were randomly assigned to experimental or control conditions, with experimentals provided jobs lasting up to 18 months. Each enrollee was scheduled to receive at least three interviews during the evaluation. The first elicited primarily demographic and background information; the rest, conducted at nine-month intervals after enrollment, procured information about respondents' experiences, circumstances, and contacts with the criminal justice system. The 3,300 offenders, addicts, and youths who completed

---

[4] The offenders participating in the evaluation were recruited in Chicago, Hartford, Jersey City, Newark, Oakland, San Francisco, and Philadelphia. Addicts were drawn from Chicago, Jersey City, Oakland, and Philadelphia. Finally, adolescent dropouts were taken from Atlanta, Hartford, Jersey City, New York, and Philadelphia.

[5] This issue of external validity is substantive: our results cannot be generalized if the cognitive processes of serious offenders in the Supported Work samples differ from their counterparts in the general population. We find this very unlikely. Participants in the Supported Work Program were selected through the sometimes haphazard and idiosyncratic procedures of numerous and widely-dispersed agents within a variety of organizations. That this disparate group of agents selected persons with uniform cognitive styles that differ substantially from other offenders, addicts, and dropouts seems improbable. We should also note that problems of sample selection and external validity are more severe in most previous individual-level research. Such studies typically drew samples from a single school or community.

the first three interviews constitute the samples for the present investigation.[6]

Descriptive statistics for these three samples appear in Table 1. Most members of the three samples have little education, meager employment histories, and extensive contacts with criminal justice agencies. Drug use is prevalent among all groups, not just among addicts. Although direct comparative data are unavailable, these characteristics paint a plausible picture of serious criminal offenders, drug addicts, and adolescent school dropouts.[7]

During the first-wave interviews, measures were obtained of key theoretical variables, including respondents' perceptions of their opportunities for, returns from, and evaluations of both legal and illegal activities. The specific questions dealt with five concepts: (1) respondents' estimates of the lowest pay they would accept from a "straight" (legal) job (MINIMUM PAY); (2) their belief that they could make more money "on the street" (illegally) than from a straight job (RELATIVE EARNING); (3) their belief that they had frequent opportunities to engage in crime (CRIME OPPORTUNITY); (4) their relative respect for a range of conventional versus illegal jobs (JOB RESPECT); (5) their estimates of the probability they would be sanctioned negatively after engaging in a $1000 crime. At the second-wave interviews, we also measured whether respondents had become involved in criminal activities, using two dichotomous indicators: self-reports of crime and self-reports of arrest. The self-report measure of crime was constructed from checklists of a variety of serious offenses.[8]

Descriptive statistics for these substantive variables parallel the portrayal of sample members painted by our background variables: most respondents perceive limited prospects for legal employment, report having been actively involved in crime, and admit having substantial contact with the criminal justice system. The mean minimum wage that respondents would accept from a legitimate job is about what they could receive from Supported Work; for most, however, this estimate is less than the wage they believe could be earned illegally. Half of them perceived frequent (daily or weekly) opportunities for generating such illegal income. Finally, between 20 percent and 30 percent of each sample reported either violating the law or being arrested in the nine months between waves. In all three samples, some respondents who reported

---

[6] In a series of separate analyses conducted for the program evaluation, Brown (1979) attempted to determine whether sample attrition was systematic, and if so, whether it biased estimates of the effects of certain background variables on criminal behavior. In the first analysis, he found that only race influenced attrition: blacks in all three samples were less likely than whites and Hispanics to drop out of the program. In the second analysis, using Heckman's (1976) procedure for estimating and correcting for sample selection bias, he found no biasing effects on selected program outcomes, including self-reported arrest. Furthermore, we initially attempted to use data from all three waves, but could not because of severe and systematic missing data. Most significantly, persons who were incarcerated at the time of their follow-up interviews were not asked several key questions about their perceived risks of sanctions. Therefore, we were forced to restrict the analyses to the first two waves.

[7] A comparison of members of the Supported Work offender sample and prisoners recently released from federal correctional institutions indicates that the Supported Work offenders are somewhat younger and more extensively involved with criminal justice agencies. Both groups are predominantly black, unmarried, and in the past heavily involved in drug use. See Administrative Office of the United States Courts (1974).

[8] The specific illegal acts included in our measure of crime ranged from continuous ongoing activities—such as drug dealing, numbers running, and gambling—to discreet activities—such as car theft, mugging, and assault. Rather than using respondents' estimates of the frequency of their crimes, we used, for two reasons, their estimates of whether or not they had engaged in the crimes. First, we are more interested in absolute deterrence—the likelihood that one will not return to a life of crime—and less concerned with restrictive deterrence—the likelihood that one will reduce his or her rate of crime. Second, we have little confidence in respondents' estimates of the frequency of their acts; we found many inadmissible responses to such estimates. Furthermore, conceptually, it may make little sense to speak of the frequency of engaging in continuous illegal activities. For example, exactly how many times in a week has a numbers runner engaged in the act of running numbers? Precisely when the activity begins and ends is unclear. On the other hand, we do feel confident in respondents' reports of whether they have ever engaged in such acts over a nine-month period.

TABLE 1   Descriptive Statistics on Sample Members' Characteristics at Enrollment in Supported Work

	Offenders		Addicts		Youth	
	Mean	**(S.D.)**	**Mean**	**(S.D.)**	**Mean**	**(S.D.)**
Average age	25.3	(6.1)	27.8	(6.7)	18.3	(1.1)
Percent male	94		80		86	
Race and ethnicity						
Percent black	84		78		78	
Percent Hispanic	9		9		16	
Percent white or other	7		14		6	
Education						
Average years of schooling	10.4	(1.8)	10.6	(1.8)	9.7	(1.1)
% with 9 years or less	25		24		39	
Household/family composition						
Percent living with spouse/ girlfriend	16		28		6	
Percent with child under 18	12		29		7	
Weeks worked in last year						
Percent with no work	64		51		43	
Percent working 1–9 weeks	16		16		22	
Percent working 10 or more weeks	20		33		35	
Average weeks worked, all respondents	6	(2.6)	10	(3.6)	9	(3.9)
Length of longest job, last 2 years						
Percent with no regular job	49		37		30	
Percent in job 1–6 months	39		40		58	
Percent in job 7 or more months	12		23		12	
Average monthly earnings during "free time" last year	$94	($22)	$111	($19)	$73	($11)
Drug use						
Percent ever used marijuana	81		91		60	
Percent ever used an opiate	53		95		12	
Percent ever used heroin	44		94		8	
Percent with "straight" best friend	77		74		82	
Illegal money-making activity						
Percent ever making money illegally	79		84		41	
Percent making money illegally in last year	41		54		34	

(continued)

TABLE 1 Continued

	Offenders		Addicts		Youth	
	Mean	**(S.D.)**	**Mean**	**(S.D.)**	**Mean**	**(S.D.)**
Arrest experience						
Percent with at least one arrest	100		90		54	
Average number, all respondents	9.2	(1.3)	8.3	(1.1)	2.2	(.5)
Conviction experience						
Percent with at least one conviction	95		75		34	
Average number, all respondents	3	(.4)	3	(.4)	.6	(.1)
Incarceration experience						
Percent with any time in jail/prison	96		70		28	
Average weeks incarcerated, ever	195		129		20	
Average weeks incarcerated, last year	31	(1.7)	6	(1.3)	4	(1.0)
Minimum acceptable pay	$110	($36)	$109	($32)	$97	($36)
Greater street relative to straight earning ability	63%		70%		50%	
Frequent criminal opportunities	48%		55%		42%	
Job respect rating	41	(30)	38	(29)	40	(28)
Risks of crime:						
Seen, if committed	3.16	(1.61)	2.99	(1.53)	3.08	(1.55)
Reported, if seen	3.59	(1.54)	3.32	(1.57)	3.31	(1.62)
Arrested, if reported	3.86	(1.48)	3.65	(1.54)	3.59	(1.50)
Job loss, if arrested	4.24	(1.33)	3.72	(1.56)	3.41	(1.60)
Prison, if arrested	4.19	(1.32)	4.00	(1.41)	3.77	(1.50)
Friend loss, if imprisoned	2.35	(1.63)	2.13	(1.53)	1.97	(1.50)
Spouse loss, if imprisoned	2.88	(1.71)	2.60	(1.69)	2.32	(1.65)
Anycrime$_{1-9}$	30%		27%		21%	
Anyarrest$_{1-9}$	33%		20%		18%	
Number in sample	1,497		974		861	

being arrested failed to admit to a crime, a attern strongest in the offender sample, leading to the unusual finding that more offenders reported an arrest than reported a crime.

Analysis of the Measurement Model

It is well known that within linear models, random measurement error in explanatory variables can attenuate estimates of substantive coefficients. This problem is particularly acute for individual-level models of deterrence since the critical variable, perceptions of the risk of sanctions—an attitudinal construct—is difficult to measure accurately. Consequently, previous research may have underestimated the impact of perceived formal sanctions on criminal behavior. To overcome this problem, and thereby provide a stronger test

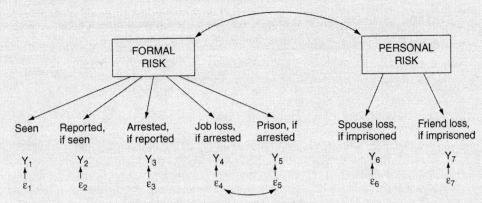

FIGURE 1 Measurement Model of Formal and Personal Risk

of the deterrence hypothesis, we attempted to estimate and statistically control for response errors in our risk construct. Using confirmatory factor analysis (Joreskog, 1969), we specified and estimated measurement models of both perceived risk of sanctions and measures of criminal activity.[9]

We examined two competing specifications of perceived risk: one in which our seven indicators are generated by a single risk construct; and another in which the risk of four events culminating in imprisonment (being seen, reported, arrested, and incarcerated), plus the risk of losing a job, reflect a formal risk construct, while fear of losing a spouse or losing friends (if imprisoned) reflect a personal risk construct (see Figure 1). The latter construct resembles, in some respects, the variable, "personal disapproval," which is firmly established in the deterrence literature (cf. Kraut, 1976; Grasmick and Green, 1980; Paternoster et al.,

1983). A test of these two nested models, which amounts to whether or not the correlation between the formal and personal risk factors is unity, supports the two-factor model in all three samples.

Standardized parameter estimates of our two-factor measurement model appear in Table 2. Validity coefficients (standardized loadings) suggest that the measures are reasonably reliable indicators of their constructs for all three samples. The risks of being reported and arrested, in particular, are very reliable indicators of persons' perceptions of the risk of formal sanctions. The correlations between factors support the discriminant validity of the two factors: while nontrivial in size, the coefficients are far from unity. We expected the measurement error of "risk of imprisonment (given arrest)" to correlate positively with the measurement error of "risk of job loss (given arrest)."[10] As indicated in Table 2, our expectations were confirmed.

Although the overall goodness-of-fit test fails to support the model in addict and offender samples, and provides only marginal support for the youth sample, we believe it represents the data adequately. An inductive search for additional significant measurement error correlations found few that could be replicated across samples; moreover, of those that could, each was trivial in

---

[9] To estimate our models, we used Joreskog and Sorbom's (1981) LISREL V program, which provides maximum likelihood estimates, asymptotic standard errors, and a likelihood ratio test statistic distributed approximately chi-square in large samples. This procedure assumes that the joint distribution of observable variables is approximately multivariate normal, an assumption that could be violated here, since some of our measures are ordinal or dichotomous. Recent Monte Carlo results suggest that the LISREL approach is reasonably robust to departures from normality given a large sample size, such as ours (Boomsma, 1983). Furthermore, however, the approach assumes that our indicators are linear functions of their latent constructs, an assumption that could be violated by our dichotomous and ordinal indicators. On the other hand, our attempts to estimate nonlinear logistic models failed to unearth any substantive differences, suggesting that if the functional form is inherently nonlinear the linear form provides a good approximation.

[10] Initially, we expected that the measurement errors of "risk of loss of spouse if imprisoned" and "risk of loss of friend if imprisoned" would also be positively correlated because each risk is conditional on imprisonment. The data did not support this hypothesis, however; in all three samples this correlation was trivial in size and produced inadmissible parameter estimates (negative variances).

TABLE 2 Standardized Factor Loadings Factor and Measurement Error Correlation[1] Offender, Addict, and Youth Samples

	Offenders	Addicts	Youths
Factor Loadings			
Formal Risk:			
Seen, if committed	.54	.57	.55
Reported, if seen	.74	.71	.73
Arrested, if reported	.70	.69	.70
Prison, if arrested	.45	.46	.52
Job loss, if arrested	.52	.51	.58
Personal Risk:			
Spouse loss, if imprisoned	.69	.70	.79
Friend loss, if imprisoned	.66	.65	.74
Factor Correlation			
Formal Risk and Personal Risk	.36	.27	.39
L^2	74.33	60.07	29.53
df	12	12	12
p	.001	.001	.003

Note: All coefficients significant at the .05 level.

[1] The measurement error correlation between "job loss, if arrested" and "prison, if arrested" is .23 for offenders, .18 for addicts, and .13 for youths.

size. Even though we could improve the fit of the model by including such correlations, our overall results remain unchanged, and we feel such a model would capitalize on chance by "over-fitting" the data. It appears that we have sufficient statistical power to detect trivial and substantively unimportant measurement error correlations (cf. Saris and Stronkhorst, 1984; Matsueda and Bielby, in Press).[11]

We also examined the hypothesis that self-reports of crime and arrest reflect a single criminal activity construct, rather than separate phenomena. The results strongly indicate that the two measures tap distinct events: when specified in a factor model, their reliabilities are unacceptably low and when entered as outcomes in regression models, the regressions are far from homogeneous. Therefore, we treat them as separate outcome variables and report both results.[12]

[11] Note that given the wording of the five measures of formal risk, they do not reflect serially conditional events. For example, respondents were asked their perceptions of risk of being reported if seen, of being arrested if reported, and so on. Thus, they are each serially independent measures of perceptions of formal risk.

[12] Although some economists have recently recommended the use of self-reports of criminal behavior in empirical tests of the rational-choice model (see Manski, 1978), some research on the use of the self-report method have questioned its use under certain circumstances. In particular Hindelang et al. (1981), in perhaps the best research on the issue, found that while self-reports appeared reasonably valid and reliable by conventional standards, they may be problematic for use on black males who have had official contact with the criminal justice system. These are not only among the most serious offenders, but they also constitute a major portion of our samples. Hindelang et al. based their conclusions on their reverse record checks: black males with an official record were significantly less likely to report having committed an illegal act. To address this issue a reverse record check for reported arrests was performed on a subsample of the offenders and addicts of the present study (Schore et al., 1979). That check found substantial underreporting of the frequency of arrests (45%) but less of prevalence of arrests (20%). Moreover, the only variable related to underreporting was race: blacks were more likely to underreport. Since blacks tend to perceive lower risks of sanctions than whites, the underreporting could attenuate the effect of risk on crime. To investigate this possibility, we followed the recommendation of Hindelang et al. and ran separate models for blacks and whites. Our results found no differences in the effect of risk on crime. This finding is consistent with Hindelang et al.'s suggestion that because validity coefficients for self-reported delinquency are of similar magnitude for blacks and whites, self reports may be valid for assessing relationships within race, but invalid for assessing differences in behavior across race.

Analysis of the Substantive Model

Specification and Hypotheses

We incorporated our measurement model of risk into a structural equation model of rational choice and crime. The model, depicted in Figure 2, is a recursive system of seven linear equations, which can be characterized by three blocks of variables—fifteen background variables, six intervening variables, and two outcome variables. The intervening variables, which measure perceived returns and costs of crime, are each functions of the background variables, and are not causally interrelated among themselves, but instead are left as unanalyzed correlations by allowing their structural disturbances (u_1–u_6) to correlate. The outcome variables—self-reported crime and arrest—are determined by the background variables plus the intervening variables.

Table 3 presents the direction of effects hypothesized by the model; the important hypotheses, derived from the rational-choice model, involve the effect of our endogenous predictors on criminal activity and appear in the last column. Focusing on these effects, we expect that perceptions of higher risks of formal (FORMAL RISK) and personal sanctions (PERSONAL RISK) will reduce the likelihood of crime. Also according to the model, persons who feel they can earn

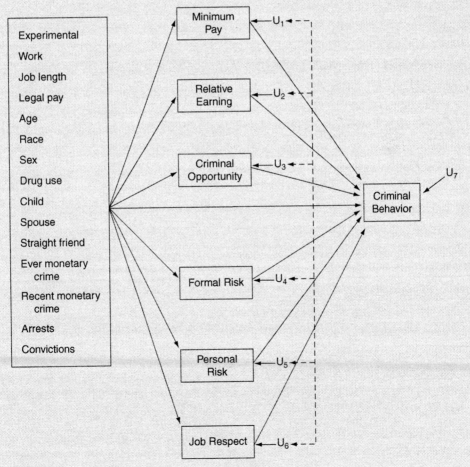

FIGURE 2 Path Diagram of the Substantive Model

TABLE 3 Hypothesized Direction of Effects for the Substantive Model

Independent Variables	Dependent Variables						
	Minimum Pay	Relative Earning	Crime Opportunity	Job Respect	Formal Risk	Personal Risk	Criminal Behavior
Experimental status	+	−		+	+		−
Work	+	−		+			−
Job length	+	−		+			−
Legal pay	+	−		+			−
Age[a]	+	−	−	−	+	+	−
Race	−	+	+	−	−	−	
Sex	+	+	+	−	−	−	+
Drug use		+	+				+
Child	+					+	−
Spouse	+					+	−
Straight friend			−	+		+	−
Ever monetary crime		+	+	−	−	−	+
Recent monetary crime		+	+	−	−	−	+
Arrests		+	+	−	+	−	+
Convictions		+	+	−	+	−	+
Minimum pay							+/−
Relative earning							+
Crime opportunity							+
Job respect							−
Formal risk							−
Personal risk							−

[a]Because of the restricted age range of the youth sample, the observed effects of age on the dependent variables may not coincide with the hypothesized effects for this sample.

more money illegally than legally (RELATIVE EARNINGS) should be more likely to succumb to criminal temptations. Similarly, persons who perceive more opportunities (CRIME OPPORTUNITY) for crimes should have greater objective opportunities and lower opportunity costs for engaging in crimes—both of which should increase their chances of illegal activity. Finally, persons holding more respect for legal jobs relative to illegal forms of work (JOB RESPECT) should have less taste for crime, greater moral inhibitions, and therefore be less likely to violate the law. Conflicting mechanisms make the direction of the impact of MINIMUM PAY on crime difficult to predict. Conceivably, persons unwilling to take low-paying conventional jobs are likely to be unemployed and willing to deviate. On the other hand, they could be simply holding out for a high-paying legitimate job, and therefore be less likely to deviate. To determine which of these competing hypotheses holds, we must turn to the data.

Estimation and Results

We estimated both the measurement model of risk and the substantive model of crime simultaneously as a single system. Again, we used the maximum likelihood estimator of Joreskog's LISREL approach (Joreskog and Sorbom, 1981). Given the large sample sizes and the large number of overidentifying restrictions, our models fit the data quite well: for the offenders, the likelihood-ratio statistic (L^2) is 405 with 183 df; for the addicts, $L^2 = 330$ with 163 df, and for the youths, $L^2 = 247$ with 169 df.[13]

Parameter estimates of the substantive model for offenders, addicts, and youths appear in Tables 4, 5, and 6, respectively. By and large these estimates depict a plausible picture of a rational choice model of crime. The last two columns describe the equations of substantive interest—self-reported crime and arrest. Across all three samples, the model explains self-reported crime better than arrest: more of the variance is explained and more of the coefficients are consistent with expectations. This suggests that the self-reported crime construct is a more valid indicator of illegal behavior (Mallar and Piliavin, 1984). We therefore emphasize the results for self-reported crime.

Of the background variables, the effects of SEX, PRIOR MONETARY CRIME and PRIOR ARRESTS are substantial and consistent across all three samples. As expected then, males, persons who have committed a monetary crime in the past, and persons who have been arrested more often, are all more likely to violate the law. Also as expected, drug users are more likely to violate the law in the offender and youth samples; but because of insufficient variance, this is not replicated in the addict sample. Finally, LAST YEAR'S

MONETARY CRIMES has a significant positive effect on crime in offender and addict samples, but not in youth samples.

Of more importance for the purpose of this article is the impact on crime of the endogenous predictors representing the rational-choice process. Here, the most dramatic finding is that across all samples and for both measures of illegal activity, both formal and personal risks of punishment have virtually no impact on criminal behavior. This finding is all the more compelling since we have attempted to correct for attenuation due to unreliability in our perceptual indicators of risk. Furthermore, our equations predicting FORMAL RISK explain a nontrivial amount of variance (about ten percent), and moreover, contain parameter estimates that coincide with our hypotheses. Our equations for PERSONAL RISK explain less variance (about seven percent), but do contain coefficients consistent with expectations. Therefore, we do not find evidence directly questioning the (criterion) validity of our risk constructs. Instead, we find that in contrast to previous research, which concludes that deterrence should be more effective in less conventional samples, in our samples containing criminally-motivated and morally-uncommitted persons, perceptions of the risk of formal and personal sanctions fail to make a difference in explaining crimes.

What does appear to make a difference is the other side of the rational-choice process—the opportunity or returns component. Specifically, CRIME OPPORTUNITY has a substantial and statistically significant effect on illegal behavior across all three samples. As expected, persons who perceive greater opportunities to earn money illegally are more likely to violate the law. Furthermore, in offender and addict samples, persons who hold more respect for illegitimate occupations relative to legitimate jobs (JOB RESPECT) have more to gain and less to lose by violating the law and therefore are significantly more likely to do so.

The variables representing the returns component of the rational-choice process mediate the

---

[13] The different degrees of freedom for offender, addict, and youth models reflect the different number of sites—a set of exogenous dummy variables not shown in the model—across samples.

TABLE 4 Unstandardized and Standardized Parameter Estimates of the Structural Model: Offender Sample (N = 1497)

Independent Variables	Minimum Pay		Relative Earning		Crime Opportunity		Personal Risk		Formal Risk		Job Respect		Any Crime$_{1-9}$		Any Arrest$_{1-9}$	
Experimental	−.005	(−.006)	.001	(.001)	—		—		−.010	(−.003)	—		−.031	(−.033)	−.016	(−.017)
Work	.024	(.052)	−.036*	(−.061)	—		—		—		.220*	(.058)	−.006	(−.011)	−.008	(−.013)
Job length	.003	(.006)	−.039*	(−.056)	—		—		—		.200	(.045)	−.011	(−.017)	−.038*	(−.055)
Legal pay	−.002	(−.010)	.011	(.049)	—		—		—		−.033	(−.024)	−.001	(−.004)	.000	(.000)
Age	.037*	(.061)	−.056**	(−.071)	−.014	(−.017)	.390***	(.198)	.210***	(.147)	.830***	(.168)	−.021	(−.027)	−.030	(−.038)
Race	.072**	(.072)	.009	(.007)	.059*	(.044)	−.360***	(−.108)	−.070	(−.030)	−.460**	(−.057)	—		—	
Sex	.105**	(.065)	−.037	(−.018)	.155**	(.072)	.630**	(.120)	.160	(.042)	−.290	(−.022)	.169***	(.085)	.172**	(.084)
Drug use	—		.111***	(.116)	.065**	(.065)	—		—		.040	(.007)	.098***	(.106)	.067**	(.071)
Spouse	.023	(.023)	—		—		−.240*	(−.073)	—		—		.038	(.031)	−.067	(−.053)
Straight friend	—		—		−.087**	(−.073)	−.090	(−.033)	—		1.07***	(.150)	−.007	(−.006)	.075**	(.067)
Ever monetary crime	−.067**	(−.074)	.144***	(.123)	.027	(.022)	−.040	(−.015)	.170**	(.078)	−.770***	(−.105)	.071**	(.063)	−.058	(−.051)
Recent monetary crime	.013	(.017)	.029	(.030)	.172***	(.168)	−.090	(−.038)	−.210***	(−.116)	−.420**	(−.068)	.124***	(.132)	.092***	(.096)
Arrests	—		.013	(.035)	.018	(.046)	.088**	(.094)	−.021	(−.031)	.044	(.019)	.018*	(.053)	.035***	(.097)
Convictions	—		.002	(.019)	.004	(.031)	−.013	(−.043)	.010	(.047)	−.070***	(−.094)	.005	(.043)	.004	(.022)
Minimum pay	—		—		—		—		—		—		−.006	(−.005)	−.006	(−.004)
Relative earning	—		—		—		—		—		—		.054*	(.056)	−.017	(−.018)
Crime opportunity	—		—		—		—		—		—		.046*	(.050)	.083***	(.088)
Personal risk	—		—		—		—		—		—		−.022	(−.057)	−.011	(−.028)
Formal risk	—		—		—		—		—		—		−.020	(−.038)	−.015	(−.027)
Job respect	—		—		—		—		—		—		−.015***	(−.099)	−.006	(−.040)
R^2	.05		.07		.07		.08		.07		.09		.15		.10	

$L^2 = 405$
$df = 183$

Note: Standardized coefficients appear in parentheses.

* $p < .05$.

** $p < .01$.

*** $p < .001$.

TABLE 5 Unstandardized and Standardized Parameter Estimates of the Structural Model: Addict Sample (N = 974)

Independent Variables	Dependent Variables							
	Minimum Pay	Relative Earning	Crime Opportunity	Personal Risk	Formal Risk	Job Respect	Any Crime$_{1-9}$	Any Arrest$_{1-9}$
Experimental	-.008 (-.012)	.013 (.014)	—	—	-.050 (-.030)	—	.003 (.003)	-.023 (-.029)
Work	-.081*** (-.227)	.005 (.010)	—	—	—	.210 (.067)	-.026 (-.052)	.005 (.012)
Job length	.018 (.043)	.001 (.002)	—	—	—	.240* (.063)	.011 (.020)	-.019 (-.037)
Legal pay	.038*** (.230)	.011 (.044)	-.049* (-.065)	.120* (.069)	.120* (.094)	-.066 (-.043)	.032*** (.139)	.002 (.009)
Age	.042** (.088)	-.058** (-.085)	.052 (.043)	-.440*** (-.156)	-.080 (-.041)	.810*** (.188)	-.054* (-.083)	-.042* (-.071)
Race	.012 (.016)	.027 (.024)	.105** (.084)	.050 (.018)	.030 (.013)	-.530*** (-.077)	.093** (.085)	.104** (.104)
Sex	.082** (.102)	-.135*** (-.117)	.235*** (.103)	.000 (.000)	—	-.830*** (-.114)	-.006 (-.003)	.090 (.049)
Drug use	—	-.090 (-.043)	—	-.410*** (-.159)	—	-.570 (-.043)	-.009 (-.009)	-.034 (-.038)
Child	-.001 (-.002)	—	—	.210* (.077)	—	—	-.040 (-.041)	-.001 (-.001)
Spouse	.030 (.042)	—	.012 (.011)	-.090 (-.028)	-.070 (-.031)	.610** (.092)	-.031 (-.031)	.007 (.008)
Straight friend	—	—	-.110* (-.079)	-.170 (-.071)	-.150* (-.087)	-.850*** (-.105)	.081* (-.066)	-.052 (-.047)
Ever monetary crime	-.011 (-.012)	.126** (.099)	.203*** (.203)	—	—	-.510** (-.087)	.066* (.075)	.091*** (.113)
Recent monetary crime	.010 (.015)	.071* (.078)	.009 (.021)	.000 (.000)	—	—	.030* (.074)	.029* (.081)
Arrests	—	.057*** (.136)	—	.075* (.070)	.040 (.051)	—	.000 (.000)	.004 (.045)
Convictions	—	.002 (.014)	.010* (.080)	—	.029* (.140)	—	-.014 (-.010)	.013 (.011)
Minimum pay							.003 (.003)	-.015 (-.018)
Relative earning							—	.020 (.025)
Crime opportunity							.090*** (.102)	.007 (.021)
Personal risk							.004 (.010)	.019 (.041)
Formal risk							-.017 (-.032)	-.009* (-.066)
Job respect							-.013** (-.084)	—
R^2	.07	.06	.06	.07	.10	.10	.11	.08

$L^2 = 330$
$df = 163$

Note: Standardized coefficients appear in parentheses.

* p < .05.
** p < .01.
*** p < .001.

TABLE 6 Unstandardized and Standardized Parameter Estimates of the Structural Model: Youth Sample (N = 861)

Independent Variables	Minimum Pay	Relative Earning	Crime Opportunity	Personal Risk	Formal Risk	Job Respect	Any Crime$_{1-9}$	Any Arrest$_{1-9}$
				Dependent Variables				
Experimental	.028 (.039)	.014 (.014)	—	—	.020 (.009)	—	−.004 (−.005)	−.001 (−.002)
Work	.006 (.015)	.009 (.017)	—	—	—	−.180 (−.057)	.043* (.092)	.040* (.092)
Job length	−.048* (−.084)	−.036 (−.046)	—	—	—	.180 (.039)	−.034 (−.052)	−.048* (−.080)
Legal pay	.010 (.051)	.007 (.027)	—	—	—	.045	−.020* (−.092)	.007 (.035)
Age	.337** (.103)	.229 (.050)	−.009 (−.002)	.310 (.028)	−.390 (−.049)	2.35* (.092)	−.211* (−.057)	−.266* (−.077)
Race	.016 (.019)	.017 (.014)	.080* (.067)	−.530*** (−.179)	−.350*** (−.163)	−.150 (−.022)	—	—
Sex	.133*** (.125)	.067 (.045)	−.092* (−.064)	−.090 (−.024)	.020 (.007)	−.470* (−.057)	.106** (.088)	.089* (.079)
Drug use	—	.140** (.092)	.136** (.092)	—	—	−.690** (−.081)	.172*** (.138)	.035 (.031)
Child	.003 (.002)	—	—	−.180 (−.038)	—	—	−.001 (−.001)	−.018 (−.012)
Spouse	.004 (.002)	—	—	.030 (.006)	—	—	−.011 (−.006)	.111* (.067)
Straight friend	—	—	−.039 (−.031)	.220* (.070)	—	—	−.026 (−.024)	.044 (.044)
Ever monetary crime	−.028 (−.038)	.002 (.002)	.169** (.169)	−.150 (−.062)	.080 (.044)	.760*** (.103)	.075 (.089)	−.009 (−.011)
Recent monetary crime	.019 (.024)	.115* (.108)	−.006 (−.006)	−.020 (−.009)	−.230* (−.124)	−.980** (−.171)	.068 (.078)	.071 (.088)
Arrests	—	.061* (.064)	.060* (.064)	.040 (.015)	.140* (.086)	−.220 (−.036)	.054* (.070)	.064** (.089)
Convictions	—	.027* (.076)	.018 (.052)	−.023 (−.027)	.007 (.011)	.130 (.025)	.030** (.102)	.310*** (.114)
Minimum pay	—	—	—	—	—	−.059 (−.030)	−.002 (−.002)	.000 (.000)
Relative earning	—	—	—	—	—	—	−.031 (−.038)	.036 (.047)
Crime opportunity	—	—	—	—	—	—	.095*** (.113)	−.006 (−.008)
Personal risk	—	—	—	—	—	—	−.012 (−.036)	−.021 (−.067)
Formal risk	—	—	—	—	—	—	−.018 (−.039)	.029 (−.068)
Job respect	—	—	—	—	—	—	.004 (−.026)	−.003 (−.020)
R^2	.08	.08	.09	.05	.07	.10	.22	.11

$L^2 = 247$
$df = 169$

Note: Standardized coefficients appear in parentheses.
* p < .05.
** p < .01.
*** p < .001.

22

impact on crime of some of our background variables. For offender and addict samples, persons who are younger and who have committed monetary crimes in the last year commit more crimes in part because they perceive greater opportunities and return to crime. In the youth sample, this mechanism holds for persons who have used drugs and who have been arrested. Overall, however, our block of endogenous variables mediates little of the total effects of our exogenous variables. Furthermore, across all three samples, the increase in explained variance is marginal at best.[14]

Could our finding that formal and personal risks fail to deter stem from a methodological artifact? We explored several possibilities. It could be that risks of formal and personal sanctions deter monetary crimes but not other crimes; in fact, this is consistent with some variants of the rational-choice explanation. To test this, we estimated our model using as an outcome variable, self-reports of committing a property crime in the previous nine months. With trivial exceptions, the parameter estimates of this model mirrored those of our earlier models. This result is not surprising since the percentage of persons reporting any crime who also report a monetary crime ranges from 77 percent (addicts) to 86 percent (offenders).

A second possible artifact involves the functional form of the relationship between sanctions and crime. Some researchers have postulated and found nonlinear effects due to diminishing returns (Logan, 1972) or threshold effects (Tittle and Rowe, 1974; Tittle, 1980). According to this hypothesis, sanctions will not deter until the perceived probability of risk reaches a certain threshold; conversely, the deterrent effect of sanctions may diminish when the

perceived probability of risk reaches a point of saturation. If true, our linear probability model may have underestimated the slope of the risk variables at moderate levels of risk. To examine this hypothesis, we estimated multivariate logistic regressions on our single-indicator variables plus factor scores of our multiple-indicator risk variables.[15] Again, for all three samples and for both self-reported crime and arrest, the results remain relatively unchanged.

Still, it could be that because the true threshold is so high, extremely high levels of perceived risk are required before sanctions deter, and consequently, the logistic functional form is unable to capture the true nonlinear relationship between sanctions and crime. We therefore estimated an extreme model, postulating that persons are not deterred until they perceive the greatest possible risk on every component of the risk construct. We constructed two dichotomous risk variables, which contrasted persons who scored highest on every indicator of FORMAL and PERSONAL RISK versus all others, and entered them into our full multivariate logit model. Again, however, the parameter estimates retained the sign and statistical significance of those of our LISREL models.

Finally, it could be that the nonlinear deterrent effect can be captured by specifying a conditional effect. That is, because the wording of our indicators of PERSONAL RISK requires that respondents hypothetically consider they have been imprisoned, it follows that PERSONAL RISK might deter only those who consider incarceration

---

[14] We arrived at these conclusions regarding indirect effects by first locating those reduced-form effects (not shown in our tables) that are substantial and statistically significant. Second, we determined which of these effects was substantially reduced in the structural form. Third, we traced the indirect effect by locating the intervening variable that had a significant effect on crime and was significantly affected by the exogenous variable in question.

[15] This strategy has the well-known additional advantages of using logistic regressions over linear probability models in predicting a dichotomous dependent variable. That is, it overcomes the problem of heteroscedastic structural disturbances and the problem of predicting inadmissible values (greater than one and less than zero) of the dependent variable. Furthermore, it relaxes the assumption of multivariate normality found in the LISREL approach. The strategy has the drawback of failing to correct for attenuated regression coefficients due to unreliability—if indeed the appropriate measurement model is a confirmatory factor model and not a weighted linear combination of indicators. The actual factor scores we used were derived from the LISREL program, based on a weighted linear combination of all observables in the model.

a likely result of crime. To test this hypothesis, we estimated the model separately for two groups: those having high scores on FORMAL RISK versus all others. Again, however, PERSONAL RISK failed to affect crime significantly in either group.

Summary and Discussion

In sum, after estimating a variety of models and examining several hypotheses, our conclusions remain unchanged: we find evidence supporting the opportunity and reward component of the rational-choice model of crime, but no evidence supporting the risk component. The null finding regarding perceived risks is consistent with findings of other individual-level studies of deterrence that have used less rigorous designs and analytical procedures. We have gone beyond previous research not only analytically, but also by extending those results to a different and significant population—namely, the population of serious and high risk offenders. Moreover, our results explicitly refute the hypothesis, proposed by Silberman (1976) and Tittle (1977, 1980), that the threat of legal punishment deters persons who are less committed to conventional morality. Furthermore, taken together with our positive results regarding opportunities and returns, these null findings suggest that the rational-choice model may oversimplify the cognitive process behind criminality. What may be needed is a more complex model that relaxes some of the stringent assumptions of the strict rational-choice approach.

For example, a greater emphasis on the limitations of human beings to acquire and process information, such as the probability of sanctions, may be warranted (cf. Simon, 1957). That is, it may be that people are insensitive to marginal changes in their perceptions of the probabilities of the consequences (sanctions) of their actions, especially when that probability is low (Kunreuther and Slovic, 1978). Instead, they may alter their behavior only after major discontinuous shifts in their perceptions of the risk of sanctions. Moreover, persons may discount the meaning or relevance of certain probabilities: when confronted with a decision, they may discount some outcomes relative to others of equal probability (Kahnemann and Tversky, 1984). For example, persons may slight those consequences or events that are either distant or beyond their direct control, and emphasize those that are immediate and within control (Kogan and Wallach, 1967; Ainslie, 1982). Furthermore, the particular style of discounting—emphasizing some options but not others—probably varies from one person to another.

We are suggesting that persons' evaluations or imputed meanings of sanctions are important in determining their behavior. These evaluations or meanings may be conditioned by elements within the immediate situation confronting the individual. For example, the persons' perceptions of the opportunity, returns, and support for crime within a given situation may influence their perceptions of risks and the extent to which those risks are discounted. This implies that the effective assessments of risk are to some extent situationally-induced, transitory, and unstable (Short and Strodtbeck, 1965). If true, this could help explain the ineffectiveness of our risk variables—that is, if persons' perceptions of risk are unstable over time, and the causally-relevant perceptions are those more proximate to crime, our distal measures of perceived risk may be irrelevant to behavior.

We can provide some indirect evidence on the last hypothesis by examining a model of the stability of our risk constructs. This model, depicted in Figure 3, is a two-wave panel version of our multiple-indicator measurement model. The model specifies that the FORMAL (PERSONAL) RISK construct at time two is a linear function of FORMAL (PERSONAL) RISK at time one and self-reported CRIME and ARREST measured at time two. Intertemporal correlations of response errors for each indicator are estimated to disentangle true stability from response effects that remain constant over time. The standardized coefficients, given in Table 7, indicate that both FORMAL and PERSONAL RISK are relatively unstable over time. For offender

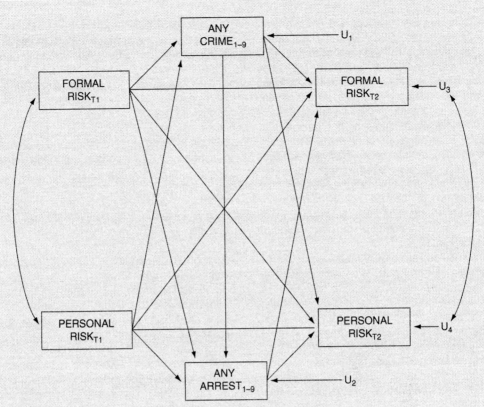

FIGURE 3 Two-Wave Panel Model of Formal and Personal Risk

TABLE 7 Standardized Parameter Estimates for a Two-Wave Panel Model of Formal and Personal Risk

Independent Variables	Offenders		Addicts		Youths	
	FORMAL RISK$_{T2}$	PERSONAL RISK$_{T2}$	FORMAL RISK$_{T2}$	PERSONAL RISK$_{T2}$	FORMAL RISK$_{T2}$	PERSONAL RISK$_{T2}$
FORMAL RISK$_{T1}$	.243	.052	.294	.093	.221	−.005
	(6.17)	(1.26)	(6.04)	(1.70)	(4.19)	(−.10)
PERSONAL RISK$_{T1}$	−.055	.443	.087	.427	.081	.286
	(−1.28)	(8.15)	(1.86)	(6.39)	(1.56)	(5.13)
ANY CRIME$_{1-9}$	−.086	−.060	−.059	−.041	−.190	−.071
	(−2.84)	(−1.81)	(−1.61)	(−1.02)	(4.83)	(−1.82)
ANY ARREST$_{1-9}$	.014	.081	.030	.017	.064	.069
	(.48)	(2.46)	(.81)	(.42)	(1.66)	(1.78)

Note: t-values appear in parentheses.

and youth samples, self-reported crime affects both FORMAL and PERSONAL RISK significantly, a result consistent with the findings by Saltzman et al. (1982) and Minor and Harry (1982) of "experiential" effects. A very small component of the total stability in perceived risk, then, works indirectly through criminal behavior.

These results suggest that persons did change their perceptions of risk substantially over the nine months between waves, and that this change was only modestly affected by crime. Therefore, we cannot rule out the possibility that in our sample, persons' perceptions of risks more proximate to their decision to engage in or refrain from crime do influence the outcome of that decision.

This issue and others raised above can be examined, at least in part, by research capitalizing on multiwave panel data. By collecting waves of data spaced closer in time, a more fine-grained temporal analysis is possible, capturing changes in perceptions of risk and the impact of those changes on criminal behavior. Furthermore, such a strategy would allow one to disentangle within-individual changes in attitudes, perceptions, and behaviors from within-time variation in such variables.

While we recognize the importance of using more sophisticated research designs and theoretical models, we nevertheless believe the present study provides the best test of the rational-choice model to date. The results of that test find that for persons at high risk of formal sanction, including addicts, and school dropouts, perceptions of the risk of both formal and personal sanctions fail to influence persons' decisions to violate the law. On the other hand, those decisions are influenced by persons' perceptions of their opportunities and respect for criminal activities.

References

Administrative Office of the United States Courts. 1974. Censuses of Persons Under Supervision of the Federal Probation System. Washington, DC: U.S. Government Printing Office.

Ainslie, George. 1982. "Beyond Microeconomics: Conflict Among Interests in a Multiple Self as a Determinant of Value." Paper presented at the Conference on the Multiple Self, Paris.

Andenaes, Johannes. 1974. *Punishment and Deterrence*. Ann Arbor: University of Michigan Press.

Anderson, Linda S., Theodore G. Chiricos, and Gordon P. Waldo. 1977. "Formal and Informal Sanctions: A Comparison of Deterrent Effects." *Social Problems* 25:103–14.

Bailey, William C. and Ruth P. Lott. 1976. "Crime, Punishment and Personality: An Examination of the Deterrence Question." *Journal of Criminal Law and Criminology* 67:99–109.

Becker, Gary S. 1968. "Crime and Punishment: An Economic Approach." *Journal of Political Economy* 78:189–217.

Block, Michael and John M. Heineke. 1973. "The Allocation of Effort Under Uncertainty: The Case of Risk Averse Behavior." *Journal of Political Economy* 81:376–85.

Boomsma, Anne. 1983. *On the Robustness of LISREL (Maximum Likelihood Estimation) Against Small Sample Size and Non-Normality*. Ph.D. Dissertation, University of Gronigen, Gronigen.

Brier, Stephen S. and Stephen E. Fienberg. 1980. "Recent Econometric Modeling of Crime and Punishment." *Evaluation Review* 4:147–91.

Brown, Randall, 1979. "Assessing the Effects of Interview Non-response on Estimates of the Impact of Supported Work." Princeton: Mathematica Policy Research.

Burkett, Steven R. and Eric L. Jensen. 1975. "Conventional Ties, Peer Influence, and the Fear of Apprehension: A Study of Adolescent Marijuana Use." *Sociological Quarterly* 16:522–33.

Chiricos, Theodore G. and Gordon P. Waldo. 1970. "Punishment and Crime: An Examination of Some Empirical Evidence." *Social Problems* 18:200–17.

Erickson, Maynard, Jack P. Gibbs, and Gary F. Jensen. 1977. "The Deterrence Doctrine and the Perceived Certainty of Legal Punishments." *American Sociological Review* 42:305–17.

Friedman, Milton and L. J. Savage. 1948. "The Utility Analysis of Choices Involving Risk." *Journal of Political Economy* 56:279–304.

Gibbs, Jack P. 1968. "Crime, Punishment, and Deterrence." *Southwestern Social Science Quarterly* 48:515–30.

——. 1975. *Crime, Punishment and Deterrence.* New York: Elsevier.

Grasmick, Harold G. and Herman M. Milligan, Jr. 1976. "Deterrence Theory Approach to Socioeconomic/Demographic Correlates of Crime." *Social Science Quarterly* 57:608–17.

Grasmick, Harold G. and Donald E. Green. 1980. "Legal Punishment, Social Disapproval, and Internalization as Inhibitors of Illegal Behavior." *Journal of Criminal Law and Criminology* 71:325–55.

Greenberg, David F. 1981. "Methodological Issues in Survey Research on the Inhibition of Crime." *Journal of Criminal Law and Criminology* 72:1094–1107.

Heckman, James J. 1976. "The Common Structure of Statistical Models of Truncation, Sample Selection, and Limited Dependent Variables and a Simple Estimator for Such Models." *Annals of Economic and Social Measurement* 5:475–92.

Heineke, J. M. 1978. "Economic Models of Criminal Behavior: An Overview," Pp. 1–34 in *Economic Models of Criminal Behavior,* edited by J. M. Heineke. New York: North Holland.

Hindelang, Michael J., Travis Hirschi, and Joseph G. Weis. 1981. *Measuring Delinquency.* Beverly Hills: Sage.

Jensen, Gary F. 1969. "Crime Doesn't Pay: Correlates of a Shared Misunderstanding." *Social Problems* 17:189–201.

Jensen, Gary F., Jack P. Gibbs, and Maynard Erickson. 1978. "Perceived Risk of Punishment and Self-Reported Delinquency." *Social Forces* 57:57–78.

Jensen, Gary F. and B. Grant Stitt. 1982. "Words and Misdeeds: Hypothetical Choices Versus Past Behavior as Measures of Deviance," Pp. 33–54 in *Deterrence Reconsidered: Methodological Innovations,* edited by J. Hagan. Beverly Hills: Sage.

Jöreskog, Karl G. 1969. "A General Approach to Confirmatory Factor Analysis." *Psychometrika* 34:183–202.

Jöreskog, Karl G. and Dag Sörbom. 1981. LISREL: *Analysis of Linear Structural Relationships by the Method of Maximum Likelihood.* University of Uppsala.

Kahneman, Daniel and Amos Tversky. 1984. "Choices, Values and Frames." *American Psychologist* 39:341–50.

Kessler, Ronald and David F. Greenberg. 1981. *Linear Panel Analysis: Models of Quantitative Change.* New York: Academic.

Kogan, Nathan and Michael A. Wallach. 1967. "Risktaking as a Function of the Situation, the Person, and the Group." *New Directions in Psychology.* Vol. III. New York: Rinehart and Winston.

Kraut, Robert E. 1976. "Deterrent and Definitional Influences on Shoplifting." *Social Problems* 23:358–68.

Kunreuther, Howard and Paul Slovic. 1978. "Economics, Psychology, and Protective Behavior." *American Economic Review* 68:64–69.

Logan, Charles. 1975. "Arrest Rates and Deterrence." *Social Science Quarterly* 56:376–89.

Mallar, Charles and Irving Piliavin. 1984. "Issues of Data Collection in Assessing Programs Involving Crime Reduction: The Job Corps and Supported Work Evaluations," in *Collecting Evaluation Data,* edited by Leigh Burstein et al. Beverly Hills: Sage.

Manski, Charles F. 1978. "Prospects for Inference on Deterrence Through Empirical Analysis of Individual Criminal Behavior," Pp. 400–24 in *Deterrence and Incapacitation: Estimating the Effects of Criminal Sanctions on Crime Rates,* edited by A. Blumstein, J. Cohen and D. Nagin. Washington, DC: National Academy of Sciences.

Matsueda, Ross L. and William T. Bielby. In press. "Statistical Power in Covariance Structure Models." In *Sociological Methodology 1986,* edited by Nancy Brandon Tuma. San Francisco: Jossey-Bass.

Meier, Robert F. and Weldon T. Johnson. 1977. "Deterrence as Social Control: The Legal and

Extralegal Production of Conformity." *American Sociological Review* 42:292–304.

Minor, W. William and Joseph Harry. 1982. "Deterrent and Experiential Effects in Perceptual Deterrence Research: A Replication and Extension." *Journal of Research in Crime and Delinquency.* 19:172–89.

Paternoster, Raymond, Linda Saltzman, Theodore G. Chiricos, and Gordon P. Waldo. 1982. "Perceived Risk and Deterrence: Methodological Artifacts in Perceptual Deterrence Research." *Criminology* 73:1238–58.

———. 1983. "Perceived Risk and Social Control: Do Sanctions Really Deter?" *Law and Society Review* 17:457–79.

Saltzman, Linda, Raymond Paternoster, Gordon P. Waldo, and Theodore G. Chiricos. 1982. "Deterrent and Experiential Effects: The Problem of Causal Order in Perceptual Deterrence Research." *Journal of Crime and Delinquency* 19:172–89.

Schore, Jennifer, Rebecca Maynard, and Irving Piliavin. 1979. *The Accuracy of Self-Report Arrest Data.* Princeton: Mathematica Policy Research.

Saris, Willem and Henk Stronkhorst. 1984. *Causal Modeling in Nonexperimental Research.* Amsterdam: Sociometric Research Foundation.

Short, James F. and Fred Strodtbeck. 1965. *Group Process and Gang Delinquency.* Chicago: University of Chicago Press.

Silberman, Matthew. 1976. "Toward a Theory of Criminal Deterrence." *American Sociological Review* 41:442–61.

Simon, Herbert A. 1957. *Models of Man.* New York: Wiley.

Teevan, James J. 1976. "Subjective Perception of Deterrence (continued)." *Journal of Research in Crime and Delinquency* 13:155–64.

Tittle, Charles R. 1969. "Crime Rates and Legal Sanctions." *Social Problems* 16:409–23.

———. 1977. "Sanction Fear and the Maintenance of Social Order." *Social Forces* 55:579–96.

———. 1980. *Sanctions and Social Deviance: The Question of Deterrence.* New York: Praeger.

Tittle, Charles R. and Alan R. Rowe. 1974. "Certainty of Arrest and Crime Rates: A Further Test of the Deterrence Hypothesis." *Social Forces* 52:455–62.

Waldo, Gordon P. and Theodore G. Chiricos. 1972. "Perceived Penal Sanctions and Self-Reported Criminality: A Neglected Approach to Deterrence Research." *Social Problems* 19:522–40.

Wrong, Dennis. 1961. "The Oversocialized Conception of Man in Modern Sociology." *American Sociological Review* 26:183–93.

Zimring, Franklin E. and Gordon Hawkins. 1973. *Deterrence: The Legal Threat in Crime Control.* Chicago: University of Chicago Press.

Conclusion

This chapter outlined deterrence and rational choice theories, both in general and with respect to racial differences in crime. This reading provided some interesting insights into the effect of race on crime and in particular, show that race is not an issue for deterrence or rational choice. However, it has some limitations. One is that it requires understanding the specific issues pertaining to the crimes. Moreover, race is not a central focus of this study, and it does not explain the data pertaining to race obtained from different populations.

Future studies on race and crime that use deterrence and rational choice theories should make race a central focus of their studies. In addition, these studies need to examine multiple forms of behaviors and use more diverse types of populations. While our knowledge base will indeed grow when future researchers take up the challenges that these studies present, for now we see that deterrence and rational choice variables trump race in the commission of crime.

Discussion Questions

1. What does rational choice theory suggest about racial differences in the planning of crime? How do rational choices influence crime rates and criminality?
2. According to Piliavin et al., what are the racial differences in the perceptions of opportunity?

What does this suggest about the racial differences in criminality and crime rates?
3. What recommendations does this selection provide that can reduce the disparities between the races with respect to crime rates and criminality?

References

Nagin, D. S., & Paternoster, R. (1991). The preventive effects of the perceived risk of arrest: Testing an expanded conception of deterrence. *Criminology, 29*, 561–587.

Paternoster, R. (1987). The deterrent effect of the perceived certainty and severity of punishment: A review of the evidence and issues. *Justice Quarterly, 4*, 173–217.

Paternoster, R., & Simpson, S. (1996). Sanction threats and appeals to morality: Testing a rational choice model of corporate crime. *Law and Society Review, 30*, 549–583.

Pogarsky, G. (2002). Identifying deterrable offenders: Implications for deterrence research. *Justice Quarterly, 19*, 431–452.

Tibbetts, S. G., & Gibson, C. L. (2002). Individual propensities and rational decision-making: Recent findings and promising approaches. In A. R. Piquero & S. G. Tibbetts (Eds.), *Rational choice and criminal behavior: Recent research and future challenges* (pp. 3–24). New York: Routledge Press.

Yu, J., & Liska, A. (1993). The certainty of punishment: A reference group effect and its functional form. *Criminology, 31*, 447–464.

CHAPTER 3

Social Disorganization

Another theory may help provide an understanding of the race-based differences in crime. According to the social disorganization theory, where an individual lives is instrumental in determining his or her propensity to commit crime. This chapter will provide a general overview of the social disorganization theory and conclude with the specific propositions that relate to race and crime.

Social disorganization theory comes from the traditions of the Chicago School's social ecology movement. In general, this theory considers several factors such as geography, usage of space, population movement, and the physical environment. Criminal behavior is a result of a combination of these factors.

Social disorganization theory sees individuals as being influenced by major social trends in the physical and social environments. An individual's morality and choices are based on the structure of their environment. Further, the theory holds that individuals are conformists and will behave in accordance with the social group that they identify themselves with.

Social disorganization theorists consider that the law reflects the values and norms of the dominant group and that criminals are individuals who are in a state of transition through a disenfranchisement of social organization.

Early social disorganization theory emphasized where individuals lived and worked. For instance, concentric zones were used to explain crime. The overall view regarding concentric zones was that the farther individuals lived from the "central business district," the less likely they were to be involved in crime. This view suggests that crime is not random but is probably based on a pattern. The pattern takes into consideration the dominant uses of land within the concentric zones. For instance, when an inner zone grows, it will take over the nearest outer zone, bringing with it its social problems including crime, as well as creating a new zone. This makes the land of the new zone less desirable, and there is a diffusion effect across the other zones. That is, all of the other zones change as well.

The first zone is usually the central business district because it houses the businesses and the factories but very few residences. The second zone is the zone of transition because the central business district zone grows and takes over this zone. This makes the land cheap, allowing immigrants and minorities to purchase land and live near places where they could work. The third zone is one that allows the individuals to move from the zone of transition and settle in it—zone of the workingmen's homes. The additional zones have comparatively less social problems and the cost of living in them is higher.

In the inner zones, individuals exhibit a sense of superficial living, anonymity, transitory relationships, and weakened bonds with family and friends. The weakening of the bonds among the individuals in the community has particular significance for social disorganization because it indicates that primary social relationships are poor and these individuals are more likely to be socially disorganized. In a socially disorganized community, people do not have a sense of loyalty to the community, neighborhoods are not stable and cohesive, and family and friendship group ties are not strong. Social disorganization has the ability to reduce opportunities for normal social control, including control of criminal and delinquent behavior.

Social disorganization theory pays special attention to the zone of transition. This zone has particular significance because it is often one of the more socially disorganized zones. This zone has a high level of mobility, neighborhood decay, and business and industry moving into the area. At the earlier stages of this social disorganization, immigrant populations would retreat to their own cultures during turbulent times in the community. This retreat causes a conflict among the cultures that further disorganizes the society. In this way, social disorganization theory helps explain the distribution of criminal behavior.

A meta-analysis by Pratt and Cullen (2005) indicates that social disorganization theory has empirical support in the literature. Further, this theory can be applied to explain racial differences in crime. Historically, racial minorities have experienced greater levels of poverty and are concentrated in geographical areas that have high rates of social disorganization. In this chapter, Sampson, Morenoff, and Raudenbush will illustrate this view.

Social Anatomy of Racial and Ethnic Disparities in Violence

Robert J. Sampson, PhD, Jeffrey D. Morenoff, PhD, and Stephen Raudenbush, EdD

We analyzed key individual, family, and neighborhood factors to assess competing hypotheses regarding racial/ethnic gaps in perpetrating violence. From 1995 to 2002, we collected 3 waves of data on 2974 participants aged 18 to 25 years living in 180 Chicago neighborhoods, augmented by a separate community survey of 8782 Chicago residents.

The odds of perpetrating violence were 85% higher for Blacks compared with Whites, whereas Latino-perpetrated violence was 10% lower. Yet the majority of the Black-White gap (over 60%) and the entire Latino-White gap were explained primarily by the marital status of parents, immigrant generation, and dimensions of neighborhood social context. The results imply that generic interventions to improve neighborhood conditions and support families may reduce racial gaps in violence.

(Am J Public Health. 2005;95:224–232. doi: 10.2105/AJPH.2004.037705)

The public health of the United States has long been compromised by inequality in the burden of personal violence. Blacks are 6 times more likely than Whites to die by homicide,[1] a crime that is overwhelmingly intraracial in nature.[2] Homicide is the leading cause of death among young Blacks,[3] and both police records and self-reported surveys show disproportionate involvement in serious violence among Blacks.[4,5] Surprisingly, however, Latinos experience lower rates of violence overall than Blacks despite being generally poorer; Latino rates have been converging with those of Whites in recent years.[6]

These disparities remain a puzzle because scant empirical evidence bears directly on the explanation of differences in personal violence by race and ethnicity. Aggregate studies based on police statistics show that rates of violent crime are highest in disadvantaged communities that contain large concentrations of minority groups,[5] but disparities in official crime may reflect biases in the way criminal justice institutions treat different racial and ethnic groups rather than differences in actual offending.[7] More important, aggregate and even multilevel studies typically do not account for correlated family or individual constitutional differences that might explain racial and ethnic disparities in violence.[8,9]

By contrast, individual-level studies tend to focus on characteristics of the offender while neglecting racial and ethnic differences associated with neighborhood contexts.[4,10,11] Individual-level surveys of self-reported violence also underrepresent Latino Americans even though they are now the largest minority group in the United States.[12] Blacks residing outside inner-city poverty areas tend to be underrepresented as well, even though there is a thriving and growing middle-class Black population.[13]

Recognizing these limitations, 2 panels from the National Research Council and other major research groups called for new studies of racial and ethnic disparities in violent crime that integrate individual-level differences with a sample design that captures a variety of socioeconomic conditions and neighborhood contexts.[5,14,15] We accomplish this objective in the Project on Human Development in Chicago Neighborhoods (PHDCN), a multilevel longitudinal cohort study that was conducted between 1995 and 2002. The study drew samples that capture the 3 major racial/ethnic groups in American society today—Whites, Blacks, and Latinos—and that vary across a diverse set of environments, from highly segregated to very integrated neighborhoods. The

analysis in this article focuses on violent offending among participants aged 8 to 25 years. We also conducted an independent survey of the respondents' neighborhoods, which, when supplemented with data from the US Census Bureau and the Chicago Police Department, provide a broad assessment of neighborhood characteristics to complement individual and family predictors.

Competing Explanations

Our theoretical framework does not view "race" or "ethnicity" as holding distinct scientific credibility as causes of violence.[16] Rather, we argue they are markers for a constellation of external and malleable social contexts that are differentially allocated by racial/ethnic status in American society. We hypothesize that segregation by these social contexts in turn differentially exposes members of racial/ethnic minority groups to key violence-inducing or violence-protecting conditions.[17] We adjudicate empirically among 3 major contextual perspectives that we derive from a synthesis of prior research.

First, the higher rate of violence among Blacks is often attributed to a matriarchal pattern of family structure; specifically, the prevalence of single-parent, female-headed families in the Black community.[18,19] Some have augmented this view by arguing that female-headed families are a response to structural conditions of poverty, especially the reduced pool of employed Black men that could adequately support a family.[20]

A second view focuses on racial differences in family socioeconomic context. Many social scientists have posited that socioeconomic inequality—not family structure—is the root cause of violence.[21,22] Black female-headed families are spuriously linked to violence, by this logic, because of their lack of financial resources relative to 2-parent families.

A third perspective is that racial and ethnic minority groups in the United States are differentially exposed to salient neighborhood conditions, such as the geographic concentration of poverty and reduced informal community controls, that cannot be explained by personal or family circumstances.[17] Prior research indicates that Blacks and, to a lesser extent, Latinos, are highly segregated residentially.[23] Although never tested directly, the implication is that neighborhood segregation may explain individual racial/ethnic gaps in violence.[24]

A prominent alternative to our approach highlights "constitutional" differences between individuals in impulsivity and intelligence (measured as IQ).[25–28] Although low IQ and impulsivity may be sturdy predictors of violence,[5,26] their potential to explain racial/ethnic disparities has rarely, if ever, been examined.[5,6] We thus assess the constitutional hypothesis that racial/ethnic differences in measured intelligence and impulsivity, more than economic, family, or neighborhood social context, stand as explanations of the observed racial/ethnic gaps in violence.

Data and Measures

The PHDCN employed a multistage sampling procedure whereby neighborhoods, families, and individual children were studied simultaneously. In the first stage, all 825 Chicago census tracts were stratified by racial/ethnic composition (7 categories) and socioeconomic status (high, medium, and low), producing 21 strata. A total of 180 tracts were selected randomly within strata. At the second stage, over 35 000 dwelling units were enumerated (or "listed") in person by our research team within each area. In most instances, all dwelling units were listed, but in particularly large tracts, the probability of a census block being listed was proportional to its size. Within each listed block, replicates (random groups of equal size) were created for all listings, and within them dwelling units were selected systematically (every nth unit) after an initial random draw. All households were then enumerated within selected dwelling units and age-eligible participants were selected with certainty. To be age eligible, a household member must have had an age within 12 months of 1 of 7 ages: 0 (or prenatal), 3, 6, 9, 12, 15, and 18 years. Respondents and caregivers were interviewed in person up to 3 times from 1995 to 2002 in intervals of about 2.5 years.

We studied the 2974 respondents from the 9-, 12-, 15-, and 18-year-old cohorts who completed the baseline interview ("wave 1" of the study). The initial response rate was 78%. Of the 2974 wave 1 participants, 85% were interviewed again at wave 2 and 77% were interviewed at wave 3. We found no evidence that the association between race/ethnicity and violence at the initial interview varied as a function of future attrition ($\chi^2 = 1.38$, P > .500). All analyses in this article nonetheless control for attrition.

Under a guarantee of confidentiality, all subjects were asked at each interview whether, during the last year, they had (a) hit someone outside of the house; (b) thrown objects such as rocks or bottles at people; (c) carried a hidden weapon; (d) maliciously set fire to a building, property, or car; (e) snatched a purse or picked a pocket; (f) attacked someone with a weapon; (g) used a weapon to rob someone; or (h) been in a gang fight. Self-reported measures of violence have the major advantage of being independent of the biases of the criminal justice system (e.g., arrests). In addition, a body of research supports the reliability and validity across racial groups of the self-reported violence items included in our survey questionnaire.[29,30]

Measures of subjects' race/ethnicity come from the primary caregiver interview for age cohorts 9, 12, and 15 years and from the subject interview for cohort 18 years. We first identified subjects as Latino or non-Latino and then categorized Latinos by country of ancestry as Mexican, Puerto Rican, or other Latino. We collapsed Puerto Ricans and other Latinos into a single category because of their relatively small sample sizes and similarity regarding sociodemographic characteristics and levels of violence. For non-Latinos, we then categorized race as being either White, Black, or other. If the parents were of different races, the subject's race was coded as the race of the mother. During the wave 2 interviews, all subjects were asked to self-identify their racial and ethnic backgrounds. Approximately 90% of subjects whom we identified as White, Black, or Latino at wave 1 self-reported the same classification at wave 2, validating our measurement scheme. In most cases where there was a discrepancy, the subjects self-identify as being of mixed race/ethnicity at wave 2.

To assess racial/ethnic disparities, we selected a set of risk factors that tap the core concepts derived from our theoretical framework and that are exogenous to violent behavior, meaning that they are determined prior to the onset of violence and are unlikely to be affected by violent offending. We thus proceed conservatively and do not control for mediating factors that might be outgrowths of participation in crime, such as drug use, affiliating with delinquent peers, or being a gang member. Research using such factors to explain racial disparities in violence begs the question of causal direction and confounds the "explainer" with the outcome.

The following sociodemographic and family background factors (listed in Table 1) were measured at the initial interview: age, sex, socioeconomic status (standardized scale of parent's income, education, and occupational status), length of residence at address, immigrant generational status (first, second, third, or higher), whether adult extended kin live in household, number of children in household, 4 indicators of family structure, and the marital status of parent(s).

To capture individual differences in IQ, we measured verbal/reading ability from the average score of 9- to 15-year-olds on the widely used Wechsler Intelligence Scale for Children vocabulary test and the Wide Range Achievement Test for reading.[31] The 18-year-old cohort received the Wechsler Adult Intelligence Scale vocabulary test (or its Spanish version).

We combined the vocabulary and reading scores using principal factor estimation and regression scoring. We then normalized the resulting scale to a mean of 100 and a standard deviation of 15. We constructed a standardized scale of impulsivity (or hyperactivity) from the Achenbach Child-Behavior CheckList; these are based on reports of the primary caregiver for cohorts 9 through 15 years and self-reports for cohort 18 years.[32] Drawing on a large body of research linking impulsivity to crime,[26,28] we averaged the following standardized items: impulsive,

acts without thinking; trouble concentrating or paying attention; cannot get mind off certain thoughts; cannot sit still, restless, hyperactive; confused or seems to be in a fog; demands a lot of attention; gets hurt a lot/accident-prone; nervous, high-strung, or tense; nervous movements or twitching; repeats certain acts over and over. These items produce a scale with a reliability of $\alpha = .78$.

Using 1990 census data and drawing on past work,[10] we constructed 3 neighborhood characteristics for each census tract: concentrated disadvantage, residential stability, and percentage professional/managerial workers (Table 1). We also examined neighborhood differences in racial/ethnic composition and immigrant concentration as measured in 1995 by aggregating the cohort samples; 1990 census data yielded similar results because of stability over time at the neighborhood level. To measure neighborhood social organization, we incorporated a separate PHDCN community survey that yielded a representative probability sample of 8782 Chicago residents in 1995, permitting construction of reliable between-neighborhood measures based on aggregating individual responses within the 180 neighborhoods that contain cohort respondents. Building on prior work, we examined validated measures of collective efficacy,[33] organizational services, social ties,[34] and moral/legal cynicism[35] (Table 1). We also examined the neighborhood's prior violent crime rate, which we constructed from incident-based records of the Chicago Police Department on murder, robbery, rape, and aggravated assault in 1993.

Statistical Methods

We formulated a multilevel logistic regression model that represents the odds that a given person living in a given neighborhood will commit a specific violent offense. This approach enabled us to combine information on all 58700 item responses to the violence questions generated by the 2925 participants living in 180 Chicago neighborhoods who were interviewed in at least 1 of 3 waves of data collection and who responded to at least 1 violence item. Our method takes into account (a) the fact that

TABLE 1 Descriptive Statistics, by Race/Ethnicity: Project on Human Development in Chicago Neighborhoods (PHDCN) Waves 1 Through 3, Age Cohorts 9 Through 18

	White (n = 445), Mean (SD)	Black (n = 1067), Mean (SD)	Mexican American (n = 976), Mean (SD)
Individual/family level			
Male, %	52 (50)	48 (50)	50 (50)
Age at wave 1, y	13.66 (3.41)	13.40 (3.33)	12.80 (3.31)
Immigrant generation, %			
First	14 (35)	2 (14)	28 (45)
Second	11 (32)	2 (15)	56 (50)
Third or higher (reference category)	75 (43)	96 (20)	16 (37)
Family structure, %			
2 parents, both biological	65 (48)	23 (42)	71 (45)
2 parents, one/both nonbiological	13 (34)	24 (43)	12 (33)
1 parent, nonbiological	2 (13)	12 (32)	2 (15)
1 parent, biological (reference category)	21 (41)	42 (49)	15 (36)
Married parents, %	66 (47)	29 (45)	70 (46)
Adult extended family, %	13 (33)	27 (45)	16 (37)
No. of children	2.75 (1.50)	3.33 (1.94)	3.78 (1.69)
Socioeconomic status	0.90 (1.36)	0.22 (1.23)	−0.59 (1.14)
Years living at same address	7.13 (5.40)	5.59 (4.92)	5.02 (4.23)
Verbal/reading ability	109.08 (15.39)	98.55 (14.09)	97.33 (14.63)
Impulsivity/hyperactivity	−0.04 (0.58)	0.06 (0.60)	−0.06 (0.55)

(continued)

TABLE 1 Continued

	White (n = 445), Mean (SD)	Black (n = 1067), Mean (SD)	Mexican American (n = 976), Mean (SD)
Neighborhood level			
Black, %	7.54 (16.69)	78.11 (25.43)	12.96 (21.01)
Mexican American, %	24.65 (17.97)	11.86 (16.45)	58.37 (25.84)
First-generation immigrant, %	15.17 (13.38)	5.81 (9.37)	23.23 (14.30)
Professional/managerial worker, %	25.80 (11.32)	19.87 (8.63)	15.55 (7.97)
Concentrated disadvantage[a]	−0.78 (0.51)	0.42 (0.95)	−0.27 (0.53)
Residential stability[b]	0.25 (0.98)	0.61 (1.20)	−0.06 (0.69)
Moral/legal cynicism[c]	−0.26 (0.69)	0.31 (0.79)	0.26 (0.73)
Collective efficacy[d]	0.61 (0.99)	−0.14 (0.80)	−0.24 (0.80)
Friend/kin ties[e]	0.23 (0.81)	−0.11 (0.69)	−0.01 (0.80)
Organizations/youth services[f]	0.00 (0.66)	0.00 (0.81)	−0.30 (0.68)
Natural log of violent crime rate, 1993[g]	7.93 (0.65)	8.91 (0.44)	8.41 (0.48)

[a] Standardized average of following variables from 1990 census: percentage of poor families, percentage of single-parent families, percentage of families on welfare, unemployment rate.

[b] Standardized average of following variables from 1990 census: percentage of residents who have lived in the same location for 5 years or more, percentage of homes that are owner occupied.

[c] Scale from PHDCN Community Survey based on agreement (on 5-point scale) with following items: laws were made to be broken; it's OK to do anything you want as long as you don't hurt anyone; to make money, there are no right or wrong ways anymore, only easy ways and hard ways; fighting between friends or within families is nobody else's business; nowadays a person has to live pretty much for today and let tomorrow take care of itself.

[d] Combination of following 2 scales from PHDCN Community Survey. Social control—assessment of how likely it is (on 5-point scale) that neighbors could be counted on to "do something" if they encountered the following situations: a group of neighborhood children skipping school; children spray-painting graffiti; a child showing disrespect to an adult; a fight in which someone was being beaten or threatened; the city was going to close down local fire station. Social cohesion—level of agreement (on 5-point scale) with following items: neighborhood is close-knit; neighbors trust each other; neighbors get along with each other; neighbors share same values; people are willing to help their neighbors.

[e] Average number of friends and relatives that respondents to PHDCN Community Survey reported to be living in the neighborhood, based on following values: 0 = none; 1 = 1 or 2; 2 = 3 to 5; 3 = 6 to 9; 4 = 10 or more.

[f] Combination of following 2 scales from PHDCN Community Survey. Neighborhood organizations—inventory of whether the following are present in respondent's neighborhood: block group/tenant association, crime prevention program/neighborhood watch, family health service, alcohol/drug treatment program, family planning clinic, mental health center, park/playground, community newspaper/newsletter. Youth services—inventory of whether following are present in respondent's neighborhood: youth center, recreational programs, after-school programs mentoring/counseling services, mental health services, crisis intervention.

[g] Incident-based reports of murder, rape, robbery, and aggravated assault from 1993 Chicago Police Department data; population data (per 100 000) from 1990 census.

some violent offenses are rarer than others, (b) changes over time within subjects in propensity to violence, and (c) the dependence of violence on individual, family, and neighborhood characteristics. Specifically, let t denote the wave of data collection ($t = 1, 2, 3$) and let i denote the specific violent offense of interest, where $i = 0, 1, 2, \ldots 7$, with item 0 denoted as the "reference item." Define $Y_{tijk} = 1$ if participant j living in neighborhood k reported committing offense i at wave t, while $Y_{tijk} = 0$ if participant did not. We are interested in the probability of such an offense, Prob ($Y_{tijk} = 1$) = ϕ_{tijk} Rather than directly modeling the probability, we model $\eta_{tijk} = \log[\phi_{tijk}/(1 - \phi_{tijk})]$, the natural logarithm of the odds ratio.

The model begins with a personal trajectory of violent behavior:

$$\eta_{tijk} = \pi_{0jk} + \pi_{1jk}d_{tjk} + \pi_{2jk}d_{tjk}^2 + \alpha_i \quad \text{(1)}$$

where d_{tjk} is the age of person jk at wave t, centered about that person's mean age over the 3 waves of data collection. According to equation 1, the log-odds that a participant will commit a given offense changes as a quadratic function of age, where α_i is a fixed effect for each item i. Thus, coefficients (π_{0jk}, π_{1jk}, π_{2jk}) are person-specific parameters of change; knowing the value of these 3 coefficients for a given person would tell us the trajectory of that person's log-odds of committing the reference offense over the course of study. Also, our model allows that when a subject has missing data due either to sample attrition or survey nonresponse, all available information on that subject is still used in the analysis.

In this article, we focus mainly on a person's log-odds of committing the reference violent offense at that person's mean age during the study. For simplicity, we refer to this quantity, π_{0jk}, as person jk's overall "propensity to violence." We model this propensity with the form

$$\pi_{0jk} = \mu + X_{jk}\beta + W_k\gamma \quad \text{(2)}$$

where X_{jk} is a vector of person and family background characteristics of participant j in neighborhood k and W_k is a vector of neighborhood

characteristics. The components of β characterize partial associations between person or family characteristics and the propensity to offend, while the components of γ characterize partial associations between neighborhood characteristics and the propensity to offend; μ is a model intercept. We also test a similar model for π_{1jk}, which captures within-person change in the log-odds of violent offending:

$$\pi_{1jk} = \mu_1 + X_{jk}\beta_1 + W_k\gamma_1 \quad \text{(3)}$$

In this model, the coefficients β_1 and γ_1 characterize the partial association between covariates and the rate of change in propensity to violence.

All models were estimated simultaneously by means of generalized estimating equations with robust standard errors, allowing for underdispersion of level-1 variance and taking into account the dependence between observations that arises from the clustering of item responses within persons and persons within neighborhoods.[36] We first estimated a 3-level random effects model and then used the results to compute a working covariance structure for Y_{tijk}.[37] Estimates and standard errors of the coefficients take this covariance structure into account.

A key assumption of the model is that the association between predictors and the log-odds of offending is invariant across items apart from the item fixed effects, α_i, in equation 1. We tested this assumption and found it to be supported,[38] consistent with past research showing that violent offenses tend to cluster together and share similar correlates.[5,8,28] We also verified that the explained reductions in racial/ethnic gaps were replicated across individual items. Other key assumptions are identical to those in standard logistic regression; namely, that the logarithm of the odds ratio is linearly associated with covariates, and that the effects of covariates are not biased by omitted variables. In results not shown here, we assessed sensitivity to the linearity assumption by testing interactions and quadratic effects of covariates; we assessed sensitivity to omitted variable bias by comparing results across a series of models.

Our analysis proceeds as follows. First, we describe the differential exposure to individual, family, and neighborhood risk factors as a function of race/ethnicity. Second, we estimate racial/ethnic disparities in the propensity to violent behavior and then consider how much these disparities are explained by immigrant status, family background, constitutional differences, and neighborhood racial/ethnic composition. Third, we investigate the mechanisms that may account for the association between neighborhood racial segregation and violence. Fourth, we consider correlates of change in the propensity to violence over the course of study.

Results

Table 1 presents summary statistics for the 3 major racial/ethnic groups in our study: Whites, Blacks, and Mexican Americans. Immigrant status varies as expected: Mexican Americans are comparatively more likely to be first- or second-generation immigrants, while Blacks are least likely to be immigrants. Family structure shows an expected pattern as well: Mexican American adolescents are likely to live with 2 biological parents and their parents are likely to be married, whereas Black adolescents are much more likely to live with a single, unmarried parent. Family socioeconomic status is highest among Whites and lowest among Mexican Americans in our sample. Whites also have longer residential tenure, on average, than do Blacks or Mexican Americans. In terms of individual differences, Whites score higher on verbal/reading ability tests than Blacks or Mexican Americans. Whites and Blacks are not statistically distinguishable in terms of impulsivity, but Blacks display higher impulsivity, on average, than Mexican Americans.

Racial/ethnic differences in neighborhood characteristics are pronounced. For example, a typical Black in Chicago lives in a neighborhood that is 78% Black, whereas Whites and Mexican Americans live in neighborhoods that are more mixed but that are still predominantly (over 85%) non-Black. Blacks are also more likely than Whites or Mexican Americans to live in neighborhoods characterized by concentrated disadvantage, high legal/moral cynicism, and low collective efficacy.

Explaining Disparities in Violence

Although 3431 violent offenses were reported, personal violence is still relatively rare overall, with the prevalence of robbery (0.3%), purse snatching (0.3%), arson (0.4%), attacking with a weapon (2.3%), and gang fighting (3.9%) all less than 5% averaged across the 3 waves of data collection. Even the most common item, hitting someone (18.7%), is reported by fewer than 20% of subjects. Carrying a hidden weapon (7.6%) and throwing objects at another person (8.2%) are in the middle. These prevalence estimates comport with national norms.[39]

Table 2 presents coefficient estimates from equation 2 for individual- and neighborhood-level predictors. Model 1 estimates racial/ethnic disparities in violence, controlling only for age and sex, providing a baseline of comparison to subsequent models that add other explanatory variables. Exponentiating the log-odds coefficient, we see that Blacks' odds of engaging in violence are $\exp(0.614) = 1.85$ those of Whites, on average (95% confidence interval [CI] for relative odds = 1.70, 2.01). Puerto Ricans' odds are 1.26 those of Whites (95% CI = 1.11, 1.42), and the odds of violence for Mexican Americans are 0.90 those of Whites (95% CI = 0.83, 0.98). The results also indicate that violence is 1.64 times higher among males than females (95% CI = 1.55, 1.74) and that violence is related to age in a curvilinear fashion.

To further clarify the relationship between age, race/ethnicity, and crime, we used the coefficients from model 1 to produce age-crime curves of violent offending from ages 8 to 25 for males of each race and ethnic group, graphically displayed in Figure 1. The curves show that the probability of violence accelerates in early adolescence for all groups, reaching a peak between the ages of 17 and 18 and then declining precipitously thereafter. The height of the curves is determined by the frequency of the reference item (hitting someone you do not know with intent to harm them), but the shape of the curves is nonetheless identical across all violence items and racial/ethnic groups because the model assumes that the covariates are related to all types of violence in the same way. Supporting this assumption, the

TABLE 2 Social Anatomy of Racial/Ethnic Disparities in Violence: Project on Human Development in Chicago Neighborhoods Waves 1–3, Age Cohorts 9–18[a]

	Model 1, Coefficient (SE)	Model 2, Coefficient (SE)	Model 3, Coefficient (SE)	Model 4, Coefficient (SE)	Model 5, Coefficient (SE)
Intercept	−1.178 (0.036)**	−1.022 (0.360)**	−1.033 (0.356)**	−1.020 (0.361)**	−1.023 (0.043)**
Race/ethnicity					
Black	0.614 (0.043)**	0.528 (0.044)**	0.401 (0.046)**	0.368 (0.047)**	0.247 (0.087)**
Mexican American	−0.101 (0.042)*	0.123 (0.052)*	0.066 (0.056)	0.065 (0.055)	0.034 (0.058)
Puerto Rican/other Latino	0.229 (0.063)**	0.228 (0.124)	0.116 (0.117)	0.100 (0.113)	0.074 (0.115)
Other race	0.190 (0.095)*	0.287 (0.093)**	0.236 (0.088)**	0.210 (0.089)*	0.139 (0.105)
Gender/age					
Male	0.495 (0.030)**	0.501 (0.030)**	0.520 (0.029)**	0.502 (0.029)**	0.507 (0.032)**
Linear age[b]	0.060 (0.004)**	0.065 (0.004)**	0.069 (0.004)**	0.059 (0.005)**	0.060 (0.005)**
Quadratic age[c]	−0.020 (0.002)**	−0.020 (0.002)**	−0.020 (0.001)**	−0.022 (0.001)**	−0.022 (0.001)**
Immigrant status					
1st-generation immigrant		−0.636 (0.052)**	−0.644 (0.056)**	−0.588 (0.056)**	−0.585 (0.057)**
Puerto Rican/other Latino[d]		0.588 (0.189)**	0.539 (0.180)**	0.449 (0.170)**	0.455 (0.145)**
2nd-generation immigrant		−0.266 (0.049)**	−0.234 (0.049)**	−0.248 (0.049)**	−0.242 (0.053)**
Puerto Rican/other Latino[e]		0.129 (0.144)	0.111 (0.138)	0.101 (0.135)	0.104 (0.116)
Family structure					
2 parents, both biological			−0.055 (0.056)	−0.029 (0.056)	−0.030 (0.057)
2 parents, 1/both not biological			0.020 (0.048)	0.023 (0.047)	0.021 (0.049)
1 parent, not biological			−0.032 (0.081)	−0.045 (0.082)	−0.050 (0.078)
Married parents			−0.215 (0.050)**	−0.203 (0.050)**	−0.204 (0.049)**
Adult extended family			0.020 (0.037)	0.013 (0.037)	0.008 (0.032)
No. of children			0.002 (0.009)	0.001 (0.009)	−0.001 (0.009)

(continued)

TABLE 2 Continued

	Model 1, Coefficient (SE)	Model 2, Coefficient (SE)	Model 3, Coefficient (SE)	Model 4, Coefficient (SE)	Model 5, Coefficient (SE)
SES/residential context					
SES			−0.019 (0.014)	−0.014 (0.014)	−0.014 (0.015)
Years at same address			−0.015 (0.003)**	−0.014 (0.003)**	−0.016 (0.004)**
Individual differences					
Verbal/reading ability				−0.004 (0.001)**	−0.004 (0.002)**
1st-generation immigrant[f]				0.017 (0.003)**	0.016 (0.003)**
2nd-generation immigrant[g]				0.009 (0.002)**	0.009 (0.002)**
Impulsivity/hyperactivity				0.280 (0.025)**	0.281 (0.025)**
Neighborhood characteristics					
% African American[h]					0.224 (0.106)*
% Mexican American[h]					0.093 (0.108)
% Puerto Rican/other Latino[h]					0.026 (0.174)
% other race[h]					0.375 (0.255)

Note: SES = socioeconomic status. Coefficients are derived from equation 2 in "Statistical Methods" section.

[a] n = 58 700 item responses (level 1), 2925 persons (level 2), 180 census tracts (level 3).

[b] Linear age is defined as the mean age of each subject averaged over 3 waves of data collection.

[c] Quadratic age is defined as the square of linear age.

[d] Interaction between first-generation immigrant and Puerto Rican/other Latino.

[e] Interaction between second-generation immigrant and Puerto Rican/other Latino.

[f] Interaction between verbal/reading ability and first-generation immigrant.

[g] Interaction between verbal/reading ability and second-generation immigrant.

[h] Coefficients and standard errors have been multiplied by 100.

* $P < .05$; ** $P < .01$.

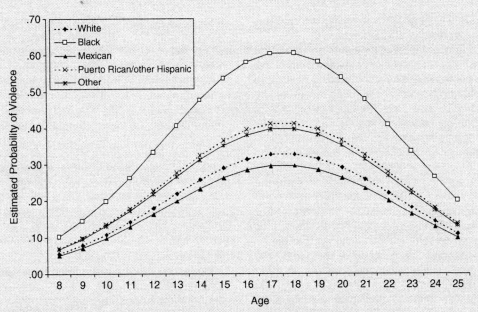

FIGURE 1   Male age-violence curves, by race/ethnicity: Project on Human Development in Chicago Neighborhoods Waves 1–3, Age Cohorts 9–18.

age–violence curve maintains approximately the same shape when it is modeled separately for each item in the violence scale and for each racial/ethnic group.

Model 2 in Table 2 adds controls for immigrant generation, revealing that the level of violence is comparatively lower for recent immigrants. First-generation immigrants' odds of violence are almost half those of third-generation immigrants (95% CI = 0.48, 0.58), and second-generation immigrants' odds are approximately three quarters those of third-generation immigrants (95% CI = 0.70, 0.85). Immigrant status is protective for all racial/ethnic groups except for Puerto Ricans/other Latinos, as indicated by the positive interaction coefficients. Controlling for immigrant generation reduces the logistic regression coefficient that describes the gap between Blacks and Whites by 14%, implying that one reason Whites have lower levels of violence than Blacks is that Whites are more likely to be recent immigrants. The odds ratio describing that gap drops from 1.85 to 1.70 (95% CI = 1.56, 1.85). Adjusting for immigrant status also changes the direction of the gap between Whites and Mexican Americans, meaning that when the comparison is restricted to third-generation immigrants (the reference category), the risk of engaging in violence is slightly higher for Mexican Americans than for Whites.

Model 3 introduces controls for family structure, socioeconomic status, and length of residence. Adding these controls reduces the logistic regression coefficient that describes the gap between Blacks and Whites by an additional 24%. The odds ratio describing that gap is now reduced from 1.70 to 1.49 (95% CI = 1.36, 1.64). Adding these controls also reduces the contrast between Mexican Americans and Whites to nonsignificance. Contrary to a major line of sociological theory,[22] however, family socioeconomic status is not directly associated with violence. What matters instead are years of residence in the neighborhood and having married parents, both of which are protective. For participants with married parents, the odds of violent offending are 0.81 times those of participants with unmarried parents (95% CI = 0.73, 0.89). Thus, among all of the dimensions of family structure, marital status alone is predictive of violence.

Model 4 assesses the explanatory power of constitutional differences between individuals, as operationalized by verbal/reading ability and impulsivity/hyperactivity. In our data, high verbal/reading ability is protective, but not for first- or second-generation immigrants, as indicated by the significant interaction terms. High impulsivity increases the risk of violence, but there are no significant interactions by race/ethnicity. Despite their significant associations with violence, the main finding is that verbal/reading ability and impulsivity explain a relatively small fraction of the gap between Blacks and Whites: the logistic regression coefficient describing the gap diminishes by only 8% in model 4 compared with model 3, while the corresponding odds ratio decreases from 1.49 to 1.44 (95% CI = 1.32, 1.59). Also, verbal/reading ability and impulsivity have no bearing on the gap between Mexican Americans and Whites, which remains virtually unchanged. Therefore, constitutional factors are significant predictors of violence but weak explainers of racial/ethnic *disparities* in violence.

Model 5 introduces neighborhood racial/ethnic composition measured from the cohort sample, allowing us to disentangle the person-level (i.e., within-neighborhood) and compositional (i.e., between-neighborhood) components of the association between race/ethnicity and violence.[40] The logistic regression coefficient describing the gap in violence between Blacks and Whites is reduced by an additional 33%. The odds ratio describing the gap decreases from 1.45 to 1.28 (95% CI = 1.08, 1.52), a 38% reduction. Note that the maximum potential reduction, or 100%, would be from 1.45 to 1.00.

Neighborhood Mechanisms

The finding that neighborhoods explain a large percentage of individual-level disparities raises a new question: What are the mechanisms that connect neighborhood characteristics to violence? To answer this question, we expanded our contextual analysis to include neighborhood factors correlated with race and ethnic composition. In Table 3, we do not present the individual-level

coefficients (β in equation 2), which are essentially identical to those shown in Table 2, and focus instead on the neighborhood-level coefficients (γ in equation 2).

We begin with a neighborhood-level model that includes percentage Black, the significant racial composition predictor in Table 2, and other neighborhood factors drawn from the Census and the PHDCN Community Survey. Model 1 in Table 3 shows that the direct effect of percentage Black is rendered nonsignificant after the introduction of immigrant concentration, percentage professional/managerial, concentrated disadvantage, and residential stability. For individuals living in neighborhoods that are 40% immigrant, the relative odds of violence are about four fifths lower (odds ratio [OR] = 0.81; 95% CI = 0.72, 0.91) than for otherwise similar individuals living in neighborhoods with no immigrants—a contrast that corresponds roughly to the 10th vs the 90th percentile. Although concentrated disadvantage is not a significant predictor, the odds of violence are about three fourths lower (OR = 0.77; 95% CI = 0.65, 0.92) in neighborhoods with a 40% higher concentration of workers in professional occupations.

In model 2, we retain the 2 significant predictors from model 1 and add measures of neighborhood social process from the community survey. Immigrant concentration and percentage professional/managerial remain significant, and a third factor, moral/legal cynicism, is significantly linked with higher odds of violence (OR = 1.05; 95% CI = 1.01, 1.09). None of the other neighborhood processes are significantly associated with levels of violence.

Robustness

It is possible that the neighborhood effects we observe in model 2 are spurious if high levels of prior neighborhood violence induced moral/legal cynicism among residents or led to demographic changes that reduced the concentration of managerial/professional workers and possibly even immigrants.[41] To assess this possibility, we introduce a control in model 3 for the logged rate of violent crime (per 100 000) in the neighborhood as of 1993. Although the odds of engaging

TABLE 3   Neighborhood Predictors of Violence: Project on Human Development in Chicago Neighborhoods Waves 1–3, Age Cohorts 9–18[a,b]

	Model 1, Coefficient (SE)	Model 2, Coefficient (SE)	Model 3, Coefficient (SE)
Intercept	−1.050 (0.043)**	−1.056 (0.044)**	−1.049 (0.043)**
% Black[c]	0.031 (0.095)		
% 1st-generation immigrant[c]	−0.524 (0.154)**	−0.563 (0.125)**	−0.532 (0.108)**
% professional/managerial occupation[c]	−0.652 (0.220)**	−0.659 (0.196)**	−0.511 (0.178)**
Concentrated disadvantage	0.027 (0.028)		
Residential stability	−0.009 (0.019)		
Moral/legal cynicism		0.045 (0.019)*	0.040 (0.019)*
Collective efficacy		0.002 (0.022)	
Friend/kin ties		−0.018 (0.022)	
Organizations/youth services		0.006 (0.021)	
Natural log violent crime rate, 1993			0.085 (0.030)**

Note: Coefficients are derived from equation 2 in "Statistical Methods" section.
[a] All models control for individual and family characteristics included in Table 2, model 5.
[b] n = 58 700 item responses (level 1), 2925 persons (level 2), 180 census tracts (level 3).
[c] Coefficients and standard errors have been multiplied by 100.
* $P < .05$; ** $P < .01$.

in violent behavior are significantly higher in neighborhoods with higher prior rates of violence (OR = 1.09; 95% CI = 1.03, 1.16), neighborhood cynicism maintains its significant independent association with cohort violence, as do immigrant concentration and percentage professional/managerial. All of the contextual effects are therefore robust to the conservative test of adding the association between the violent behavior of the subject and prior neighborhood violence. In model 3, the individual-level coefficient for Black respondents drops to 0.22 (OR = 1.25; 95% CI = 1.11, 1.40), a 64% reduction from the original coefficient of 0.614 in model 1 of Table 2.

To further probe the sensitivity of results to selection bias, we reestimated models with controls for individual-level measures of paternal and maternal history of criminality, substance abuse, and history of depression. Both maternal depression and father's criminality significantly predicted a subject's violence when added to

model 3 (*t* ratios = 3.66 and 3.86, respectively). Although potentially caused by neighborhood characteristics, neither maternal depression nor father's criminality materially altered the magnitude, direction, or statistical significance of the neighborhood-level findings in Table 3.

Change Over Time

As a final step in our analysis, we examined person- and neighborhood-level predictors of subject-specific change in violence over time, as specified in equation 3. The question is whether Blacks, Whites, and Latinos differ in their developmental profiles of violence with respect to age. The answer from our data is that there are no significant unadjusted differences between Blacks and Whites in changes over time in violence. Moreover, once the full set of neighborhood covariates in Table 3 was introduced, there were no remaining differences between Latinos and Whites. The results showed that average linear change (π_{1jk}) was negative, meaning that most subjects were reducing their involvement in violent behavior (overall, a 3% reduction with each year). This finding is consistent with the secular decreases in violence that Chicago and other large cities experienced during the late 1990s.[42]

Discussion

The gap between Whites and Blacks in levels of violence has animated a prolonged and controversial debate in public health and the social sciences. Our study reveals that over 60% of this gap is explained by immigration status, marriage, length of residence, verbal/reading ability, impulsivity, and neighborhood context. If we focus on odds ratios rather than raw coefficients, 70% of the gap is explained. Of all factors, neighborhood context was the most important source of the gap reduction and constitutional differences the least important.

We acknowledge the harsh and often justified criticism that tests of intelligence have endured, but we would emphasize 2 facts from our findings. First, measured verbal/reading ability, along with impulsivity/hyperactivity, predicted violence, in keeping with a long line of prior research.[25-28] Second, however, neither factor accounted for much in the way of racial or ethnic *disparities* in violence. Whatever the ultimate validity of the constitutional difference argument, the main conclusion is that its efficacy as an explainer of race and violence is weak.

Our findings are consistent with the hypothesis that Blacks are segregated by neighborhood and thus differentially exposed to key risk and protective factors, an essential ingredient to understanding the Black-White disparity in violence.[17] The race-related neighborhood features predicting violence are percentage professional/managerial workers, moral/legal cynicism, and the concentration of immigration. We found no systematic evidence that neighborhood- or individual-level predictors of violence interacted with race/ethnicity. The relationships we observed thus appeared to be generally robust across racial/ethnic groups. We also found no significant racial or ethnic disparities in trajectories of change in violence.

Similar to the arguments made by William Julius Wilson in *The Truly Disadvantaged*,[20] these results imply that generic interventions to improve neighborhood conditions may reduce the racial gap in violence. Policies such as housing vouchers to aid the poor in securing residence in middle-class neighborhoods[43] may achieve the most effective results in bringing down the long-standing racial disparities in violence. Policies to increase home ownership and hence stability of residence may also reduce disparities (see model 3, Table 2).

Family social conditions matter as well. Our data show that parents being married, but not family configuration per se, is a salient factor predicting both the lower probability of violence and a significant reduction in the Black-White gap in violence. The tendency in past debates on Black families has been either to pathologize female-headed households as a singular risk factor or to emphasize the presence of extended kin as a protective factor. Yet neither factor predicts violence in our data. Rather, being reared in married-parent households is the distinguishing factor for children, supporting recent work on the social influence of marriage[44,45] and calls for renewed attention to the labor-market contexts that support stable marriages among the poor.[46]

Although the original gap in violence between Whites and Latinos was smaller than that between Whites and Blacks, our analysis nonetheless explained the entire gap in violence between Whites and Latino ethnic groups. The lower rate of violence among Mexican Americans compared with Whites was explained by a combination of married parents, living in a neighborhood with a high concentration of immigrants, and individual immigrant status. The contextual effect of concentrated immigration was robust, holding up even after a host of factors, including the immigrant status of the person, were taken into account.

The limitations of our study raise issues for future research. Perhaps most important is the need to replicate the results in cities other than Chicago. The mechanisms explaining the apparent benefits to those living in areas of concentrated immigration need to be further addressed, and we look to future research to examine Black–White differences in rates of violence that remain unexplained. As with any nonexperimental research, it is also possible we left out key risk factors correlated with race or ethnicity. Still, to overturn our results any such factors would have to be correlated with neighborhood characteristics and uncorrelated with the dozen-plus individual and family background measures, an unlikely scenario. Even controlling for the criminality of parents did not diminish the effects of neighborhood characteristics. Finally, it is possible that family characteristics associated with violence, such as marital status, were themselves affected by neighborhood residence. If so, our analysis would mostly likely have underestimated the association between neighborhood conditions and violence.

We conclude that the large racial/ethnic disparities in violence found in American cities are not immutable. Indeed, they are largely social in nature and therefore amenable to change.

References

1. Fox JA, Zawitz MW. *Homicide Trends in the United States: 2000 Update*. Washington, DC: Bureau of Justice Statistics; 2003. Publication NCJ 197471.

2. Rennison C. *Violent Victimization and Race, 1993–98*. Washington, DC: Bureau of Justice Statistics; March 2001. Publication NCJ 176354.

3. Anderson RN. *Deaths: Leading Causes for 2000*. Hyattsville, Md: National Center for Health Statistics; 2002.

4. Hawkins DF, Laub JH, Lauritsen JL. Race, ethnicity and serious juvenile offending. In: Loeber R, Farrington DP, eds. *Serious and Violent Juvenile Offenders: Risk Factors and Successful Interventions*. Thousand Oaks, Calif: Sage Publications; 1998: 30–46.

5. Reiss AJ, Roth JA, eds. *Understanding and Preventing Violence*. Vol 1. Washington, DC: National Academy Press; 1993.

6. Morenoff, JD. Racial and ethnic disparities in crime and delinquency in the US. In: Tienda M, Rutter M, eds. *Ethnicity and Causal Mechanisms*. New York, NY: Cambridge University Press. In press.

7. Tonry M. *Malign Neglect: Race, Crime, and Punishment in America*. New York, NY: Oxford University Press; 1995.

8. Farrington DP, Loeber R, Stouthamer-Loeber M. How can the relationship between race and violence be explained? In: Hawkins DF, ed. *Violent Crime: Assessing Race and Ethnic Differences*. New York, NY: Cambridge University Press; 2003: 213–237.

9. McNulty T, Bellair P. Explaining racial and ethnic differences in serious adolescent violent behavior. *Criminology*. 2003;41:709–748.

10. Sampson RJ, Morenoff JD, Gannon-Rowley N. Assessing neighborhood effects: social processes and new directions in research. *Annu Rev Sociol*. 2002;28:443–478.

11. Peeples F, Loeber R. Do individual factors and neighborhood context explain ethnic differences in juvenile delinquency? *J Quant Criminol*. 1994; 10(2):141.

12. Miller S. *Hispanics Replace African-Americans as Largest US Minority Group*. Washington, DC: US Dept of State; 2003.

13. Farley R. *The New American Reality: Who We Are, How We Got Here, Where We Are Going*. New York, NY: Russell Sage Foundation; 1996.

14. McCord J, Widom CS, Crowell NA, eds. *Juvenile Crime, Juvenile Justice*. Washington, DC: National Academy Press; 2001.

15. Loeber R, Farrington DP, Kerr CA, Allen-Hagen B. *Serious and Violent Juvenile Offenders. US Department of Justice, Juvenile Justice Bulletin*. Washington, DC: Bureau of Justice Statistics; 1998.

16. Kaufman JS, Cooper RS. Commentary: use of racial/ethnic classification in etiologic research. *Am J Epidemiol*. 2001;154:291–298.

17. Sampson RJ, Wilson WJ. Toward a theory of race, crime, and urban inequality. In: Hagan J, Peterson R, eds. *Crime and Inequality*. Stanford, Calif: Stanford University Press; 1995:37–56:37–56.

18. Monahan T. Family status and the delinquent child. *Soc Forces*. 1957;35:250–258.

19. Moynihan DP. *The Negro Family: The Case for National Action*. Washington, DC: Office of Policy Planning and Research, US Dept of Labor; 1965.

20. Wilson WJ. *The Truly Disadvantaged: The Inner City, the Underclass, and Public Policy*. Chicago, Ill: University of Chicago Press; 1987.

21. Blau JR, Blau PM. The cost of inequality: metropolitan structure and violent crime. *Am Social Rev.* 1982;47:114–129.

22. Messner S, Rosenfeld R. *Crime and the American Dream.* Belmont, Calif: Wadsworth; 1997.

23. Massey DS, Denton. NA. *American Apartheid: Segregation and the Making of the Underclass.* Cambridge, Mass: Harvard University Press; 1993.

24. Krivo L, Peterson RD. The structural context of homicide: accounting for racial differences in process. *Am Sociol Rev.* 2000; 65:547–559.

25. Wilson JQ, Herrnstein RJ. *Crime and Human Nature.* New York, NY: Simon and Schuster; 1985.

26. Farrington DP. Individual differences and offending. In: Tonry M, ed. *The Handbook of Crime and Punishment.* New York, NY: Oxford University Press; 1998:241–268.

27. Wolfgang ME, Figlio RM, Sellin T. *Delinquency in a Birth Cohort.* Chicago, Ill: University of Chicago Press; 1972.

28. Gottfredson M, Hirschi T. *A General Theory of Crime.* Stanford, Calif: Stanford University Press; 1990.

29. Farrington DP, Loeber R, Stouthamer-Loeber M, Kammen WBV, Schmidt L. Self-reported delinquency and a combined delinquency seriousness scale based on boys, mothers, and teachers: concurrent and predictive validity for African-Americans and Caucasians. *Criminology.* 1996;34(4):493–518.

30. Thornberry TP, Krohn MD. Comparison of self-report and official data for measuring crime. In: Pepper JV, Petrie CV, eds. *Measurement Problems in Criminal Justice Research: Workshop Summary.* Washington, DC: National Academies Press; 2002:43–94.

31. Wilkinson G. *WRAT-3: Wide-Range Achievement Test, Administration Manual.* Wilmington, Del: Wide-Range Inc; 1993.

32. Achenbach TM. *The Young Adult Self-Report-Revised and the Young Adult Behavior Checklist.* Burlington, Vt: University of Vermont, Dept of Psychiatry; 1993.

33. Sampson RJ, Raudenbush SW, Earls F. Neighborhoods and violent crime: a multi-level study of collective efficacy. *Science.* 1997;277:918–924.

34. Morenoff JD, Sampson RJ, Raudenbush S. Neighborhood inequality, collective efficacy, and the spatial dynamics of urban violence. *Criminology.* 2001;39:517–560.

35. Sampson RJ, Bartusch D. Legal cynicism and (subcultural?) tolerance of deviance: the neighborhood context of racial differences. *Law Soc Rev.* 1998;32:777–804.

36. Raudenbush S, Bryk A, Cheong FW, Congdon R. *HLM 5: Hierarchical Linear and Nonlinear Modeling.* Chicago, Ill: Scientific Software Inc; 2000.

37. Zeger SL, Liang K-Y, Albert PS. Models for longitudinal data: a generalized estimating equation approach. *Biometrics.* 1988;44(4):1049–1060.

38. Raudenbush SW, Johnson C, Sampson RJ. A multivariate, multilevel Rasch model for self-reported criminal behavior. *Sociol Methodol.* 2003;33:169–211.

39. Brener N, Simon T, Krug E, Lowry R. Recent trends in violence-related behaviors among high school students in the United States. *JAMA.* 1999;281:440–446.

40. Raudenbush SW, Bryk AS. *Hierarchical Linear Models: Applications and Data Analysis Methods.* 2nd ed. Thousand Oaks, Calif: Sage Publications; 2002:139–141.

41. South SJ, Messner SF. Crime and demography: multiple linkages, reciprocal relations. *Annu Rev Sociol.* 2000;26:83–106.

42. Blumstein A, Wallman J. *The Crime Drop in America.* New York, NY: Cambridge; 2000.

43. Goering J, Feins J. *Choosing a Better Life? Evaluating the Moving to Opportunity Social Experiment.* Washington, DC: Urban Institute Press; 2003.

44. Kiecolt-Glaser JK, Newton TL. Marriage and health: his and hers. *Psychol Bull.* 2001;137:472–503.

45. Waite LJ. Does marriage matter? *Demography.* 1995;32:483–507.

46. Wilson WJ. *When Work Disappears.* New York, NY: Knopf; 1996.

Conclusion

Social disorganization theory takes a land usage approach to explaining criminal behavior. In particular, this theory suggests that racial minorities are highly concentrated in geographical areas that are riddled with social and economic inequality. This inequality develops mistrust among its residents, which forces them to rely on cultural similarities for survival.

While the reading presented has shown that social disorganization theory can explain the race–crime connection, it does have some limitations. One limitation is that it considers only a few versions of social disorganization. Most of the social disorganization literature represents studies confined to only a few locations. Rarely are national-level studies offered. Future research should take up this view and reexamine already existing findings using broader versions of social disorganization that go beyond a few locations. However, for now, social disorganization theory does have some support in understanding racial differences in crime.

Discussion Question

1. How do Sampson et al. extend social disorganization? What are the racial implications of this extension for crime rates and criminality?

Reference

Pratt, T. C., & Cullen, F. T. (2005). Assessing macro-level predictors and theories of crime: A meta-analysis. In M. Tonry (Ed.), *Crime and justice: A review of research* (pp. 373–450). Chicago: University of Chicago Press.

CHAPTER 4

Differential Association and Social Learning Theories

In criminology, there has traditionally existed a view that individuals learn to commit crime. Differential association and social learning theories are helpful in understanding this perspective. This chapter provides an overview of both theories, lists the specific propositions that these theories have to help us understand the connection between race and crime, and presents two articles that examine these views.

Sutherland (1947) differential association theory is the first criminological theory to explicitly focus on the learning process, and it later evolved into social learning theory. This theory suggests that individuals can learn criminal behavior just as an individual can learn any other type of behavior. In general, the theory posits that individuals learn criminal behavior as a result of their exposure to others' ideas and rationalizations that are favorable to violating the law.

According to the differential association theory, individuals are social blanks that need socialization. The socialization takes place in the context of family, friends, society, and education. This theory does not see criminals and noncriminals as being different in their ability to learn, but they are different in the groups with which they socialize and which provide the information that is learned. For instance, criminals socialize with individuals who do not follow the rules, whereas noncriminals socialize with individuals who do follow the rules. Thus, criminals and noncriminals will have differing values: Noncriminals will see the criminal law as a set of behavioral prohibitions, but criminals will see the violation of these laws as acceptable under certain conditions.

Differential association theory puts forth nine major points:

1. Criminal behavior is learned.
2. Criminal behavior is learned during interactions with other people.
3. The principal part of the learning of criminal behavior occurs within intimate groups.
4. When criminal behavior is learned, it includes learning techniques of committing the crime that are sometimes very complicated, sometimes very simple.
5. The specific direction of motives and drives is learned from definitions that are favorable or unfavorable toward the violation of the law.

6. A person becomes delinquent because of exposure to an excess of opinions favorable to violation of the law over opinions unfavorable to violation of the law.
7. Differential associations may vary in frequency, duration, priority, and intensity.
8. The process of learning criminal behavior involves all of the mechanisms that are involved in any other learning.
9. While criminal behavior is an expression of certain general needs and values, it is not explained by those general needs and values alone, since noncriminal behavior is an expression of the same needs and values.

In short, differential association theory suggests that individuals are more likely to become criminal or delinquent when they gain knowledge of the "hows" (i.e., techniques, drives, and rationalizations) and the "whys" (i.e., the definitions of criminal behavior). As Sutherland believed, the knowledge to perform criminal behavior did not usually exceed the knowledge of most things in daily life. However, the role of criminal definitions, definitions of crime, is crucial to differential association theory. The theory does not focus on the number of definitions, but on the weight that is given to the different definitions. That is, the weight of the definitions is the result of the quality of the association with others. Overall, differential association theory is not concerned so much with who the individual associates with but is more concerned about the quality of the relationship because it has implications for the transmission of definitions. The individual may learn the techniques and definitions of criminal behavior from anyone. Therefore, differential association can be seen as the differential exposure to individuals or groups that have varying views on the importance of the law.

Social learning theory has evolved from differential association theory, with connections to psychological theories. This theoretical basis builds on Sutherland's efforts by focusing on the role of reinforcements. Burgess and Akers (1966) presented the "differential association reinforcement theory," where the environment is the most important source of reinforcement. Akers (1985, 1998) has continued to develop social learning theory.

In a later development of the theory, Akers (1998) noted that "learning" is not restricted to the novelty of criminal behavior. However, social learning theory was developed in a way that would explain the motives of crime and the control of criminal behavior. Specifically, the individual would be propelled toward or repelled from criminal behavior due to these variables. Put another way, the same social learning process that brings out conforming behavior also serves to bring out criminal behavior, except that the direction of the learning, in the context of the law, is direction. However, the probability of criminal, delinquent, or deviant behavior is increased when an individual associates with others who harbor definitions favorable to the violation of the law, define the deviant behavior as proper to perform, and have received or anticipate some form of reward for performing the behavior.

Social learning theory has been developed around four key components:

1. **Differential association** refers to an individual's exposure to criminal behavior and criminal attitudes through association with others who are involved in crime (e.g., being exposed to others who download illegally from the Internet).
2. **Definitions** refer to an individual's positive or negative attitudes toward criminal behavior that are either rationalizations or neutralizations about the attributes of the criminal behavior (e.g., positive or negative attitudes toward digital piracy).
3. **Imitation** refers to an individual engaging in behavior that he or she has witnessed (e.g., committing digital piracy in a way that was shown by a friend).

4. Differential reinforcement refers to the rewards (i.e., social and nonsocial rewards) that come from performing a behavior (e.g., the ability to garner a friendship because of digital piracy).

At the individual level, social learning theory is very complex. These variables work together in a series of reciprocal effects. That is, learned definitions, imitation, and differential reinforcement work together back and forth over time to produce a criminal, delinquent, or deviant act. After the act has been performed, imitation becomes less important in this process. Once the behavior has been performed, reinforcement becomes dominant in determining if the behavior will be continued and at what frequency. As the individuals continue to perform the action, they define it as the proper way to behave. Therefore, when an individual is faced with an opportunity to engage in the behavior, he or she will do so based on their past experiences and reinforcement. Finally, it should be noted that differential association with family or friends typically precedes the individual's committing the act.

According to Akers (1998) and Warr (2002), differential association and social learning theories have empirical support in the literature. However, the majority of the studies have examined issues other than race–crime connections.

On one hand, differential association would assume that individuals across races are likely to be subject to strong influences toward crime. On the other hand, Akers (1998) modified social learning theory to take into account the structure of society. Akers's (1998) theory uses the differential location of individuals in the social structure to explain racial differences in crime. According to the theory, the primary socialization across the races is systematically different. Because of these differences, blacks are more likely to associate with deviant peers and whites are less likely to associate with deviant peers. Akers's version of social learning theory can be used to examine the differences in association, definitions, and behaviors among different races. Matsueda and Heimer have done such an examination.

Race, Ethnicity, and Deviance: A Study of Asian and Non-Asian Adolescents in America

Sung Joon Jang

This study shows that Asian American adolescents commit less deviance in the form of school misbehavior than white, black, Hispanic, or Native American adolescents. Social control and social learning theories receive support as the observed differences are explained primarily by race/ethnic differences in family backgrounds and school bonding. These variables' explanatory ability tends to be invariant across four regional groups of Asian Americans. This study applies OLS regression to self-reported data from a nationally representative sample.

Introduction

In the midst of the ongoing debate over the arbitrariness of race categorization and changes in the social conception and significance of race and ethnicity (Alba, 1990; Barringer et al., 1993; Lieberson and Waters, 1988; Peterson and Hagan, 1984; Wilson, 1980), sociological criminologists have regarded race/ethnicity as a major demographic correlate of deviance and crime. While early self-report studies argued that racial/ethnic differences in crime observed in official data primarily reflect bias in the justice system against racial/ethnic minorities (e.g., Chambliss and

Nagasawa, 1969), victimization studies, as well as later self-report studies, find that the system-bias factor cannot explain most of the observed differences (Hindelang et al., 1979; Sampson and Lauritsen, 1997). Cross-national studies generally concur with this finding (Tonry, 1997).

Previous researchers, however, have given most attention to white–black comparisons, whether they examine the race/ethnicity–crime bivariate relationship or its theoretical explanations, using official or unofficial data (e.g., Elliott et al., 1989; Hindelang et al., 1979; Matsueda and Heimer, 1987; Sampson and Lauritsen, 1997). Asian Americans have rarely been a focus of interest in comparative etiological research. Even in gang studies, they tend to receive less attention compared to other racial groups (Toy, 1992), and discussion of the etiology of Asian American criminality largely remains sketchy and often speculative (e.g., Flowers, 1988).

This general lack of interest in Asian Americans among criminologists may be partly due to their low visibility not only in demographic data[1] but also in crime statistics, which might have led scholars to feel less urgency to study Asian Americans than other racial/ethnic minorities whose criminality tends to be higher. However, their low criminality itself warrants systematic examination of Asian Americans, as much as high criminality warrants the study of other racial/ethnic minorities. Another possible reason might be simply the unavailability of data collected from a representative sample that includes a relatively large number of Asian American respondents. Whatever the reason, few criminologists have conducted comprehensive research that compares Asian Americans and non-Asian Americans in deviance and crime.

To fill this gap in knowledge, the present study focuses on adolescent deviance, primarily misbehavior at school. Specifically, it first examines the empirical validity of the popular image of Asian American adolescents as well behaved compared to other racial/ethnic groups, using self-reported data from a national survey, unlike previous studies that rely on official data, especially police-arrest data or self-reported data with limited generalizability. Second, and more important, it investigates theoretical explanations of differences in deviant behavior between Asian and non-Asian American adolescents, using two major social psychological theories of delinquency. Before I describe my theoretical model, I briefly summarize official statistics on crimes and arrests of Asian immigrants in America and other Western countries.

Crimes and Arrests of Asian Immigrants: Official Statistics

Like early arrest data on "Orientals" in the United States (Hayner, 1933, 1938; Lind, 1930), recent data show relatively low arrest rates among those of Asian origin for all types of offenses. For example, a 17-year trend of racial differences in juvenile arrests based on the Uniform Crime Reports (UCR), 1982–98 (not presented in a table), reveals that "Asian or Pacific Islander" juvenile arrest rate (1201.0) for total crime (i.e., what the UCR calls "Part I" and "Part II" offenses) is, on average, almost a half of white (2499.6) and "American Indian or Alaskan Native" (2493.9) rates and one fourth of the black rate (4,800.5).

The low crime rates among Asian immigrants and their children are also observed in other Western countries like England (Smith, 1997), France (Tournier, 1997), the Netherlands (Junger-Tas, 1997), and Sweden (Martens, 1997). Cross-national studies suggest that cultural as well as structural factors should be considered as an explanation of racial/ethnic differences, given the substantially different crime patterns between structurally similarly situated immigrants (Tonry, 1997). For example, Batta et al. (1981) attribute lower crime rates among Asian immigrants in England to their effective social control through strong family units based within a wider kinship network, family stability, and traditional moral values supported by shared religious beliefs.

---

[1] The March 1999 supplement to the Current Population Survey shows that Americans of Asian or Pacific origin numbered 10.9 million, constituting 4% of the U.S. total population (Humes and McKinnon, 2000).

Wilson and Herrnstein (1985) suggest that racial discrimination had an unintended crime-control function for "Orientals" in America during early 1900s by forcing them to live in socially isolated but culturally protected communities, which helped maintain social order within the community and controlled community members through the processes of family socialization.[2]

Theoretical Model

Social psychological theories of delinquency identify key concepts to explain behavioral differences not only between individuals but also between groups of individuals. Thus, such theories have been used to explain demographic group differences in delinquency (e.g., Hagan *et al.*, 1985). In such "post hoc" applications (Sampson and Lauritsen, 1997:330), researchers make a general-theory assumption that those theoretical concepts are universally applicable to all groups under consideration, while their explanatory abilities might vary across the groups.

At least implicitly, all major social psychological theories of delinquency are claimed to be general theories. Among them, Hirschi's social bonding theory posits that deviant motivation is universal to all humans, and that deviance is a behavioral outcome of the adolescent's weak or broken bonds to conventional society (Hirschi, 1969). As specific concepts of the bond, he emphasizes four elements, three of which concern an adolescent's relations with immediate social environments like family and school: *attachment* (i.e., the extent to which an adolescent shows sensitivity to others' opinions), *commitment* (i.e., the extent to which an adolescent's social rewards are tied to conformity), and *involvement* (i.e., the extent to which an

adolescent engages in conventional activities). On the other hand, the last element, *belief* (i.e., the extent to which conventional norms are internalized), is an attitudinal concept. Hirschi argues that adolescents who score high on the four social bonding elements will exhibit low levels of deviance because they are constrained by their close relationships with conventional surroundings and their favorable attitudes toward the moral validity of social rules.

Like Hirschi (1969), Akers (1985) presents his social learning theory as general theory. However, unlike Hirschi, who argues that the very bonds an adolescent has to others decrease deviance regardless of the moral content of the bonds, Akers argues that deviance is a function of the extent to which an adolescent is associated with deviant versus conventional significant others who influence the adolescent's behavior through various learning mechanisms. Thus, social learning theory posits that the adolescent's association with deviant peers increases deviance. Previous studies, whether cross-sectional or longitudinal, generally provide empirical support for social bonding as well as social learning theory (Akers, 1997; Elliott *et al.*, 1985, 1989; Hirschi, 1969; Krohn and Massey, 1980; Wiatrowski *et al.*, 1981).

Without claiming to fully integrate these two theories, the present study includes social bonding and social learning variables in the same theoretical model to explain differences in deviant behavior between Asian and non-Asian American adolescents. Specifically, I hypothesize that Asian American adolescents are less likely to commit deviant acts than non-Asian American adolescents because the former are more likely than the latter to be *attached* to conventional institutions of informal social control and their authority figures (i.e., family/parents and school/teachers), *committed* to conventional goals (e.g., academic achievement), *involved* in conventional activities (e.g., schoolwork), socialized to hold conventional *belief* (e.g., respect for authority), and *associated* with conventional friends.

Consistent with the general-theory assumption made by Hirschi and Akers, previous studies report that the effects of social bonding and social

---

[2] Other researchers sometimes attribute the low crime rates among Asian Americans partly to the "closeness" (Flowers, 1988:135) or "insularity" (Poole and Pogrebin 1990:57) of the Asian American community. Although this speculation seems based on Asian cultural emphasis on reticence and in-group orientation, it seems more applicable to internalized deviance like mental illness (Berg and Jaya, 1993; Kim-Raynor and Nakasone, 1981) than externalized, especially serious forms of deviance that are hard to simply cover up to "save face."

learning variables on adolescent deviance are significant across different racial/ethnic groups, while finding some interaction between their effects and racial/ethnic group membership (Cernkovich and Giordano, 1992; Junger and Marshall, 1997; Lee, 1998; Matsueda and Heimer, 1987; Okada, 1987; Sheu, 1986; Wong, 1997, 1999; Yue, 1993). Thus, I postulate here that racial/ethnic differences in adolescent deviance are in part due to differences in the extent to which members of each racial/ethnic group are, on average, controlled by conventional society and exposed to deviant peers.

The present study focuses on the relational or social process variables derived from social bonding and social learning theory. However, those variables are examined in the context of family and school backgrounds because both theories emphasize that the variables have significant effects on adolescent deviance above and beyond the adolescent's structural location in family and school contexts, which previous research tends to support (e.g., Elliott et al., 1985, 1989; Sampson and Laub, 1993). Thus, the present theoretical model includes such background variables for two reasons: first, to indicate that they are antecedent to the social-process variables, which in turn explain variations in adolescent deviance; and, second, to estimate the social process variables' explanatory abilities after adjusting for racial/ethnic differences in the adolescent's location in the structure of social roles and statuses in family and school.

Prior Research

Family ethnicity researchers tend to agree that the family is the key social agent that perpetuates the diversity of ethnic cultures through its primary socialization function (Kendall, 1988; London and Devore, 1988; McAdoo, 1993; Taylor et al., 1991; Wilkinson, 1993). Ethnic families commonly emphasize the importance of family relations, respect for authority, a strong work ethic, and personal virtues, while they are different in various ways, including their central unit (e.g., nuclear vs. extended family) and cultural

orientation (e.g., collectivism vs. individualism). Despite such commonality, the extent to which ethnic families succeed in socializing children and controlling their behaviors according to their ideals tends to vary across racial/ethnic groups, partly because of their different socioeconomic conditions and cultural beliefs as well as historical experiences.[3]

Prior research indicates that Asians living in the United States hold, on average, higher socioeconomic status than do blacks, Hispanics, and Native Americans, and that they are becoming increasingly similar to whites, partly because of their selective immigration, the presence of more wage-earners in a family, and their willingness to work longer hours (Hirschman, 1983; Waters and Eschbach, 1995). Family stability among Asian Americans is also higher than among non-Asian Americans, especially blacks, partly because of their collectivist culture and limited acculturation due to their relatively short immigration history (Barringer et al., 1993; Kitano and Daniels, 1995). The high family stability provides Asian American children with favorable environments for fostering conventional behaviors.

Research on ethnic families tends to report differences in family socialization practices and cultural values taught at home between Asian and non-Asian Americans (Kim-Raynor and Nakasone, 1981; Lin and Liu, 1993; Yamamoto and Wagatsuma, 1980). For example, because of their beliefs in an Eastern Worldview (e.g., Confucianism or Hinduism), Asian American

---

[3] While the present study focuses on *current* differences in the degree of success in ethnic family socialization and social control among race/ethnic groups as the key explanations of race/ethnic differences in adolescent deviance, it recognizes the importance of placing the current differences in a historical context. For example, all racial minorities have been subject to racial prejudice and discrimination throughout American history, but they tend to differ in the intensity of racism they experienced and the way they became members of American society both of which might have affected their mode of adaptation and coping strategies (Kitano and Daniels, 1995; Ogbu, 1990; Unger, 1977). Although a direct examination of the historical impact on the current state of racial minorities' family socialization and social control is beyond the scope of the present study, the causal link between the past and the present is assumed.

parents tend to instill in their children collectivism rather than the individualism of the mainstream American culture. Specifically, they emphasize the importance of following group norms, obeying group authority, enhancing group honor, and strengthening group harmony, rather than expressing individual autonomy, which has been related to adolescent deviance (e.g., Agnew, 1990). Research also finds that Asian American parents consciously discourage assertive and aggressive behaviors that are disrespectful of parental authority (Ou and McAdoo, 1993; Yue, 1993).

Asian American parents socialize their children to regard their relationships with teachers at school as an extension of their relationships with parents at home; thus, they are encouraged to obey their authority and behave respectfully toward them (Kim and Chun, 1994). Asian American parents also motivate and often pressure their children to "bring honor" to their families through educational achievements. So, they tend to be more willing to sacrifice their lives as well as resources for their children's best possible education. They are more likely to be involved in their children's schoolwork, but less likely to be pleased with their academic performance, than non-Asian American parents (Hieshima and Schneider, 1994; Shoho, 1994; Yee, 1992; Yue, 1993). Previous research tends to confirm this parental influence on higher educational achievement among Asian than non-Asian American students (Choi et al., 1994; Kim and Chun, 1994; Yee, 1992).

Although few researchers have examined whether social bonding and social learning theories explain differences in deviant behavior between Asian and non-Asian American adolescents, previous research tends to indicate the applicability of those theories to Asian American adolescents. For example, researchers attribute the development of youth gangs among Asian American immigrants' children to the breakdown of the family brought about by the disruptive processes of migration and adaptation to a new country as well as by intergenerational conflicts caused by differential pace of acculturation and different

reactions to its pressure among parents and their children (Bankston, 1998; Chin, 1990; Sanders, 1994; Vigil and Yun, 1990). Others report that social bonding and social learning theories significantly explain non-gang delinquency among Asian American adolescents (Lee, 1998; Okada, 1987; Sheu, 1986; Wong, 1997, 1999; Yue, 1993).

Previous researchers have also examined the concept of cultural assimilation in relation to social bonding and social learning theories (Lee, 1998; Wong, 1999; Yue, 1993). Specifically, cultural assimilation among Asian immigrants' children is likely to weaken traditional, hierarchical parent–child relations as they increasingly challenge the cultural mandate that children are to submit to parental authority and control without question (Lin and Liu, 1993; Yamamoto and Wagatsuma, 1980). Such weakening parental control will also be translated into an increase in children's associations with deviant friends. Then cultural assimilation is likely to be positively related to adolescent deviance, which is consistent with some previous findings (Barringer et al., 1993; Wong, 1999).

In sum, previous research shows that Asian American adolescents tend to be less deviant than their non-Asian American counterparts in their behavioral patterns, which suggests that these racial/ethnic differences can be attributed to between-group differences in social process (e.g., socialization and social control) and social structural variables (e.g., family structure). Before describing data and measures to estimate the present theoretical model, it is worthwhile to discuss briefly Asian Americans as a heterogeneous as well as a homogeneous group.

Asian Americans: Who Are They?

In this study "Asia begins with Pakistan on the west and includes all countries lying east of Pakistan, including the countries of South Asia, Southeast Asia, and East Asia, but not including Mongolia or the Soviet Union" (Barringer et al., 1993:2). An "Asian American" is defined here as someone living in the United States who specifies his or her racial/ethnic background by choosing one of the countries mentioned above. Asian Americans in this study include immigrants, native-born Americans of Asian descent, students, refugees, and other citizens of foreign countries residing in the United States (e.g., permanent residents). However, those of Pacific or Middle Eastern origins, who are often lumped together with Asian-origin groups in an "Asian or Pacific Islander" category (e.g., in the U.S. Census or the Uniform Crime Reports), are not included.

While the above definition provides a basis for constructing a reasonably homogeneous group of Asian Americans, this study also recognizes within-group heterogeneity, especially the diversity of cultural and historical backgrounds, as well as the context of and experiences with immigration itself among Americans of Asian origin.[4] Specifically, I divide Asian Americans into four regional groups: Far East, East, Southeast, and South Asian Americans. First, Far East Asian Americans include Chinese, Japanese, and Koreans, who not only share common cultural/religious backgrounds (i.e., Confucianism and Buddhism, primarily Mahayana Buddhism) but also have similar immigration histories (Kitano and Daniels, 1995). Second, East Asian Americans comprise the Filipinos, whose history (including American imperialism) and religion (Catholicism) are different from those of all other Asian racial/ethnic groups. Third, Southeast Asian Americans (Vietnamese, Laotian, Cambodian, Thai, etc.) differ from other Asian immigrants in that most of them came to the United States in a desperate, sudden move to a foreign country as refugees. Their two dominant religions are Catholicism and Buddhism, primarily Hinayana Buddhism. Finally, South Asian Americans, whose major religions are Hinduism and Islam, come from India, Pakistan, Bangladesh, and Sri Lanka.

Asian Indians, who are the majority of this regional group, show a better profile than other Asian Americans in terms of socioeconomic status and family stability (Kitano and Daniels, 1995).

The relative homogeneity and within-group heterogeneity of Asian Americans imply that the present model needs to be examined not only for a total sample but also separately for the regional groups of Asian American adolescents. In addition, the relatively short immigration history of many Asian Americans and their within-group variations (Humes and McKinnon, 2000; Kitano and Daniels, 1995) suggest that an adolescent's cultural assimilation and his or her family's immigrant status should be considered when the present model is estimated. Control for this variable is also important, given the positive relationships between deviant behavior and the degree of assimilation as well as the length of immigration (e.g., first- vs. second-generation immigrants; see Barringer et al., 1993; Hayner, 1938; Lee, 1998; Rutter and Giller, 1983; Tonry, 1997; Wong, 1999; Yue, 1993).

Data

I analyze the first follow-up data from the National Educational Longitudinal Study of 1988 (NELS:88), collected in 1990 when the survey respondents were in middle adolescence (i.e., tenth grade), a period when their nondrug, deviant behavior is expected to be at the highest level (Jang, 1999)[5]. For the initial study, the National Center for Education Statistics of the U.S. Department of Education conducted a two-stage sampling procedure (i.e., schools were first randomly selected, and then students within the schools were sampled) to draw a large, nationally representative sample of boys and girls in eighth grade in the spring of 1988. A nationally representative sample would typically be unsuitable for my comparative research because of the relatively small number of Asian American respondents in the sample (e.g., Elliott et al., 1985, 1989). However, the NELS:88

---

[4] Scholars of race/ethnicity have already recognized similar problems encountered even when they focus on a "single" racial/ethnic group, whether they study white Americans, African Americans, Hispanic Americans, Native Americans, or Asian Americans (Alba, 1990; Barringer et al., 1993; Kitano and Daniels, 1995; Portes and Truelove, 1987; Taylor et al., 1991; see also Waters and Eschbach, 1995, for a discussion of within-group heterogeneity in terms of socioeconomic inequality in the United States).

[5] Besides this substantive reason, I decided to analyze the first follow-up data because they include more variables of social bonding and social learning as well as deviant behavior than any other wave of data collected so far.

included a disproportionately large number of Asian American (and Hispanic) respondents in its sample. To correct for this oversampling, the present sample is weighted in the following analyses.

Measurement

For the present analysis, three groups of variables were constructed: background, process, and outcome variables. Items measuring these variables all come from the student survey, except the proxy measure of cultural assimilation, whose items come from the parent survey. When multiple items were used to construct a variable's measure, maximum-likelihood exploratory factor analysis and inter-item reliability analysis were conducted to see whether the items load on a common factor with high (at least 0.40) loadings and an acceptable (at least 0.60) Cronbach's alpha. If they do, then a respondent's score on that variable was calculated as the multiple items' average. . . . In the following description, variable names are italicized.

Background Variables

DEMOGRAPHIC BACKGROUND A respondent's race/ethnicity is measured by using two items. The first item asks respondents to identify themselves by selecting one of five ethnic categories: "Asian or Pacific Islander," "Hispanic, regardless of race," "Black, not of Hispanic origin," "White, not of Hispanic origin," and "American Indian or Alaskan Native." A second item asks those who identified themselves as "Asian or Pacific Islander" to specify their ethnic background by choosing 1 of 10 categories. Six of the 10 categories are consistent with the present definition of Asian Americans, covering all the four regions (Far East, East, Southeast, and South) of Asia.[6] To compare Asian American

adolescents with their *white, black, Hispanic,* and "American Indian or Alaskan Native" (henceforth, *Native American*) counterparts, four dummy variables are constructed, using Asian American as the reference category. In addition, a respondent's self-reported sex is dummy-coded (female = 0, male = 1), whereas *age* is calculated by using a respondent's birth year. In addition, three dummy variables for region-of-residence are constructed, *Northeast, Midwest,* and *South,* using West as the reference category.

FAMILY BACKGROUND First, *family SES* is measured by the NELS:88 composite measure of family socioeconomic status. Second, family size is operationalized by the *number of children* living at a respondent's home. Third, family intactness is measured by its relational as well as structural dimensions: a respondent's perceived *marital harmony* of his or her parents and the presence of *both parents,* specifically, biological parents at home (no = 0, yes = 1).[7] Finally, a proxy measure of cultural *assimilation* was constructed so that a higher score indicates higher levels of assimilation on the part of a respondent.[8]

SCHOOL BACKGROUND First, *school size* is measured by total enrollment in a respondent's school. Second, a dummy variable was constructed to measure whether a respondent attends a *public school* (=1) or nonpublic school (=0). Third, two dummy variables, *urban school* and *suburban school,* were constructed, with rural school as the omitted category. Students are likely to be differentially exposed to social control

---

[6] The six categories are (1) Chinese, (2) Japanese, (3) Korean, (4) Filipino, (5) Southeast Asian (Vietnamese, Laotian, Cambodian/Kampuchean, Thai, etc.), and (6) South Asian (Asian Indian, Pakistani, Bangladeshi, Sri Lankan, etc.), whereas the four excluded are (1) Pacific Islander (Samoan, Guamanian, etc.), (2) West Asian (Iranian, Afghan, Turkish, etc.), (3) Middle Eastern (Iraqi, Israeli, Lebanese, etc.), and (4) Other Asian.

[7] Because the marital harmony and family process variables are both perceptual in nature and measured concurrently, causal order between the two is less clear than that between the structural family intactness and family process variables. The present study assumes that marital harmony affects family process rather than vice versa, given that good marital relations are likely to result in good parent–child relations and close monitoring by parents rather than the other way around.
[8] Four different levels of cultural assimilation were constructed as follows: respondent and both of his or her parents are foreign-born (=1); respondent and at least one of his or her parents are foreign-born (=2); respondent and at least one of his or her parents are native-born (=3); and respondent and both of his or her parents are native-born (=4).

and peer relations at and around school, depending on the type of school they attend in terms of teacher–student ratio and location. Thus, these variables are included to control for spuriousness due to the self-selection process, which is likely to vary across racial/ethnic groups, given their differences in socioeconomic status and place of residence.

Process Variables

FAMILY PROCESSES Family bonding variables focus on Hirschi's concept of attachment to parents, which includes three key dimensions: affective relations, close communication, and parental supervision. First, an adolescent's affective relations with his or her parents are operationalized by a single-item measure of a respondent's perceived *parental trust* in him or her and a five-item measure of the respondent's *affective ties* with his or her parents. Second, *close communication* is measured by three items about how often a respondent discusses things like course selection with his or her parents. Lastly, to construct a measure of parental supervision, four items of *parental monitoring* are employed.

SCHOOL PROCESSES School bonding variables tap three concepts: attachment to school, commitment to education, and involvement in school-related activities. First, a measure of *attachment to school* is based on eight items about a respondent's perceptions of his or her school and teachers. Second, two variables are constructed to measure commitment to education: *school grades* and *educational expectation*. . . . Lastly, the concept of involvement is measured by a respondent's *time spent on homework*.

PEER PROCESSES The present data include five items asking about a respondent's close friends' attitudes toward school and education. These items tap the moral content of peer relations, not the number of bonds to peers, thereby measuring Akers's association with peers, specifically, *conventional peers*, rather than Hirschi's attachment to peers. While measuring friends' attitudes indirectly via a respondent is less than ideal, the current measure of peer relations seems to have construct validity, given its significant relationship with the dependent variable in the expected direction (see below).

COGNITIVE PROCESSES To measure Hirschi's concept of belief, this study employs the 16 items of the survey that ask each respondent how often he or she feels that it is okay for him or her to commit deviant behaviors, ranging in seriousness from cutting classes to bringing weapons to school. The 16 items are combined into an index of *conventional attitudes*.

Outcome Variable

DEVIANT BEHAVIOR The present study conceptualizes deviance as a general, not directly observable, underlying propensity to commit deviant *"acts, the detection of which is thought to result in punishment of the person committing them by agents of the larger society"* (Hirschi, 1969:47; emphasis in original) or *"disapproved behavior considered serious enough to warrant major societal efforts to control them, using strong negative sanctions or treatment-corrective techniques"* (Akers, 1985:9; emphasis in original). The present study focuses on an omnibus measure of *general deviance*, given that the present theories focus on a general conception of adolescent behavior and do not make causal distinctions based on the type of deviance. However, two nonschool deviance items (i.e., *runaway* and *arrest*) are separated from the general-deviance items to see whether the independent variables' effects on general deviance largely reflect those on *school deviance*, given that most deviance items measure misbehavior and sanctioning at school. . . .[9] Since the

---

[9] A preliminary analysis was conducted to examine whether the inclusion of societal reaction items (i.e., school disciplinary measures and police arrest) in the measure of deviance would introduce any bias into data analysis because of potential redundancy (i.e., double counting) and/or different sources of measurement error. Correlations between the deviance measure without societal reaction items and the independent variables are found to be not substantially different from those involving the measure with the items. In addition, the alternative measures of deviance are highly correlated with each other ($r = 0.87$), while the measure without the items has smaller Cronbach's alpha ($\alpha = 0.64$) primarily because of fewer items included than the one with the items ($\alpha = 0.78$).

deviance items do not have the same response categories, they were standardized before being combined into a composite measure. Consistent with the general conception of adolescent behaviors, the reliability coefficient of general-deviance items was found to be relatively high (0.76).

Results

The present analysis is based on the weighted total sample of 18,132 respondents who provided valid information about their racial/ethnic backgrounds. The weighted sample closely represents the racial/ethnic distribution of the total youth population in the survey year of 1990: 71.6% white ($n = 12989$), 13.4% black ($n = 2424$), 11.0% Hispanic ($n = 1997$), 1.3% Native American ($n = 231$), and 2.7% Asian American ($n = 490$). The total Asian American group consists of four regional groups consists of four regional groups of 43.5% Far East ($n = 213$), 25.7% East ($n = 126$), 19.2% Southeast ($n = 94$), and 11.6% South ($n = 57$) Asian Americans. Also, Far East Asian Americans are 56.3% Chinese ($n = 120$), 28.6% Korean ($n = 61$), and 15.1% Japanese ($n = 32$).

Table 1.1 summarizes results from conducting an analysis of variance (ANOVA) to compare white, black, Hispanic, and Native American adolescents with all Asian American adolescents as well as each regional group. First, Asian American adolescents, whether we look at the total or any regional group, report significantly lower levels of general deviance than their non-Asian American counterparts. A major exception is East Asian American adolescents (Filipinos), whose mean is not significantly different from any group of non-Asian American adolescents. An almost identical pattern of racial/ethnic differences is observed for school deviance, which most items of general deviance include. On the other hand, Asian American adolescents are not consistently less deviant than non-Asian American adolescents for runaway and arrest. Specifically, the only significant difference is observed for self-reported arrest between Native American and Asian American (except East Asian American) adolescents. General and school

deviance measures are based on standardized scores (i.e., z-scores).

Second, with few exceptions, Asian American adolescents tend to come from families of higher socioeconomic status, smaller numbers of children, and greater stability than non-Asian American adolescents (see also Waters and Eschbach, 1995).[10] As expected, Asian American parents and their children are more likely to be foreign-born, so Asian American adolescents can be assumed to have been significantly less assimilated to American culture than their non-Asian American counterparts (Barringer et al., 1993). Third, Asian American adolescents are more likely to attend not only relatively large, urban, or suburban (rather than rural) schools but also private (24%) schools as compared to their non-white, non-Asian American peers. Lastly, Asian American adolescents tend to report stronger attachment to school, higher school grades and educational expectations, more time spent on homework, and association with more conventional friends, as hypothesized. On the other hand, they are generally no different from their non-Asian American peers in attachment to parents.

Table 1.1 also shows that Asian American adolescents are not a completely homogeneous group, as suspected. Specifically, coming from the most advantaged family/school environments (Kitano and Daniels, 1995), South Asian American adolescents tend to report the lowest levels of deviance and the highest levels of bonding to conventional society of all regional groups. Far East Asian American adolescents are ranked as the second most advantaged and conventional group, followed by Southeast and East Asian American adolescents. However, results from another ANOVA that included only Asian American adolescents (not presented in a table)

---

[10] Although Southeast Asian American families report, on average, the lowest socioeconomic status and the largest number of children of all Asian American families, their stability (0.63) is not significantly different from white (0.65), Hispanic (0.61), and Native American (0.58) families' and even significantly higher than black (0.34) families' despite their predominantly refugee backgrounds.

TABLE 1.1 Comparison of Means Between Asian and Non-Asian American Adolescents

Variable name	Non-Asian American adolescents				Asian American adolescents				
	White (n = 12,989)	Black (n = 2,424)	Hispanic (n = 1,997)	Native American (n = 231)	Far East (n = 213)	East (n = 126)	South-east (n = 94)	South (n = 57)	Total (n = 490)
General deviance[a]	−0.01*⁺	0.12*⁺	(0.18)*⁺	(0.35)*⁺	−0.28	0.03	(−0.18)	−0.48⁺	−0.21*
School deviance[a]	−0.01*⁺	0.13*⁺	(0.19)*⁺	(0.34)*⁺	−0.29	0.03	(−0.20)	−0.48⁺	−0.21*
Runaway	0.06	0.04	0.08	0.06	0.03	0.06	0.10	0.00	0.05
Arrest	0.04	0.04	0.04	(0.13)*⁺	0.05	0.04	(0.02)	0.00⁺	0.04*
Male	0.51	0.50	0.49	0.49	0.53	0.54	0.54	0.41	0.52
Age	(16.35)⁺	16.54*⁺	16.47⁺	16.51⁺	16.44	16.30	(16.60)	16.07⁺	16.39*
Northeast	0.21⁺	0.14⁺	0.14⁺	0.19⁺	0.23	0.07	0.12	0.46⁺	0.20
Midwest	(0.30)*	0.14	0.10	0.09	0.11	0.10	(0.13)	0.21	0.13*
South	0.33*	(0.64)*⁺	0.32*	0.24	0.15	0.18	(0.17)	0.19⁺	0.17*
Family SES	(0.11)*⁺	−0.39*⁺	−0.54*⁺	−0.41*⁺	0.27	0.33	(−0.40)	0.80⁺	0.23*
Number of children	(2.34)⁺	3.13*⁺	3.16*⁺	3.41⁺	2.25	2.21	3.27	1.65⁺	2.36*
Marital harmony	4.66⁺	4.42*	4.61	4.75	4.63	4.85	4.33	5.18⁺	4.71*
Both parents	0.65*⁺	(0.34)*⁺	0.61*⁺	0.58*⁺	0.79	0.77	(0.63)	0.91⁺	0.77*
Assimilation	(3.94)*⁺	(3.91)*⁺	(3.30)*⁺	(3.89)*⁺	1.98	1.93	(1.39)	1.33⁺	1.76*
School size	(4.37)*⁺	(5.25)*	6.20	(4.38)*⁺	6.34	5.59	(6.12)	5.55⁺	6.00*

(continued)

TABLE 1.1 Continued

Variable name	Non-Asian American adolescents				Asian American adolescents				
	White (n = 12,989)	Black (n = 2,424)	Hispanic (n = 1,997)	Native American (n = 231)	Far East (n = 213)	East (n = 126)	South-east (n = 94)	South (n = 57)	Total (n = 490)
Public school	0.86	0.93*+	0.91*+	0.96*+	0.90	0.80	0.89	0.77+	0.86*
Urban school	(0.21)*	0.53+	0.48+	(0.20)*	0.43	0.55	(0.54)	0.28+	0.46*
Suburban school	0.45	0.26*+	0.30*+	0.25*+	0.44	0.37	0.40	0.59+	0.44*
Parental trust	0.82	0.76	0.74	0.85	0.77	0.74	0.75	0.88	0.77
Affective ties	4.81	4.79	4.78	4.85	4.62	4.75	4.45	5.00	4.67
Close communication	2.05*	2.02*	1.92	1.99	1.89	1.95	1.90	2.09	1.93*
Parental monitoring	2.67	2.74	2.72	2.65	2.70	2.68	2.75	2.89	2.73
Attachment to school	2.80*+	2.82	2.84*	2.81	2.83	2.92	2.92	2.98+	2.89*
School grades	3.59*+	(3.43)*+	(3.38)*+	(3.33)*+	4.02	3.76	(3.84)	4.33+	3.95*
Educational expectation	4.52*+	4.45*+	(4.22)*+	(3.93)*+	5.10	4.88	(4.69)	5.60+	5.02*
Time on homework	(1.29)*+	(1.39)*+	(1.32)*+	(1.19)*+	1.79	1.58	(1.80)	1.99+	1.76*
Conventional peers	(2.47)*+	2.61	(2.51)*	(2.47)*	2.68	2.56	(2.66)	2.66+	2.64*
Conventional attitudes	3.58*	3.69	3.64	3.58	3.68	3.62	3.65	3.72	3.66*

Note: Different symbols are used to indicate statistically significant ($\alpha = 0.05$) differences between non-Asian and Asian Americans (total or regional group) as follows: (1)*; total Asian Americans; (2) boldface, Far East Asian Americans; (3) underline, East Asian Americans; (4) (parenthesis), Southeast Asian Americans; and (5)+, South Asian Americans.

General and school deviance measures are based on standardized scores (i.e., z-scores).

indicated relatively small within-group variation, thereby providing support for this study's combining adolescents of various Asian origins into a single ethnic group.

Significant differences of primary interest among Asian American adolescents are mostly observed in family background, commitment to education (i.e., school grades and educational expectation), and general deviance (see Table 1.1). Moreover, the rank-order of the four regional groups' mean scores is internally consistent across these variables; that is, the more advantaged is the background and the more conventional are the relations with family, school, and peers that a regional group of Asian Americans has, the less is the deviant behavior reported by the group. In addition, I examined within-group variation among Far East Asian American adolescents (not presented in a table). Results showed that most of observed differences among Chinese American, Japanese American, and Korean American adolescents failed to be statistically significant.

The above results from ANOVA generally indicate that Asian American adolescents tend to report more advantaged family backgrounds, more conventional relations with the institution of school and peer networks, and less deviant behavior than their non-Asian American counterparts, while the former are not very different from the latter in other variables, including attachment to parents and conventional attitudes. These findings suggest that differences in deviance between Asian American and non-Asian American adolescents are more likely to be explained by family backgrounds, school bonding, and association with peers than other variables included in the present theoretical model. To test the explanatory ability of the theoretical variables in a multivariate context, controlling for the sources of spuriousness, I conducted ordinary least squares (OLS) regression analysis.

The following analysis is based on those respondents who provided valid data on the two key variables, race/ethnicity and general deviance, employing mean-substitution of missing data

on most of the other variables ($n = 17,074$).[11] Specifically, "hierarchical analysis" was conducted to compare contributions made by different groups of variables to the explanation of racial/ethnic differences (Cohen and Cohen, 1983). First, the model was estimated with only demographic background variables (i.e., race/ethnicity, sex, age, and region-of-residence) included (initial model). Second, family and school background variables were added to the initial model separately (family and school background model, respectively) as well as jointly (combined background model). Third, four process models were estimated by adding four groups of social bonding and social learning variables to the combined background model, one group at a time (family, school, peer, and cognitive process models). Finally, a model including all independent variables was estimated (full model). For statistical significance, one-tailed tests ($\alpha = 0.05$) are conducted, given the hypothesized directions of relationships, while a two-tailed test ($\alpha = 0.05$) is applied to any significant coefficient in the unexpected directions.

Table 1.2 summarizes results from regressing general deviance on background and process variables for the total sample, with the total Asian American group as the reference category. The initial model confirms significantly higher levels of general deviance among non-Asian than Asian American adolescents, with the demographic correlates of deviant behavior held constant. When family background variables are entered into the model, the racial/ethnic differences reduce in a varying degree for different comparisons. Specifically, the largest reduction in the size of

---

[11] The model was initially estimated using listwise deletion ($n = 11,520$). To minimize the number of excluded cases, however, the present study decided to estimate the model by substituting mean for missing data. To correct for the nonrandomness of missing data, the present study also constructed a dummy variable (1 = missing, 0 = not missing) for each independent variable whose missing data are replaced by its mean to include it in regression equation. The dummy variables' coefficients are not shown in the table below for simpler presentation. The overall results were substantively similar between the methods of missing-data treatment, and major conclusions of the present study remain the same.

TABLE 1.2 Unstandardized and Standardized (in Parentheses) Coefficients for OLS Regression of General Deviance on Background and Process Variables for Total Sample With Total Asian American Group as Reference Category (n = 17, 074)

Variable name	Background model				Process model				
	Initial model	Family	School	Combined	Family	School	Peer	Cognitive	Full model
White	0.22* (0.09)	0.17* (0.07)	0.28* (0.12)	0.21* (0.09)	0.26* (0.11)	0.04 (0.02)	0.13* (0.05)	0.11* (0.05)	0.04 (0.02)
Black	0.39* (0.13)	0.22* (0.07)	0.40* (0.13)	0.21* (0.07)	0.28* (0.09)	0.10* (0.03)	0.22* (0.07)	0.26* (0.09)	0.20* (0.07)
Hispanic	0.40* (0.12)	0.26* (0.08)	0.40* (0.12)	0.23* (0.07)	0.29* (0.09)	0.11* (0.03)	0.19* (0.06)	0.20* (0.06)	0.14* (0.04)
Native American	0.49* (0.05)	0.37* (0.04)	0.57* (0.06)	0.43* (0.05)	0.52* (0.06)	0.23* (0.03)	0.39* (0.04)	0.36* (0.04)	0.28* (0.03)
Male	0.28* (0.14)	0.32* (0.16)	0.28* (0.14)	0.32* (0.16)	0.29* (0.14)	0.21* (0.10)	0.22* (0.11)	0.11* (0.05)	0.08* (0.04)
Age	0.13* (0.08)	0.08* (0.05)	0.13* (0.08)	0.08* (0.05)	0.06* (0.04)	0.01 (0.01)	0.08* (0.05)	0.09* (0.05)	0.04* (0.02)
Northeast	-0.14* (-0.06)	-0.19* (-0.08)	-0.11* (-0.04)	-0.09* (-0.04)	-0.12* (-0.05)	-0.11* (-0.04)	-0.09* (-0.04)	-0.14* (-0.06)	-0.14* (-0.05)
Midwest	-0.18* (-0.08)	-0.28* (-0.13)	-0.13* (-0.06)	-0.14* (-0.06)	-0.17* (-0.07)	-0.18* (-0.08)	-0.16* (-0.07)	-0.16* (-0.07)	-0.17* (-0.07)
South	-0.28* (-0.13)	-0.08* (-0.06)	-0.26* (-0.12)	-0.25* (-0.12)	-0.24* (-0.12)	-0.25* (-0.12)	-0.26* (-0.12)	-0.20* (-0.09)	-0.20* (-0.09)
Family SES		-0.08* (-0.06)		-0.10* (-0.08)	-0.05* (-0.04)	0.04* (0.03)	-0.06* (-0.05)	-0.09* (-0.07)	0.01 (0.01)
Number of children		0.04* (0.06)		0.04* (0.06)	0.03* (0.05)	0.03* (0.05)	0.04* (0.06)	0.03* (0.05)	0.03* (0.04)
Marital harmony		-0.10* (-0.14)		-0.10* (-0.14)	-0.03* (-0.05)	-0.05* (-0.08)	-0.07* (-0.11)	-0.04* (-0.06)	-0.02* (-0.03)
Both parents		-0.15* (-0.07)		-0.14* (-0.07)	-0.15* (-0.07)	-0.13* (-0.06)	-0.14* (-0.07)	-0.14* (-0.07)	-0.13* (-0.06)
Assimilation		0.04* (0.02)		0.06* (0.03)	0.06* (0.03)	0.02 (0.01)	0.04* (0.02)	0.04* (0.02)	0.02* (0.01)
School size			0.03* (0.06)	0.03* (0.06)	0.03* (0.05)	0.01* (0.03)	0.02* (0.06)	0.03* (0.05)	0.02* (0.04)
Public school			0.10* (0.03)	0.01 (0.00)	0.01 (0.00)	-0.07* (-0.02)	0.00 (0.00)	0.02 (0.01)	-0.01 (0.00)
Urban school			0.12* (0.05)	0.13* (0.06)	0.13* (0.06)	0.18* (0.08)	0.15* (0.07)	0.15* (0.07)	0.17* (0.07)
Suburban school			0.08* (0.04)	0.11* (0.05)	0.11* (0.05)	0.13* (0.06)	0.12* (0.06)	0.10* (0.05)	0.11* (0.05)
Parent trust					-0.22* (-0.08)				-0.09* (-0.03)
Affective ties					-0.15* (-0.16)				-0.02* (-0.03)
Close communication					-0.21* (-0.10)				-0.02 (-0.01)
Parental monitoring					-0.13* (-0.08)				-0.04* (-0.02)
Attachment to school						-0.56* (-0.23)			-0.14* (-0.06)
School grades						-0.29* (-0.23)			-0.21* (-0.17)
Educational expectations						-0.08* (-0.11)			-0.05* (-0.06)
Time spent on homework						-0.08* (-0.06)			
Conventional peers							-0.63* (-0.28)		-0.01* (-0.01)
Conventional attitudes								-1.52* (-0.55)	-0.08* (-0.03)
Constant	-2.38*	-1.23*	-2.71*	-1.59*	0.20	3.01*	0.11	3.82*	-1.23* (-0.44)
Adjusted R²	0.04*	0.09*	0.05*	0.10*	0.17*	0.27*	0.17*	0.38*	0.43*

* $p < 0.05$ (one-tailed test); $^+ p < 0.05$ (two-tailed test).

unstandardized regression coefficient is observed for the black-Asian comparison (0.17 = 0.39 − 0.22, 44% reduction), followed by Hispanic-Asian (0.14 = 0.40 − 0.26, 35% reduction), Native American–Asian (0.12 = 0.49 − 0.37, 24% reduction, henceforth, Native- Asian), and white-Asian (0.05 = 0.22 − 0.17, 23% reduction) comparisons.

However, when school instead of family background variables are added to the initial model, the racial/ethnic differences are little explained in black-Asian and Hispanic-Asian comparisons, and even become larger in white-Asian (from 0.22 to 0.28, 27% increase) and Native-Asian (from 0.49 to 0.57, 16% increase) comparisons. These widened gaps can be attributed to the school size and urban school variables that suppress the white-Asian and Native-Asian differences until they are controlled for and their suppressor effects are removed. In other words, if white and Native American respondents attended no more advantaged schools than their Asian American peers in terms of school size and location,[12] white-Asian and Native-Asian differences in general deviance would be larger than those observed in the initial model. The coefficients of racial/ethnic dummy variables in the combined background model reflect the differences between Asian American and non-Asian American adolescents after taking all the background explanatory variables and suppressors into account.

The school process model explains racial/ethnic differences better than the other three process models, showing that all racial/ethnic differences dramatically reduce in size and even become nonsignificant. Specifically, white-Asian difference decreases from 0.22 to 0.04 (82%), becoming nonsignificant, and black-Asian, Hispanic-Asian, and Native-Asian differences

also substantially reduce (74, 72, and 53%, respectively), while they remain significant. Similar patterns of explanation, though to a lesser extent, are observed in the peer process and cognitive process models as well. On the other hand, in the family process model racial/ethnic differences become slightly larger than the differences in the combined background model, indicating the suppressor effect of the family bonding variables.

When all process variables are simultaneously entered into the regression equation (i.e., the full model), the white-Asian difference becomes nonsignificant (.04, $p > 0.05$), but the model explains the initially observed black-Asian (49%), Hispanic-Asian (65%), and Native-Asian (43%) differences less than the school process model (see above). This differential improvement in explanatory ability can be attributed to the suppressor effects of the family and cognitive process variables. Specifically, adding attachment to parents and conventional attitudes to the combined background model increases, rather than decreases, black-Asian difference by 33% (from 0.21 and 0.28) and 24% (from 0.21 to 0.26). Similarly, Hispanic-Asian and Native-Asian differences in the family process model become 26% (from 0.23 to 0.29) and 21% (from 0.43 to 0.52) larger, respectively, than the differences in the combined background model. This finding that the same domain may differentially improve the explanation of racial/ethnic differences, depending on which aspect it is focused on (e.g., the suppressor effects of family *process* variables versus the significant explanation of family *background* variables for the black-Asian difference), highlights the importance of separately examining the ability of structural and relational variables to explain racial/ethnic differences in adolescent deviance.

As expected, the explained variance in the dependent variable gradually increases as blocks of independent variables are entered into the initial model ($R^2 = 0.04$) until it reaches a maximum in the full model ($R^2 = 0.43$). While the direct effects of background variables on general deviance remain significant in the final

---

[12] As far as the two school background variables are concerned, Asian American adolescents, on average, can be said to be less advantaged than their white and Native American peers in that the former are more likely than the latter to attend large, urban schools (see Table 1.1), which tend to be weakly but positively correlated with general deviance (0.05 and 0.10, respectively, $p < 0.05$)

model, most of them become smaller as a result of controlling for social bonding and social learning variables, meaning that the effects of background variables on deviance are partly explained by the social process variables. A similar pattern is observed for the social process variables themselves, which indicates that their effects on deviance are partly indirect via other social process variables, as previous studies show (e.g., Elliott et al., 1985, 1989; Matsueda and Heimer, 1987; Thornberry, 1987), and Hirschi himself acknowledges (Wiatrowski et al., 1981, see note 5).

Of the social bonding variables, belief (i.e., conventional attitudes) has the largest direct effect on general deviance ($\beta = -.44$), followed by commitment to education (i.e., school grades, $\beta = -.17$; educational expectation, $\beta = -.06$) and attachment to school ($\beta = -.06$). This relatively large effect might have been, at least partly, due to respondents reporting their attitudes so that they would be consistent with their behaviors. However, such self-attribution is unlikely to have taken place among the majority of respondents, given the lack of evidence of colinearity involving the belief and deviance variables. In addition, it is not unusual to find stronger effects of belief on deviance than other social bonding variables because the attitudinal measure is a more proximate "cause" of deviance than are relational measures (e.g., Wiatrowski et al., 1981). On the other hand, the direct effects of family, school, and belief variables on deviance remain significant even after controlling for association with conventional peers (Sampson and Laub, 1993; Sheu, 1986).[13]

Finally, to see whether the present model's explanation of racial/ethnic differences varies across regional groups of Asian American adolescents, the same regression analysis is repeated by using each regional group alternately as the reference category. Table 1.3 shows only the coefficients of race/ethnic dummy variables across models. The initial models show that all racial/ethnic differences are significant in the expected direction with one exception, specifically, the nonsignificant difference between white and East Asian American adolescents.[14] Also, consistent with the above ANOVA results, South Asian American adolescents show the least deviant behavioral patterns of all regional groups (with non-Asian American groups as reference point), being followed, in order, by Far East, Southeast, and East Asian American adolescents.

With a few exceptions, each model's relative standing in the explanatory ability for racial/ethnic differences in general deviance does not change much across the analyses using different regional groups of Asian American adolescents as the reference group. That is, the school process model is still the best in accounting for differences in deviance between Asian American and non-Asian American adolescents, making the differences nonsignificant in the comparisons of South, Southeast (with one exception), and East Asian American with non-Asian American adolescents. Also, school background, family process, and, to a lesser degree, cognitive process variables suppress some differences between Asian American and non-Asian American adolescents. Finally, in the full model, white-Asian differences become nonsignificant for all the subgroup analyses and—unlike in the analysis including the total Asian American group—black-Asian and Hispanic-Asian differences also become nonsignificant when South Asian American adolescents are used as the

---

[13] First, all the models presented above were replicated for the submeasures of deviance: school deviance, runaway, and arrest. Not surprisingly, results from estimating the regression models of school deviance are very similar to those presented above for general deviance, which primarily consists of the items of misbehavior and sanctioning at school. On the other hand, estimated models of runaway and arrest are different from those of either general or school deviance. As indicated by the ANOVA results (see Table 1.1), there is no significant difference in runaway and arrest to explain between Asian American and non-Asian American adolescents with one exception (i.e., Native American adolescents' higher levels of arrest than Asian American adolescents'). Second, the present study reestimated the general deviance model (presented in Table 1.2) without the total sample weighted. No substantial difference is observed between model estimation with and without weighting.

[14] While the above bivariate analysis (see Table 1.1) showed no significant difference in general deviance between East Asian and non-Asian American adolescents, three of the four differences between the two groups are found to be significant in the expected direction after controlling for sociodemographic characteristics.

TABLE 1.3 Unstandardized and Standardized (in Parentheses) Race/Ethnicity Dummy Coefficients for OLS Regression of General Deviance on Background and Process Variables for Total Sample With Regional Group of Asian Americans as Reference Category

Variable name	Initial model	Background model			Process model				
		Family	School	Combined	Family	School	Peer	Cognitive	Full model
Far East Asian American: Chinese, Japanese, and Korean (n = 16,816)									
White	0.29* (0.13)	0.24* (0.10)	0.36* (0.16)	0.29* (0.12)	0.36* (0.15)	0.12* (0.05)	0.17* (0.07)	0.17* (0.07)	0.08 (0.04)
Black	0.46* (0.15)	0.29* (0.10)	0.48* (0.16)	0.29* (0.10)	0.38* (0.13)	0.17* (0.06)	0.26* (0.09)	0.31* (0.10)	0.24* (0.08)
Hispanic	0.47* (0.14)	0.33* (0.10)	0.48* (0.14)	0.32* (0.09)	0.39* (0.12)	0.19* (0.06)	0.23* (0.07)	0.25* (0.08)	0.18* (0.05)
Native American	0.56* (0.06)	0.44* (0.05)	0.65* (0.07)	0.52* (0.06)	0.62* (0.07)	0.31* (0.03)	0.43* (0.05)	0.41* (0.05)	0.32* (0.03)
East Asian American: Filipino (n = 16,749)									
White	0.05 (0.02)	−0.02(−.01)	0.09 (0.04)	0.01 (0.00)	0.08 (0.04)	−0.08 (−0.03)	−0.02 (−0.02)	−0.02 (−0.01)	−0.04 (−0.02)
Black	0.21* (0.07)	0.03 (0.01)	0.21* (0.07)	0.00 (0.00)	0.10 (0.03)	−0.02 (0.01)	0.07 (0.02)	0.12 (0.04)	0.11 (0.04)
Hispanic	0.22* (0.07)	0.07 (0.02)	0.20* (0.06)	0.02 (0.01)	0.10 (0.03)	−0.01 (0.00)	0.03 (0.01)	0.06 (0.02)	0.05 (0.01)
Native American	0.31* (0.03)	0.18 (0.02)	0.37* (0.04)	0.23* (0.03)	0.34* (0.04)	0.11 (0.01)	0.24* (0.03)	0.22* (0.02)	0.19* (0.02)
Southeast Asian American: Vietnamese, Laotian, Cambodian, Thai, etc. (n = 16,711)									
White	0.22* (0.09)	0.24* (0.10)	0.29* (0.12)	0.30* (0.13)	0.35* (0.15)	0.09 (0.04)	0.18* (0.08)	0.22* (0.10)	0.12 (0.05)
Black	0.38* (0.13)	0.29* (0.10)	0.40* (0.14)	0.29* (0.10)	0.36* (0.12)	0.14 (0.05)	0.27* (0.09)	0.37* (0.12)	0.27* (0.09)
Hispanic	0.38* (0.12)	0.33* (0.10)	0.40* (0.12)	0.32* (0.10)	0.37* (0.11)	0.15 (0.05)	0.24* (0.07)	0.31* (0.09)	0.21* (0.06)
Native American	0.48* (0.05)	0.44* (0.05)	0.58* (0.06)	0.53* (0.06)	0.60* (0.07)	0.28* (0.03)	0.44* (0.05)	0.47* (0.05)	0.35* (0.04)
South Asian American: Indian, Pakistani, Sri Lankan, etc. (n = 16,682)									
White	0.40* (0.17)	0.24* (0.10)	0.45* (0.19)	0.25* (0.11)	0.25* (0.11)	−0.01 (−0.01)	0.19 (0.08)	0.09 (0.04)	−0.02 (−0.01)
Black	0.57* (0.19)	0.29* (0.10)	0.56* (0.19)	0.25* (0.08)	0.27* (0.09)	0.04 (0.01)	0.28* (0.10)	0.24* (0.08)	0.13 (0.04)
Hispanic	0.57* (0.17)	0.33* (0.10)	0.56* (0.17)	0.27* (0.08)	0.27* (0.08)	0.05 (0.02)	0.25* (0.08)	0.18 (0.05)	0.07 (0.02)
Native American	0.67* (0.07)	0.43* (0.05)	0.73* (0.08)	0.48* (0.05)	0.51* (0.06)	0.18 (0.02)	0.45* (0.05)	0.34* (0.04)	0.21* (0.02)

$* p < 0.05$ (one-tailed test).

reference category.[15] The overall findings show that the explanatory ability of the theoretical model and the relative importance of submodels in accounting for racial/ethnic differences in adolescent deviance are largely invariant across the four subgroups of Asian Americans, indicating similarity rather than dissimilarity among those groups.

Discussion and Conclusion

This study finds that Asian American adolescents generally report less deviance than their white, black, Hispanic, and Native American peers, but the difference is observed primarily for school deviance. Asian American adolescents are no less likely than non-Asian American adolescents to report having run away from home, perhaps because running away is a deviant behavior that is less serious than violent and felony property offenses, and thus one that exhibits smaller racial/ethnic differences than those serious offenses (Hindelang et al., 1979). Also, Asian and non-Asian American adolescents are generally similar in self-reported arrest. This might be partly because of its limited measurement (i.e., a single item for all types of arrest) and/or to the underreporting bias that previous research tends to find among non-whites for measures of serious deviance like police arrest (Bachman et al., 1991; Hindelang et al., 1981).

Another reason for the lack of difference in self-reported arrest might have to do with the present sample, which is school-based and thus does not include dropouts and those who were absent on the day of the survey. Specifically, the present data might underestimate racial/ethnic differences in arrest given that (1) those who were excluded, especially school dropouts, are more likely than graduates to engage in higher levels of delinquency, including violence, and

(2) dropout rates among blacks and Hispanics are disproportionately higher than among other groups (Jarjoura, 1993; Kaufman et al., 2000). While all the above discussion remains speculative without additional data, the null finding is likely to be suspect rather than reflecting reality, given that the recent UCR data consistently show substantial differences in arrest rates between Asian and non-Asian juveniles.[16]

This study also finds that the observed racial/ethnic differences in adolescent deviance are substantially explained primarily by their differences in family backgrounds and school bonding. In addition, as hypothesized, the effects of most background variables on deviance are partly mediated by process variables. Another important finding is that a similar pattern of the same variables' explanatory ability is observed across different regional groups of Asian American adolescents. The present findings of significant differences between Asian and non-Asian American adolescents *and* more similarities than dissimilarities among Asian American adolescents themselves generally validate the way this study has constructed the racial/ethnic category of "Asian Americans," while within-group heterogeneity still needs to be recognized. Specifically, Asian American adolescents tend to differ from their non-Asian, especially non-white American peers (1) in their location in the structure of family (i.e., socioeconomic status, family size, family intactness) and school (i.e., the size, location, and type of school); and (2) in their relations with school/education (i.e., attachment to school and commitment to education) and friends (i.e., conventional peer networks), as well as in their behavioral patterns. On the other hand, comparisons of

---

[15] While differences between black and Hispanic adolescents, on the one hand, and East Asian American adolescents, on the other, are also found to be nonsignificant in the final model, the racial/ethnic differences were already explained by the family background model unlike the black-Asian and Hispanic-Asian comparisons where South Asian American adolescents are used as the reference group.

[16] Alternatively, the observed discrepancy in Asian vs. non-Asian differences in arrest between the UCR and the NELS data can be interpreted as evidence of favorable treatment which Asian American juveniles receive by the juvenile justice system because of the police image of Asian Americans as more law-abiding and less crime-prone than their non-Asian Americans (Chambliss and Nagasawa, 1969). However, previous researchers tend to agree that racial/ethnic differences in crime and delinquency cannot be fully explained by differential treatment by the justice system (Hindelang et al., 1979; Sampson and Lauritsen, 1997; Tonry, 1997; Wilson and Herrnstein, 1985).

the four regional groups of Asian American adolescents show a general pattern of within-group homogeneity, whereas the observation of within-group heterogeneity tends to be confined to some of the family structural characteristics (i.e., socioeconomic status and family size), commitment to education, and, to a lesser extent, behavioral patterns.

What deserves further discussion concerns the relative explanatory power of two social bonding variables; that is, school bonding variables substantially explain differences in general deviance between Asian and non-Asian American adolescents, whereas family bonding variables do not.[17] This explanatory power of school bonding variables, especially commitment to education (measured by school grades), is consistent with previous studies that tend to find that the dimension of commitment explains adolescent deviance better than any other dimension of social bonding (e.g., Krohn and Massey, 1980). Also, the greater explanatory ability of school bonding compared to that of other variables might be attributed to the greater salience of the school as a "locus of interaction and control" (Thornberry, 1987:879) during middle adolescence, the period that this study focuses on. Previous research on the age-varying effects of commitment to school on delinquency tends to find that school influence peaks during middle adolescence (Jang, 1999; Thornberry et al., 1991).

Unlike school bonding variables, family bonding variables failed to explain differences in deviance between Asian and non-Asian American adolescents, while the lack of explanatory ability was a posteriori expected based on the ANOVA results. Specifically, Asian and non-Asian American adolescents were found to be not significantly different in all the measures of attachment to parents except close communication. Even in that exception, Asian (specifically, Far East Asian) American adolescents reported a significantly lower mean score than their non-Asian (i.e., white and black) counterparts. The present finding that Asian American adolescents are not necessarily more attached to their parents than their non-Asian American peers is somewhat surprising, given the more traditional parent–child relationships in Asian than non-Asian American families.[18]

While it is difficult to fully explain this unexpected finding without additional data that include expanded measures of attachment to parents for the entire period of adolescence, the finding could be attributed to the present study's focus on adolescent data. Specifically, it is likely that Asian American children become similar to their non-Asian American peers in their relations with parents during the developmental period of adolescence, which is characterized by various changes in expected social roles and self-identity. That is, such developmental changes might increase cultural conflicts between Asian American parents and adolescent children, thereby weakening their previously strong relations and thus making Asian American adolescents similar to their non-Asian counterparts in attachment to parents.

Alternatively, some indication of Asian American adolescents' relatively low levels of close communication with parents as well as the observed lack of difference in parental trust and affective ties between Asian and non-Asian American adolescents might reflect the collectivist

---

[17] The ability of school bonding variables in explaining the racial/ethnic differences might have been an artifact of the skewed composition of the general deviance measure because it primarily captures behavioral patterns at school. While the present data include two nonschool deviance items (i.e., runaway and arrest), it is difficult to examine whether the same explanatory power of school bonding variables will be observed for nonschool as well as school deviance measure because nonschool deviance items are limited.

[18] Given the cultural significance of the extended family among ethnic minorities including Asian Americans (Yue, 1993) and the present finding of the generally higher levels of parental monitoring among Asian than non-Asian American adolescents, I examined whether any possible Asian vs. non-Asian difference in the presence of grandparents and other relatives at home might have resulted in the different levels of parental monitoring as respondents treated their grandparents and other relatives as additional source of "parental" monitoring. Analysis of variance results, however, showed that Asian and non-Asian American respondents are not significantly different in the number of grandparents and other adult relatives living in the same household.

Asian culture. That is, Asian cultural precepts do not necessarily emphasize affective closeness and its expressions between parents (especially the father) and children as much as children's absolute submission to parental authority (e.g., Yue, 1993). Similarly, traditional Asian parent–child communication relies on "tacit understandings" rather than direct, verbal expression (Hieshima and Schneider, 1994:320; Yue, 1993). Alternately, the relatively low levels of Asian American adolescents' close communication might be due to language barriers and/or cultural distance between parents and children (e.g., Lin and Liu, 1993; Shoho, 1994).

Unlike family process variables, family background variables substantially explain the observed differences in deviance between Asian and non-Asian American adolescents. This tends to suggest that the family-related advantage that Asian American adolescents have over their non-Asian American peers is likely to be their living in families of high socioeconomic status and stability (i.e., living with both biological parents) rather than their relations with parents perse. In addition, this study finds that Asian American adolescents' limited assimilation, usually considered as an obstacle to their full participation in the mainstream American society, might be an "advantage" as far as its effects on their behavioral patterns are concerned. Perhaps their limited assimilation means their limited exposure to the American cultural element of "ontological individualism" (Bellah et al., 1985:143), which encourages youth to consider themselves free to cultivate and express themselves against societal constraints and conventions, exploring their own identity and experimenting with deviance. These family structural factors are likely to provide favorable environments for fostering conventional behaviors, including educational achievements, which in turn reduces deviant behavior among Asian American adolescents.

Several limitations of this study need to be acknowledged. First, although I analyzed data collected from a nationally representative sample, its failure to include school dropouts and other than tenth graders suggests that the present findings can be generalized only to the population of middle adolescents who stay in school. Future research needs to investigate racial/ethnic differences in deviance among school dropouts and to apply comparative analysis to youths in early and later adolescence to examine the age-(in)variance of the racial/ethnic differences. Second, the limited measure of deviance, which primarily taps misbehavior at school, implies another constraint on the generalizability of the present findings. Existing theories and research tend to suggest that these findings are likely to be replicated when adolescent deviance occurring in other social contexts than school is examined (Akers, 1985; Gottfredson and Hirschi, 1990; Jessor and Jessor, 1977; Loeber and Farrington, 1998). Third, given the present analysis of contemporaneous effects of social bonding and social learning variables on deviance, their causal interpretation should be made with caution.[19] Finally, future research should extend the present analysis to examine American adolescents of Pacific or Middle Eastern origin, which is another neglected ethnic group in criminological research.

In conclusion, despite their cultural diversity, this study shows that American adolescents of all racial/ethnic backgrounds are likely to engage in deviant behavior when they (1) fail to have their basic needs for proper socialization and adequate social control met within their families for some reason like family disruption or poverty; (2) are neither encouraged to do nor supported for doing their best at school, so that they have few "stakes in conformity"; (3) associate with friends who see

---

[19] Additional analyses were conducted by regressing general deviance on social bonding and social learning variables of the base year (i.e., 2 years prior to the first follow-up when the dependent variable was measured) to see whether results would change when lagged instead of contemporaneous effects are estimated. Although a full and direct comparison is impossible because of the inconsistency of measures across the two waves (e.g., no peer and attitudinal data available at the base year), the overall pattern of the effects of social bonding and social learning variables on general deviance tends to remain the same.

little relevance of education for their lives; and (4) believe that it is acceptable to violate social norms. This general finding suggests that delinquency prevention programs focusing on the adolescent's relations with the key social domains (i.e., the family, school, and peer group) and cognitive ability (e.g., moral reasoning) are likely to help adolescent children of all racial/ethnic groups to avoid engaging in deviant activities. A consistent policy for the successful operation of such programs would probably gradually reduce racial/ethnic differences in deviant and criminal behaviors among American adolescents.

References

Agnew, Robert
1990   "Adolescent resources and delinquency." Criminology 28:535–566.

Akers, Ronald L.
1985   Deviant Behavior: A Social Learning Approach, 3rd edn. Belmont, CA: Wadsworth.
1997   Criminological Theories: Introduction and Evaluation, 2nd edn. Los Angeles: Roxbury.

Alba, Richard D.
1990   Ethnic Identity: The Transformation of White America. New Haven, CT: Yale University Press.

Bachman, Jerald G., John M. Wallace Jr., Patrick M. O'Malley, Lloyd D. Johnston, Candace L. Kurth, and Harold W. Neighbors
1991   "Racial/ethnic differences in smoking drinking, and illicit drug use among American high school seniors, 1976–89." American Journal of Public Health 81:372–377.

Bankston, Carl L., III
1998   "Youth gangs and the new second generation: A review essay." Aggression and Violent Behavior 3:35–45.

Barringer, Herbert, Robert W. Gardner, and Michael J. Levin
1993   Asians and Pacific Islanders in the United States. New York: Russell Sage Foundation.

Batta, I. D., R. I. Mawby, and J. W. McCulloch
1981   "Crime, social problems, and Asian immigration: The Bradford experience." International Journal of Contemporary Sociology 18:135–168.

Bellah, Robert N., Richard Madsen, William M. Sullivan, Ann Swidler, and Stephen M. Tipton
1985   Habits of the Heart: Individualism and Commitment in American Life. Berkeley: University of California Press.

Berg, Insoo Kim, and Ajakai Jaya
1993   "Different and same: Family therapy with Asian-American families." Journal of Marital and Family Therapy 19:31–38.

Cernkovich, Stephen, and Peggy Giordano
1992   "School bonding, race, and delinquency." Criminology 30:261–291.

Chambliss, William J., and Richard H. Nagasawa
1969   "On the validity of official statistics: A comparative study of White, Black, and Japanese high-school boys." Journal of Research in Crime and Delinquency 6:71–77.

Chin, Ko-Lin
1990   "Chinese gangs and extortion." In Ronald C. Huff (ed.), Gangs in America: 129–145. Newbury Park, CA: Sage.

Choi, Y. Elsie, Janine Bempechat, and Herbert P. Ginsburg
1994   "Educational socialization in Korean American children: A longitudinal study." Journal of Applied Developmental Psychology 15:313–318.

Cohen, Jacob, and Patricia Cohen
1983   Applied Multiple Regression/Correlation Analysis for the Behavioral Sciences, 2nd edn. Hillsdale, NJ: Erlbaum.

Elliott, Delbert S., David Huizinga, and Suzanne S. Ageton
1985   Explaining Delinquency and Drug Use. Newbury Park, CA: Sage.

Elliott, Delbert S., David Huizinga, and Scott Menard
1989   Multiple Problem Youth: Delinquency, Substance Use and Mental Health Problems. New York: Springer.

Flowers, Ronald Barri
1988   Minorities and Criminality. New York: Greenwood Press.

Gottfredson, Michael R., and Travis Hirschi
1990   A General Theory of Crime. Stanford, CA: Stanford University Press.

Hagan, John, A. R. Gillis, and John Simpson
1985   "The class structure of gender and delinquency: Toward a power-control theory of common delinquent behavior." American Journal of Sociology 90:1151–1178.

Hayner, Norman S.
1933   "Delinquency areas in the Puget Sound." American Journal of Sociology 39:314–328.
1938   "Social factors in oriental crime." American Journal of Sociology 43:908–919.

Hieshima, Joyce, and Barbara Schneider
1994   "Intergenerational effects on the cultural and cognitive socialization of third- and fourth-generation Japanese Americans." Journal of Applied Developmental Psychology 15:319–327.

Hindelang, Michael J., Travis Hirschi, and Joseph G. Weis
1979   "Correlates of delinquency: The illusion of discrepancy between selfreport and official measures." American Sociological Review 44:995–1014.
1981   Measuring Delinquency. Beverly Hills, CA: Sage.

Hirschi, Travis
1969   Causes of Delinquency. Berkeley: University of California Press.
1979   "Separate and unequal is better." Journal of Research in Crime and Delinquency 16:34–37.

Humes, Karen, and Jesse McKinnon
2000   The Asian and Pacific Islander Population in the United States: March 1999 (U.S. Census Bureau, Current Population Reports, Series P20–529). Washington, DC: U.S. Government Printing Office.

Jang, Sung Joon
1999   "Age-varying effects of family, school, and peers on delinquency: A multilevel modeling testing of interactional theory." Criminology 37:643–685.

Jarjoura, G. Roger
1993   "Does dropping out of school enhance delinquent involvement? Results from a large-scale national probability sample." Criminology 31:149–172.

Jessor, Richard, and Shirley Jessor
1977   Problem Behavior and Psychosocial Development: A Longitudinal Study of Youth. New York: Academic Press.

Junger, Marianne, and Ineke Haen Marshall
1997   "The interethnic generalizability of social control theory: An empirical test." Journal of Research in Crime and Delinquency 34:79–112.

Junger-Tas, Josine
1997   "Ethnic minorities and criminal justice in the Netherlands." In Michael Tonry (ed.), Ethnicity, Crime, and Immigration: Comparative and Cross-National Perspectives, Vol. 21: Crime and Justice: A Review of Research: 257–310. Chicago: University of Chicago Press.

Kaufman, Phillip, Jin Y. Kwon, Steve Klein, and Christopher D. Chapman
2000   Dropout Rates in the United States: 1999 (National Center for Education Statistics, Statistical Analysis Report. NCES 2001-022). Washington, DC: U.S. Government Printing Office.

Kendall, Katherine A.
1988   "The evolving family: An international perspective." International Social Work 31:81–93.

Kim, Uichol, and Maria B. J. Chun
1994   "Educational 'success' of Asian Americans: An indigenous perspective." Journal of Applied Developmental Psychology 15:329–343.

Kim-Raynor, Soonja, and Tazuko Shibusawa Nakasone
1981   "Social work practice with Asian American families." Social Work Papers 16:33–42.

Kitano, Harry H. L., and Roger Daniels
1995 Asian Americans: Emerging Minorities, 2nd edn. Englewood Cliffs, NJ: Prentice Hall.

Krohn, Marvin D., and James L. Massey
1980 "Social control and delinquent behavior: An examination of the elements of the social bond." Sociological Quarterly 21:529–543.

Lee, Yoon Ho
1998 "Acculturation and delinquent behavior: The case of Korean American youths." International Journal of Comparative and Applied Criminal Justice 22:273–292.

Lieberson, Stanley, and Mary C. Waters
1988 From Many Strands: Ethnic and Racial Groups in Contemporary America. New York: Russell Sage Foundation.

Lin, Chien, and William T. Liu
1993 "Intergenerational relationships among Chinese immigrant families from Taiwan." In Harriette Pipes McAdoo (ed.), Family Ethnicity: Strength in Diversity: 271–286. Newbury Park, CA: Sage.

Lind, Andrew W.
1930 "Some ecological patterns of community disorganization in Honolulu." American Journal of Sociology 26:206–220.

Loeber, Rolf, and David P. Farrington
1998 Serious and Violent Juvenile Offenders: Risk Factors and Successful Interventions. Thousand Oaks, CA: Sage.

London, Harlan, and Wynetta Devore
1988 "Layers of understanding: Counseling ethnic minority families." Family Relations 37:310–314.

Martens, Peter L.
1997 "Immigrants, crime, and criminal justice in Sweden." In Michael Tonry (ed.), Ethnicity, Crime, and Immigration: Comparative and Cross-National Perspectives, Vol. 21: Crime and Justice: A Review of Research: 183–255. Chicago: University of Chicago Press.

Matsueda, Ross L., and Karen Heimer
1987 "Race, family structure, and delinquency: A test of differential association and social control theories." American Sociological Review 52:826–840.

McAdoo, Harriette Pipes
1993 "Ethnic families: Strengths that are found in diversity." In Harriette Pipes McAdoo (ed.), Family Ethnicity: Strength in Diversity: 3–14. Newbury Park, CA: Sage.

Ogbu, John U.
1990 "Minority education in comparative perspective." Journal of Negro Education 59:45–57.

Okada, Daniel William
1987 "Japanese American juvenile delinquency: An analysis of control theory in a Japanese American community." PhD dissertation, University of Maryland, College Park.

Ou, Young-Shi, and Harriette Pipes McAdoo
1993 "Socialization of Chinese American children." In Harriette Pipes McAdoo (ed.), Family Ethnicity: Strength in Diversity: 245–270. Newbury Park. CA: Sage.

Peterson, Ruth D., and John Hagan
1984 "Changing conceptions of race: Toward an account of anomalous findings of sentencing research." American Sociological Review 49:56–70.

Poole, Eric D., and Mark R. Pogrebin
1990 "Crime and law enforcement policy in the Korean American community." Police Studies 13:57–66.

Portes, Alejandro, and Cynthia Truelove
1987 "Making sense of diversity: Recent research on Hispanic minorities in the United States." Annual Review of Sociology 13:359–385.

Rutter, Michael, and Henri Giller
1983 Juvenile Delinquency: Trends and Perspectives. Harmondsworth, UK: Penguin Books.

Sampson, Robert J., and John H. Laub
1993 Crime in the Making: Pathways and Turning Points Through Life. Cambridge, MA: Harvard University Press.

Sampson, Robert J., and Janet L. Lauritsen
1997 "Racial and ethnic disparities in crime and criminal justice in the United States." In Michael Tonry (ed.), Ethnicity, Crime, and Immigration: Comparative and Cross-National Perspectives, Vol. 21: Crime and Justice: A Review of Research: 311–374. Chicago: University of Chicago Press.

Sanders, Williams B.
1994   Gangbangs and Drive-Bys: Grounded Culture and Juvenile Gang Violence. New York: Aldine De Gruyter.

Sheu, Chuen-Jim
1986   Delinquency and Identity: Juvenile Delinquency in an American Chinatown. New York: Harrow and Heston.

Shoho, Alan R.
1994   "A historical comparison of parental involvement of three generations of Japanese Americans (Isseis, Niseis, Sanseis) in the education of their children." Journal of Applied Developmental Psychology 15:305–311.

Smith, David F.
1997   "Ethnic origins, crime, and criminal justice in England and Wales." In Michael Tonry (ed.), Ethnicity, Crime, and Immigration: Comparative and Cross-National Perspectives, Vol. 21: Crime and Justice: A Review of Research: 101–182. Chicago: University of Chicago Press.

Taylor, Robert Joseph, Linda M. Chatters, M. Belinda Tucker, and Edith Lewis
1991   "Developments in research on Black families: A decade review." In Alan Booth (ed.), Contemporary Families: Looking Forward, Looking Back: 275–296. Minneapolis, MN: National Council on Family Relations.

Thornberry, Terence P.
1987   "Toward an interactional theory of delinquency." Criminology 25:863–891.

Thornberry, Terence P., Alan J. Lizotte, Marvin D. Krohn, Margaret Farnworth, and Sung Joon Jang
1991   "Testing interactional theory: An examination of reciprocal causal relationships among family, school, and delinquency." Journal of Criminal Law and Criminology 82:3–35.

Tonry, Michael
1997   "Ethnicity, crime, and immigration." In Michael Tonry (ed.), Ethnicity, Crime, and Immigration: Comparative and Cross-National Perspectives, Vol. 21: Crime and Justice: A Review of Research: 1–27. Chicago: University of Chicago Press.

Tournier, Pierre
1997   "Nationality, crime, and criminal justice in France." In Michael Tonry (ed.), Ethnicity, Crime, and Immigration: Comparative and Cross-National Perspectives, Vol. 21: Crime and Justice: A Review of Research: 523–551. Chicago: University of Chicago Press.

Toy, Calvin
1992   "A short history of Asian gangs in San Francisco." Justice Quarterly 9:647–665.

Unger, Steven
1977   The Destruction of American Indian Families. New York: Association on American Indian Affairs.

Vigil, James Diego, and Steve Chong Yun
1990   "Vietnamese youth gangs in southern California." In Ronald C. Huff (ed.), Gangs in America: 146–162. Newbury Park, CA: Sage.

Waters, Mary C., and Karl Eschbach
1995   "Immigration and ethnic and racial inequality in the United States." Annual Review of Sociology 21:419–446.

Wiatrowski, Michael D., David B. Griswold, and Mary K. Roberts
1981   "Social control theory and delinquency." American Sociological Review 46:525–541.

Wilkinson, Doris
1993   "Family ethnicity in America." In Harriette Pipes McAdoo (ed.), Family Ethnicity: Strength in Diversity: 15–59. Newbury Park, CA: Sage.

Wilson, William Julius
1980   The Declining Significance of Race: Blacks and Changing American Institutions, 2nd edn. Chicago: University of Chicago Press.

Wilson, James Q., and Richard J. Herrnstein

1985   Crime and Human Nature. New York: Simon and Schuster.

Wong, Siu Kwong

1997   "Delinquency of Chinese-Canadian youth: A test of opportunity, control, and intergeneration conflict theories." Youth and Society 29:112–133.

1999   "Acculturation, peer relations, and delinquent behavior of Chinese-Canadian youth." Adolescence 34:107–119.

Yamamoto, Joe, and Hiroshi Wagatsuma

1980   "The Japanese and Japanese Americans." Journal of Operational Psychiatry 11:120–135.

Yee, Albert H.

1992   "Asians as stereotypes and students: Misperceptions that persist." Educational Psychology Review 4:95–132.

Yue, Ma

1993   "Family relationships, broken homes, acculturation and delinquency in Chinese-American communities." PhD dissertation, Rutgers, State University of New Jersey–Newark.

Race, Family Structure, and Delinquency: A Test of Differential Association and Social Control Theories*

Ross L. Matsueda
Karen Heimer, *University of Wisconsin–Madison*

Studies of the relationship between race and delinquency have typically found that broken homes lead to greater delinquency among blacks than whites, but have not demonstrated empirically why this is so. This paper derives theoretical mechanisms from differential association theory and social control theory, specifying how broken homes may influence delinquency among both blacks and nonblacks. The analysis specifies a structural equation model of delinquency (Matsueda 1982), derives competing hypotheses from the two theories, and estimates a cross-population model for blacks and nonblacks using data from the Richmond Youth Project. Consistent with previous research, we find that broken homes have a larger impact on delinquency among blacks than nonblacks, but, unlike previous studies, our model explains this effect completely. In both populations, the effects of broken homes and attachment to parents and peers are mediated by the learning of definitions of delinquency, a finding that supports differential association over social control theory.

* Direct all correspondence to Ross L. Matsueda, Department of Sociology, University of Wisconsin, Madison, WI 53706.

This is a revised version of a paper prepared for presentation at the 1987 Annual Meetings of the American Sociological Association, Chicago. The research was partially supported by the Graduate School of the University of Wisconsin–Madison. For their insightful comments on an earlier draft, we thank William T. Bielby, Rosemary Gartner, Charles N. Halaby, and two anonymous ASR reviewers. We also thank Travis Hirschi, Joseph G. Weis, and Carol A. Zeiss for making the data available.

Although race is a critical variable in many theories of crime, little empirical research has examined competing explanations of the race-delinquency relationship. There are perhaps three reasons for this. First, given the history of racial discrimination in the United States, any examination of black-white differences in unlawful behavior is likely to be politically sensitive and controversial (Wilson and Herrnstein 1985; Wilson 1985). Second, differences in criminal and delinquent behavior, as measured by official statistics, have been attributed to racial bias in the criminal justice system. Third, racial disparities in delinquency have been difficult to measure reliably. Indeed, researchers disagree over the extent to which rates of unlawful behavior vary by race: official statistics and victimization surveys show wide disparities, while self-report surveys show few differences (Hindelang 1978; Hindelang, Hirschi, and Weis 1979, 1981). Moreover, because the responses of blacks to survey questions contain more random variability than those of whites, some have cautioned against making racial comparisons with delinquency data (Hirschi 1969). This implies that any cross-race comparison must consider differential errors of measurement (Bielby, Hauser, and Featherman 1977).

Most previous research on black-white differences in delinquency has focused on the structure of the family. Stimulated by the Moynihan Report (1965), which hypothesized that black youths commit more delinquent acts in part because of a tangle of pathology originating in female-headed households, unemployment, illegitimacy, and differential socialization, such research has examined the joint relationships among race, broken homes, and delinquency. The conclusions have been mixed: most researchers find that broken homes have a larger effect on delinquency among blacks (Monahan 1957; Moynihan 1965; Rosen, Lalli, and Savitz 1975); some find a greater effect among whites (Toby 1957; Chilton and Markle 1972; Austin 1978); still others find little difference by race (Tennyson 1967; Berger and Simon 1974). This literature has been preoccupied with the demographic question of whether the effect of broken homes on delinquency varies by race. From a theoretical standpoint, a more significant question concerns the causal mechanisms intervening between broken homes and delinquency for both races. What is needed, then, is a theoretical model that can explain these relationships.

This paper examines delinquent behavior among blacks and nonblacks using a causal model derived from two dominant sociological theories of delinquency: differential association theory and social control theory. The model builds on a statistical model previously estimated to test differential association against control theory (Matsueda 1982). We use the model to examine differences in parameters across populations of black and nonblack youth, to focus on the relationship between family structure and delinquency, and to test the efficacy of differential association versus social control theory across race. The first section discusses the implications of differential association and social control theories for explaining the relationships among race, broken homes, and delinquency. Here we derive several testable hypotheses from the competing theories. The second section presents a structural equation model of these relationships, estimates the model's parameters, and tests key hypotheses. The third section discusses the implications of the results for theorizing about race, social structure, and delinquency.

Modeling Racial Differences: Differential Association Versus Social Control Theory

Our task is to develop a social-psychological explanation of the joint relationships among race, broken homes, and delinquency. Two distinct mechanisms can explain such relationships. First, race and broken homes could interact in their effects on delinquency: the effect of broken homes and other determinants of delinquency could be greater among blacks. Second, race could influence delinquency indirectly through its effects on broken homes. The latter assumes that the effect of broken homes on delinquency does not vary by race; consequently, testing the interaction effect is logically prior. For this reason, and because prior studies suggest that both measurement and substantive processes vary by race, we will examine a cross-race model of delinquency. Previous research suggests that the effects of race and broken homes must be disentangled from the influences of socioeconomic status and neighborhood processes (Shaw and McKay 1969; Monahan 1957; Moynihan 1965; Berger and Simon 1974). Therefore, we need to locate those intervening social-psychological processes explaining such relationships.

According to Sutherland's (1947) theory of differential association, delinquency is rooted in normative conflict. Modern industrial societies contain conflicting structures of norms, behavior patterns, and definitions of appropriate behavior that give rise to high rates of crime. At the *group* level of explanation, Sutherland posited that normative conflict is translated into group rates of delinquency through differential social organization: the extent to which a group is organized for or against delinquency determines its rate of law violation. This differential organization consists of neighborhood organization, family processes, peer relationships, and the distribution of age, race, and class.

At the *individual* level, Sutherland maintained that normative conflict is translated into individual acts of delinquency through differential association. Definitions favorable and unfavorable to delinquent behavior are learned through communication, primarily in intimate groups. Whether delinquency occurs depends on the ratio of learned definitions favorable and unfavorable to that act. Moreover, each definition is weighed by four modalities: frequency, duration, priority, and intensity. Definitions presented more frequently, for a longer time, earlier in life, and from a more prestigious source receive more weight.

Taken together, the individual and group components of differential association explain the organizational and learning mechanisms by which race and family status influence delinquent behavior. The learning mechanism (differential association process) should be invariant across race, although the context or source of that learning, such as parents, peers, or neighborhoods (differential social organization), may vary by race. For example, if a broken home impedes parental supervision and attachment, it could indirectly increase a child's contact with prodelinquent definitions from delinquent boys and other influences outside the home (Sutherland and Cressey 1978, p. 219–24; Shaw and McKay 1931). Furthermore, broken homes may hamper the formation of attachments to parents (prestige) and the transmission of antidelinquent definitions from parent to child; thus, the prodelinquent organization of the community or neighborhood would not be offset by antidelinquent influences within the home. Since racial segregation often limits blacks to inner-city neighborhoods with low socioeconomic status and abundant definitions favorable to street crimes (Sutherland and Cressey 1978, p. 220), the influence of broken homes on delinquency may be particularly acute for blacks. The important point is that for both blacks and nonblacks, structural variables such as broken homes and neighborhood organization affect delinquency by influencing the dynamic process of learning definitions favorable and unfavorable to crime.

In contrast to differential association, Hirschi's (1969) social control theory denies the existence of normative conflict and ignores the importance of motives for delinquency, such as prodelinquent definitions. Control theory posits a single conventional moral order in society and assumes that the motivation for delinquency is invariant across persons. The question is not, "Why do some people violate the law?" since we are all equally motivated to do so, but rather, "Why do most people refrain from law violation?" Hirschi's answer is that they are dissuaded by strong bonds to conventional society: attachment, commitment, involvement, and belief.

Attachment to others dissuades persons from delinquency through a moral process: those with warm relationships with their parents or friends are likely to consider their reactions to the unlawful act. Because only a single moral order exists, that reaction will always be negative. Commitment to conventional lines of action reflects an investment of time and energy in procuring an education, developing a business, or building a virtuous reputation. The greater the investment, the less likely the person will jeopardize it by violating the law. Involvement in conventional activities simply limits one's time to contemplate and execute illegal acts. Finally, belief in the moral order directly taps an individual's internalization of conventional morality. Here, Hirschi reconceptualizes Sutherland's definitions of delinquency to conform to the assumptions of control theory: since there is only one moral order, beliefs concerning delinquency are all conventional, and the greater the belief the less likely the deviation.

Each of these components of the bond, while intercorrelated, are said to affect delinquency independently and additively (Hirschi 1969, pp. 27–30). While differential association theory implies that attachments, involvements, and commitments will affect delinquency only indirectly through their effects on definitions (belief), control theory maintains that each element of the bond *itself* affects delinquency directly (Jensen 1972; Kornhauser 1978; Matsueda 1982).

Control theory implies that the causes of delinquency (social bonding) are the same for all racial groups (Hirschi 1969, p. 80). The theory would receive strong support if the absolute effect on delinquency of each element of the bond were identical for all races. This would imply that the theory describes a deep invariant structure that persists in the face of racial segregation and discrimination. But confirming control theory may not require such invariance, instead requiring only that the elements of the bond explain the probability of delinquent behavior. Thus, we might expect socialization practices or belief systems to vary across racial groups, causing attachment, commitment, involvement, and belief to affect delinquency differently by race.

Furthermore, the relative strength of structural determinants of social bonding may also vary by race. Here, we are on less-solid ground, since Hirschi (1969, p. 113) had little to say about factors affecting the strength of elements of the bond. Nevertheless, if we conceptualize the structural-level counterpart of bonding as social disorganization—a community's inability to control the behavior of juveniles because of weak and unlinked institutions—we can hypothesize about racial differences in bonding and its

determinants (Kornhauser 1978; Shaw and McKay 1969). Broken homes, lower socioeconomic classes, and high-crime neighborhoods (disorganization) should influence delinquency by impeding the formation of strong attachments, commitments, involvements, and beliefs. Because nonintact homes undermine parent-child relations, attachment to parents—perhaps the most important element of the bond—should be the principal intervening variable between broken homes and delinquency (Hirschi 1969, 1983).[1] In turn, attachments to parents should generalize, allowing attachments to form among peers and reinforcing strong moral beliefs. If Moynihan and others are correct that blacks are ensnarled in a tangle of pathology, then social control theory would claim that this pathology is a reflection of disorganization and that broken homes, social class, and neighborhood delinquency will produce more delinquency among blacks by inhibiting the formation of strong attachments and beliefs.

In sum, control theory and differential association make different predictions of the causes of delinquency among black and nonblack males. Social control theory predicts that, for both blacks and nonblacks, delinquency is determined by the independent effects of the elements of the social bond. Family structure may affect the elements of the social bond differently across race, but each element of the bond should exert a unique effect on delinquency for both races. The relative importance of these bonds, however, may vary across race, due to a different emphasis on socialization practices, which in turn stems from social disorganization. Differential association, however, predicts that, for both blacks and nonblacks, delinquency is determined by learning definitions of the legal code (beliefs), which mediate the influence of attachments, commitments, and involvements. The sources of that learning,

---

[1] Hirschi (1969, 1983) has argued that single-parent families should have similar rates of delinquency as intact families, since, all things being equal, one parent should be as effective as two in socializing children. Nevertheless, all things are never equal, and logically, for social control theory, if broken homes influence delinquency, they do so by attenuating the elements of the social bond.

however, are determined by individuals' group location in the social structure, which organizes their patterns of interactions, and which may differ by race. This implies that the determinants of a person's learned definitions, such as being from a broken home, a trouble-ridden neighborhood, a close family unit, or a delinquent peer group, may vary across race, but the determinant of delinquency—an excess of definitions favorable to delinquency—will not.

A Cross Population Model of Race and Delinquency

Our investigation analyzes Matsueda's (1982) causal model of differential association, control theory, and delinquency by replicating the model on the black population of the Richmond Youth Project. We first examine whether the model as a whole varies across race, then test key hypotheses about substantive parameters both within and across groups. We examine two substantive issues: (1) the model's ability to explain the influence of family structure on delinquency; and (2) the relative efficacy of differential association versus social control theory.

The data were collected in 1965 as part of the Richmond Youth Project, which sampled a large number of students in 11 junior and senior high schools of Contra Costa County in California (Wilson 1965). These data are particularly well suited to the issues at hand: 1965 marked the publication of Moynihan's report; the population is a large heterogeneous metropolitan area containing substantial numbers of lower-income, inner-city blacks; and the random sample was stratified by race, as well as school, sex, and grade. Our analyses will focus on the 1,588 nonblack males and 1,001 black males.[2]

Self-report measures . . . were obtained through questionnaires administered in schools.[3] (For further details of the data collection procedures and characteristics of the sample, see Hirschi 1969.)

Our causal model of delinquency, depicted in Figure 2.1, consists of a substantive model of the mechanisms generating delinquent behavior and a measurement model of the process by which underlying substantive concepts generate observable measures. The measurement model, indicated by the paths connecting latent variables to observable indicators, allows us to estimate and control statistically for the biasing effects of measurement error in substantive constructs.[4] Such a model can be crucial for cross-population analyses because it can reveal differential measurement processes across populations, which, if not dealt with, can obscure cross-population comparisons. Therefore, before we proceed to our hypotheses derived from differential association and social control theory, we will examine our measurement models for the two populations.

The substantive component of our model consists of three blocks of variables: four exogenous background variables describing demographic characteristics of individuals, four intervening variables representing the social control and differential association processes, and an outcome variable of self-reported

---

[2] The response rate for nonblacks was 75 percent, for blacks, 68 percent. Hirschi (1969) examined potential bias due to non-response, finding that nonresponse was evenly distributed among permission denied by parent, no response by parent, transfers and dropouts, and absentees. Furthermore, while respondents were less likely than nonrespondents to have a police record, this effect did not vary much by race. Therefore, nonresponse should not bias our cross-population results appreciably. (Upon request, covariance matrices of observable variables are available from the authors.)

[3] In using a sample stratified by race, estimating separate models for nonblacks and blacks, and fixing the validity coefficient of self-reported delinquency to be larger for nonblacks than blacks, we are following the recommendations of Hindelang et al. (1981), who argue that, after taking these steps, self-reports of minor forms of delinquency are reasonably reliable and valid for testing theories.

[4] The measurement model of definitions of delinquency conceptualizes Sutherland's concept of a ratio of definitions favorable and unfavorable to delinquency as a unidimensional construct, which generates fallible indicators. Each indicator, measured on a single continuum from highly antidelinquent to highly prodelinquent, is assumed to capture one domain of the ratio of definitions. After controlling statistically for response errors, the common variation across our measures should adequately tap such a construct (see Matsueda 1982 for details).

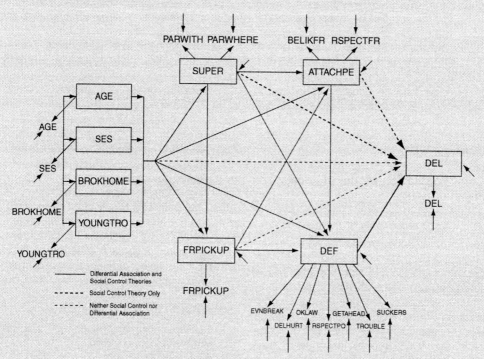

FIGURE 2.1 Path Diagram of the Full Structural Equation Model of Delinquency

delinquency.[5] We specify the intervening variables—parental supervision (attachment to parents), delinquent friends, attachment to peers, and definitions of delinquency—as linear functions of our background variables: age, socioeconomic status, broken homes, and neighborhood trouble (see Figure 2.1). In both social control and differential association theories, these effects, representing the influence of social structure on socialization processes, may vary by race.

HYPOTHESIS 1. *The effects of background variables, including family structure, on social bonding(attachment and belief) vary by race.*

In addition, differential group organization predicts that attachment to parents and peers and delinquent friends may influence definitions differently by race:

HYPOTHESIS 2. *The effects of background variables and parental and peer processes on definitions of delinquency vary by race.*

According to both theories, the total impact of broken homes and other background variables on delinquency may differ by race. For example, as some previous research has found, broken homes may exert a larger effect on delinquency for blacks than for nonblacks. Whatever the magnitude, however, social control and differential association

---

[5] The causal ordering among our variables within a cross-sectional design follows previous research using these data (Hirschi 1969; Jensen 1972; Matsueda 1982). This ordering is consistent with both differential association theory and social control theory. Some recent evidence on this issue within a longitudinal framework confirms the causal priority of attachment to parents on delinquency (Liska and Reed 1985; Agnew 1985) and definitions of delinquency (belief) (Agnew 1985; Elliott, Huizinga, and Ageton 1985), but see also Minor (1984).

theories specify intervening mechanisms to account for the total effects. The most significant hypotheses for social control theory are that attachment to parents, attachment to peers, and belief in morality each have a direct effect on delinquency and together should mediate the influence on delinquency of background characteristics such as broken homes, age, SES, and neighborhood trouble. These hypotheses should hold equally for blacks and nonblacks. Furthermore, control theory allows the relative effects of these variables on delinquency to differ by race, reflecting, for example, differential socialization practices across racial groups. The foregoing can be expressed as two hypotheses:

> **HYPOTHESIS 3**. *The effects on delinquency of broken homes and the other background variables are mediated by variables representing social bonding.*

> **HYPOTHESIS 4**. *Attachment to parents, attachment to peers, and belief all have significant effects on delinquency.*

In contrast, the crucial proposition of differential association theory is that the effects of definitions of delinquency on delinquent behavior should be racially invariant and, for both blacks and nonblacks, should mediate the effects on delinquency of all other variables (see Figure 2.1). The antecedent variables, including background characteristics and other elements of the social bond, reflect elements of social organization that structure the differential learning of behavior patterns. Consequently, if age, broken homes, or parental supervision have large total effects on delinquency, it is because they represent an important source of learning definitions of delinquency. These propositions translate into two testable hypotheses:

> **HYPOTHESIS 5**. *For both blacks and non-blacks, a person's learned ratio of definitions mediates the effects of other antecedent variables in the model, including the effect of broken homes.*

> **HYPOTHESIS 6**. *The effect of definitions of the law on delinquency is racially invariant.*

Results

We estimated the parameters of our measurement and substantive models jointly as a single system using the maximum likelihood estimator of Joreskog's LISREL V program (Joreskog and Sorbom 1984). Our analysis of the measurement models . . . reveals larger measurement errors for blacks than nonblacks. Thus, the failure to correct for attenuation due to unreliability could lead to greater downward biases in regression coefficients among blacks than nonblacks. Overall, the model fits better for nonblacks ($L^2 = 129.04$ d.f. = 71) than blacks ($L^2 = 216.22$; d.f. = 71).[6] Both findings are consistent with other similar response models (Bielby et al. 1977).

Estimation of the Model for Nonblacks

Our discussion of the substantive model will focus on the above six hypotheses. We first highlight the results for nonblacks, then present the findings for blacks in more detail, emphasizing differences across race. Table 2.1 presents the unstandardized parameter estimates of our baseline model for nonblacks in their reduced, semireduced, and structural forms; their standardized counterparts appear in Table 2.2. These estimates reveal four principal findings. First, the model explains substantial variation in definitions of delinquency ($R^2 = .66$). Friends picked up by the police, attachment to peers, and parental supervision exert substantial direct effects on the learned ratio of definitions (line 10 of Table 2.2) and also mediate the effects of certain background variables. More precisely, the total effect of neighborhood trouble is mediated by supervision and delinquent friends (compare line 7 with lines 8 and 9). Thus, living in a troubled neighborhood exposes nonblacks to more delinquent

---

[6] this holds even though we have a larger sample of nonblacks, and, thus, greater statistical power to detect departure from the hypothesized model. For comparability, the model for blacks includes the same measurement error correlations specified by Matsueda (1982) for the nonblacks—some of which were nonsignificant. A sensitivity analysis, however, revealed that a better-fitting model did not alter the substantive picture in any meaningful way. Thus, it appears that the overall goodness-of-fit statistic is sensitive to trivial departures from uninteresting restrictions.

TABLE 2.1 Unstandardized Parameter Estimates of the Substantive Model: Nonblack Males ($N = 1,558$)

Dependent Variables	Predetermined Variables								Components of Variation			
	AGE	SES	BROKHOME	YOUNGTRO	SUPER	FRPICKUP	ATTACHPE	DEF	R^2	Residual	Explained	Total
1. SUPER	-.031 (.008)	.004 (.008)	-.154 (.043)	-.107 (.020)					.089	.389	.120	.407
2. FRPICKUP	.157 (.024)	-.022 (.026)	.033 (.132)	.426 (.062)					.121	1.148	.427	1.225
3. FRPICKUP	.134 (.024)	-.019 (.025)	-.082 (.132)	.345 (.063)	-.715 (.122)				.178	1.110	.518	1.225
4. ATTACHPE	.020 (.009)	.015 (.008)	.031 (.041)	-.076 (.020)					.062	.303	.084	.315
5. ATTACHPE	.025 (.010)	.015 (.008)	.055 (.042)	-.059 (.020)	.159 (.041)				.089	.298	.100	.315
6. ATTACHPE	.035 (.010)	.013 (.008)	.050 (.042)	-.035 (.021)	.107 (.040)	-.069 (.016)			.161	.288	.126	.315
7. DEF	.037 (.010)	-.013 (.009)	.111 (.045)	.182 (.025)					.208	.336	.170	.377
8. DEF	.025 (.009)	-.011 (.009)	.052 (.043)	.140 (.023)	-.387 (.053)				.367	.300	.228	.377
9. DEF	.003 (.009)	-.008 (.009)	.065 (.041)	.082 (.021)	-.261 (.045)	.169 (.019)			.614	.235	.295	.377
10. DEF	.012 (.010)	-.004 (.009)	.080 (.041)	.072 (.021)	-.231 (.045)	-.149 (.019)	-.282 (.071)		.660	.219	.307	.377
11. DEL	.062 (.018)	.000 (.020)	.227 (.101)	.365 (.047)					.123	.877	.327	.936
12. DEL	.043 (.018)	.002 (.019)	.133 (.101)	.299 (.048)	-.613 (.094)				.188	.844	.405	.936
13. DEL	-.017 (.018)	.011 (.018)	.169 (.096)	.144 (.048)	-.275 (.091)	.450 (.033)			.473	.680	.643	.936
14. DEL	-.011 (.019)	.013 (.018)	.179 (.096)	.137 (.048)	-.254 (.092)	.437 (.035)	-.189 (.151)		.476	.677	.646	.936
15. DEL	-.026 (.021)	.019 (.019)	.083 (.099)	.050 (.052)	.024 (.112)	.257 (.056)	.152 (.180)	1.208 (.292)	.557	.623	.699	.936

Note: Standard errors appear in parentheses.

TABLE 2.2 Standardized Parameter Estimates of the Substantive Model: Nonblack Males (*N* = 1,558)

Dependent Variable	AGE	SES	BROK-HOME	YOUNG-TRO	SUPER	FRPICKUP	ATTACHPE	DEF
				Predetermined Variables				
1. SUPER	−.123	.017	−.140	−.210				
2. FRPICKUP	.208	−.033	.010	.278				
3. FRPICKUP	.178	−.029	−.025	.225	−.250			
4. ATTACHPE	.106	.092	.037	−.193				
5. ATTACHPE	.132	.088	.066	−.150	.206			
6. ATTACHPE	.180	.080	.059	−.089	.138	−.271		
7. DEF	.160	−.063	.109	.384				
8. DEF	.109	−.056	.051	.296	−.419			
9. DEF	.011	−.040	.064	.173	−.282	.548		
10. DEF	.054	−.022	.078	.152	−.249	.484	−.235	
11. DEL	.108	.000	.090	.311				
12. DEL	.075	.005	.052	.255	−.267			
13. DEL	−.030	.022	.067	.123	−.120	.589		
14. DEL	−.018	.027	.071	.117	−.111	.572	−.063	
15. DEL	−.044	.037	.033	.043	.011	.336	.051	.487

definitions by attenuating parental supervision and increasing the number of delinquent companions. Also, the total effect of broken homes on definitions, modest in size but statistically significant, is mediated by parental supervision.

Second, the model also does well in explaining variation in delinquent behavior (R^2 = .56): every variable in the model except socioeconomic status has a significant total effect on delinquency. The largest total effect is exerted by delinquent friends, followed by definitions of delinquency, supervision, and neighborhood trouble. Broken homes exert a small but statistically significant total effect.

Consistent with social control theory (Hypothesis 3), our third finding is that the significant total effects of age, broken homes, and neighborhood trouble are mediated by the joint effects of attachment to parents, delinquent friends, attachment to peers, and moral beliefs (line 15). Thus, being older, from a broken home, and from a troubled neighborhood increases the

likelihood of delinquency by attenuating attachments to parents and peers, increasing the number of delinquent friends, and reducing the strength of conventional beliefs.

Nevertheless, our fourth finding, which addresses our crucial test of differential association versus social control theory (Hypothesis 4), supports differential association theory. Both attachment to parents and peers have substantial and statistically significant indirect effects on delinquency through definitions. Moreover, the remaining unmediated direct effects of the attachment variables are not only nonsignificant and small in magnitude, but, from the standpoint of social control theory, implausibly positive in sign (line 15 of Table 2.1). Thus, as differential association predicts, youths who are closely supervised and develop warm friendships commit fewer delinquent acts because they are exposed to fewer prodelinquent definitions.

In addition, none of the background variables has a significant direct effect on delinquency in the structural form (Hypothesis 5). The number of delinquent friends, however, does have a substantial and statistically significant influence on delinquency.[7] This direct effect is smaller than the effect of definitions, and about as large as the indirect effect of delinquent friends through definitions of delinquency; nevertheless, the result provides some negative evidence for differential association.[8] Although irrelevant to the debate between Hirschi and Sutherland, the finding supports a group process explanation of delinquency (Short and Strodtbeck 1965; Briar and Piliavin 1965).

Estimation of the Model for Blacks

Parameter estimates of our substantive model for blacks appear in Table 2.3 in unstandardized form, and Table 2.4 in standardized form. Our discussion will focus on our cross-population hypotheses. To test these hypotheses, we use likelihood-ratio statistics, which are distributed chi-square in large samples and are obtained by subtracting the pooled likelihood-ratio statistic of our baseline model ($L^2 = 345.26$; d.f. = 142) from that of the model with cross-group constraints. Using the overall test of invariance, we reject the hypothesis that all substantive parameters are the same for blacks and nonblacks ($L^2 = 427.79$; d.f. = 82; $p < .001$) and then proceed to more specific cross-group comparisons. Our first comparison hypothesizes that the determinants of the processes of social bonding and differential association vary by race. For the social control process, the effects of background variables on elements of the social bond (Hypothesis 1) appear invariant across groups ($L^2 = 20.13$; d.f. = 12; $p > .05$). For the differential association process, however, we find that the determinants of definitions of the legal code vary by race ($L^2 = 18.37$; d.f. = 7; $p < .01$). This finding (Hypothesis 2) is due primarily to the larger effects of broken homes, parental supervision, and neighborhood trouble on the process of learning definitions among blacks (compare line 10 in Tables 2.3 and). Thus, from the standpoint of differential association, the neighborhood and family organization of blacks is most telling in the process producing definitions of delinquency.

Turning to the equations predicting delinquent behavior, we first examine the total effects of our substantive variables and then the causal structure explaining those total effects. Note that delinquent friends have a slightly larger total effect in our model for nonblacks than for blacks. Perhaps the most striking racial difference, however, is in the reduced-form effects of broken homes and neighborhood trouble: the former is three times larger among blacks, while the latter is five times smaller. Thus, consistent with much previous research, broken homes are more influential in producing delinquency among blacks than nonblacks.

Paralleling our findings for nonblacks, we find that, along with delinquent peers, the elements of the social bond—attachments to parents and peers and belief in morality—collectively mediate the influence of our background variables on delinquency (line 15). The indirect effects of age, broken homes, and neighborhood trouble are substantial, while the remaining unmediated effects are either trivial in size (broken homes) or opposite in sign than anticipated (age and neighborhood trouble). Again, this is consistent with social control theory (Hypothesis 3).

We can assess Hypotheses 4 and 5, which test control theory against differential association, by comparing lines 11–15 in Tables 2.3 and 2.4. Line 14 reveals that before adding definitions

---

[7] This is the only finding inconsistent with Matsueda (1982), who found that the influence of delinquent friends on delinquent behavior was mediated by definitions. The discrepancy between our model for nonblacks and Matsueda's (1982) is due to a different method of handling missing values. Here, to insure comparability with the sample of blacks, we used pairwise deletion for nonblacks, while Matsueda (1982) used listwise deletion. We also estimated cross-population models using listwise deletion for both groups, and, while the sample size was reduced by 40 percent, the results were identical for blacks. Thus, missing values do not substantially influence the overall pattern of results.

[8] This direct effect of delinquent friends on delinquent behavior also results in three variables having indirect effects on delinquency through delinquent friends, not definitions of delinquency. The effects are modest in size, however, particularly in comparison to similar indirect effects through definitions. The relative indirect effects through delinquent friends and definitions, respectively, are: .07 and .08 for age, .09 and .19 for neighborhood trouble, and −.07 and −.20 for supervision.

TABLE 2.3 Unstandardized Parameter Estimates of the Substantive Model: Black Males ($N = 948$)

Dependent Variable	Predetermined Variables								Components of Variation			
	AGE	SES	BROKHOME	YOUNGTRO	SUPER	FRPICKUP	ATTACHPE	DEF	R^2	Residual	Explained	Total
1. SUPER	-.015 (.008)	.010 (.014)	-.178 (.058)	-.057 (.025)					.066	.332	.084	.344
2. FRPICKUP	.112 (.033)	-.032 (.056)	.347 (.221)	.190 (.096)					.063	1.108	.288	1.145
3. FRPICKUP	.097 (.032)	-.022 (.055)	.166 (.223)	.132 (.096)	-1.021 (.200)				.151	1.055	.445	1.145
4. ATTACHPE	.001 (.011)	.029 (.017)	.041 (.065)	-.050 (.029)					.035	.324	.063	.330
5. ATTACHPE	.004 (.011)	.027 (.017)	.072 (.068)	-.040 (.029)	.175 (.063)				.066	.318	.008	.330
6. ATTACHPE	.012 (.011)	.025 (.017)	.087 (.068)	-.029 (.029)	.086 (.065)	-.088 (.026)			.145	.305	.126	.330
7. DEF	.073 (.024)	.037 (.030)	.531 (.119)	.243 (.052)					.326	.437	.303	.532
8. DEF	.063 (.023)	.044 (.029)	.409 (.114)	.204 (.050)	-.688 (.123)				.509	.373	.379	.532
9. DEF	.049 (.024)	.047 (.029)	.384 (.112)	.184 (.049)	-.534 (.122)	.150 (.038)			.598	.338	.411	.532
10. DEF	.053 (.024)	.056 (.029)	.414 (.114)	.174 (.049)	-.504 (.121)	.119 (.041)	-.349 (.136)		.638	.319	.425	.532
11. DEL	.003 (.024)	.060 (.041)	.697 (.164)	.075 (.071)					.096	.794	.258	.835
12. DEL	-.007 (.024)	.067 (.041)	.576 (.166)	.037 (.071)	-.681 (.146)				.170	.761	.345	.835
13. DEL	-.034 (.024)	.073 (.041)	.530 (.165)	.000 (.071)	-.394 (.157)	.281 (.056)			.295	.701	.454	.835
14. DEL	-.030 (.024)	.082 (.041)	.560 (.167)	-.011 (.071)	-.364 (.156)	.250 (.060)	-.353 (.198)		.312	.693	.467	.835
15. DEL	-.082 (.041)	.026 (.051)	.149 (.245)	-.183 (.106)	.136 (.253)	.131 (.077)	-.007 (.255)	.992 (.371)	.456	.616	.565	.835

Note: Standard errors appear in parentheses.

TABLE 2.4   Standardized Parameter Estimates of the Substantive Model: Black Males (N = 948)

Dependent Variable			Predetermined Variables					
	AGE	SES	BROK-HOME	YOUNG-TRO	SUPER	FRPICKUP	ATTACHPE	DEF
1. SUPER	−.070	.039	−.180	−.135				
2. FRPICKUP	.162	−.039	.106	.136				
3. FRPICKUP	.141	−.027	.051	.094	−.306			
4. ATTACHPE	.006	.121	.043	−.125				
5. ATTACHPE	.019	.114	.076	−.100	.183			
6. ATTACHPE	.062	.106	.092	−.071	.089	−.306		
7. DEF	.228	.097	.348	.372				
8. DEF	.197	.115	.268	.312	−.444			
9. DEF	.151	.123	.252	.281	−.345	.323		
10. DEF	.165	.146	.272	.266	−.325	.257	−.216	
11. DEL	.006	.101	.291	.074				
12. DEL	−.014	.112	.241	.036	−.280			
13. DEL	−.068	.122	.221	.000	−.162	.385		
14. DEL	−.059	.137	.234	−.010	−.150	.342	−.139	
15. DEL	−.164	.044	.062	−.178	.056	.180	−.003	.632

of the legal code into the equation, our model accounts for a substantial amount of variation in delinquency (R^2 = .31). Thus, our test of differential association—the extent to which definitions mediate the effects of other variables on delinquency—is a strong one, since substantial total effects must be mediated. As noted above, in the black sample, the reduced-form effect of broken homes on delinquency is substantial (line 11 of Table 2.4), as is the semi-reduced form (line 14). Before adding definitions into the equation, then, broken homes have a large and significant effect on delinquency. After adding definitions, however, that effect becomes trivial in size and statistically indistinguishable from zero (line 15 of Table 2.3). As differential association predicts, broken homes influence delinquency by impeding the transmission of antidelinquent definitions and increasing the transmission of prodelinquent patterns. Similarly, in accord with control theory, attachment to parents (supervision) has a large total effect on delinquency that works partly indirectly through delinquent friends and partly directly before adding our definitions variable. But the structural form (line 15) reveals that, after adding definitions into the equation, the effect

of supervision becomes nonsignificant, and, from the standpoint of control theory, implausibly positive. Again, this is consistent with differential association theory: supervision influences delinquency by influencing the ratio of learned definitions of delinquency. Furthermore, delinquent friends exert a large and significant effect on delinquency before adding definitions, but a comparatively small and nonsignificant effect in the presence of our definitions construct (compare lines 14 and 15). Thus, in contrast to our findings for nonblacks, delinquent friends influence delinquency by presenting definitions of the legal code; this finding supports differential association theory over group process theories.[9] While the

[9] The nonsignificance of this parameter estimate for blacks could be due to type II error, given the smaller size of the black sample. To investigate this, we conducted a power analysis, following the recommendation of Matsueda and Bielby (1986). We found that the model for blacks had ample statistical power (.95) to detect a metric coefficient the size of the estimate for nonblacks. But, although we cannot detect, with reasonable power, a standardized coefficient of .20 (power = .50), we can detect a standardized coefficient of .23 (power = .65). Thus, we have sufficient protection against type II error, assuming a nontrivial (larger than .20) effect of delinquent friends on delinquency in our black population.

total effect of attachment to peers is small and statistically nonsignificant, the indirect effect through definitions is significant, rendering the direct effect on delinquency virtually nonexistent. Differential association is again supported over control theory.

Finally, we tested Hypothesis 6, derived from differential association theory, which postulates that the effect of definitions on delinquency is invariant across race. That test confirmed the hypothesis: the point estimates are indistinguishable from one another at conventional levels of significance ($L^2 = .17$; d.f. $= 1$; $p > .50$). Thus, differential association theory again receives strong support.

Discussion

For both black and nonblack samples, our models support differential association theory over social control theory. Contrary to Hirschi's (1969) postulate that each element of the social bond shows a unique and substantial effect on delinquency, we find that the effects of attachment to parents and peers operate indirectly through the process of learning an excess of definitions favorable to delinquency. This finding is consistent with differential association theory, as are the findings that across racial groups, the effect of definitions on delinquency is invariant, and within groups, definitions mediate the influence on delinquency of our other explanatory variables.

Of more interest are the differences between our models for blacks and nonblacks. The most striking difference is that the total effect of broken homes on delinquency is much larger for blacks than nonblacks. Yet in both racial groups nonintact homes influence delinquency through a similar process—by attenuating parental supervision, which in turn increases delinquent companions, prodelinquent definitions, and, ultimately, delinquent behavior. But to a much greater extent, broken homes *directly* foster an excess of definitions favorable to delinquency, which then increases delinquent behavior. This effect, being much larger among blacks, accounts for the greater total effect of broken homes on delinquency among blacks.

A second racial difference is the total effect of neighborhood trouble on delinquency, which

is much larger in the model for nonblacks. Among nonblacks, that effect works partly through delinquent friends, but largely through definitions of delinquency; among blacks, a large indirect effect operates solely through definitions. We also examined an interaction hypothesis between neighborhood trouble and broken homes: Do broken homes influence delinquency only in the context of a trouble-ridden, high delinquency neighborhood? Entering a product variable representing the interaction effect, we found evidence of a conditional effect among blacks but not nonblacks. Blacks from broken homes who also live in troubled neighborhoods are more likely than those residing in troublefree neighborhoods to associate with delinquents, learn an excess of definitions favorable to delinquency, and, consequently, voilate the law. We were unable to locate such an interaction in the nonblack model, perhaps due to multicollinearity among main and interaction effects.[10]

We should note that, following a long history of research on family structure and delinquency, we have used a single dichotomous variable to distinguish intact from nonintact homes. Recently, some have argued that the impact of family structure on delinquency may vary depending on the nature of that structure, such as whether a step-parent is present or whether the mother or father is absent (Rankin 1983; Johnson 1986; Wells and Rankin 1986). We were unable to examine the joint relationships among different forms of family structure, our intervening variables, race, and delinquency because the small number of cases falling into each category of family status led to multicollinearity and unstable estimates. Other research suggests that the etiology of the break, such as death, divorce, or desertion, can influence subsequent behavior (McLanahan 1985). Furthermore, many argue that the pertinent

---

[10] Large bivariate correlations between product variables and their constituents suggest the problem of multicollinearity in disentangling interaction effects from main effects in both samples. Thus, we treat these results with caution. We also failed to unearth interaction effects among SES, broken homes, and neighborhood trouble, which was expected, given the null effects of SES on the endogenous variables.

variable is marital and familial discord, which could have an adverse effect on intimacy, supervision, and the transmission of antidelinquent behavior patterns, and which could also cause a marital breakup. Since marital severance is also likely to cause discord, cross-sectional research designs are likely to confound the causes and consequences of family disruption. Longitudinal designs are needed to disentangle the reciprocal effects of family process, family structure, and delinquent behavior. Based on the results of our models, we expect that the key intervening mechanism explaining the effects on delinquency of such family processes is the learning of delinquent and antidelinquent definitions.

But the link between definitions of delinquency and social structure may be more complex than implied thus far and may suggest another empirically testable divergence between the theories of differential association and social control. More precisely, social control theory, based on a consensus model of social order, denies the efficacy of competing subcultural norms and assumes that only conventional norms and definitions of morality influence behavior. In contrast, differential association theory, based on a group conflict model of social organization, specifies that subcultural groups may differ on two dimensions of definitions of delinquency—the dimension of the weight of the definition, and, more importantly, the dimension of the meaning or content of the definition (Matsueda 1982). The latter implies that groups located at different junctures in the social structure may communicate and behave according to very different definitions of unlawful behavior. In particular, the content of definitions of delinquency may vary by race, neighborhood, and social class.[11] To explore this issue, researchers must first use in-depth interviews to induce the

content of such definitions for distinct communication groups and then develop empirical measures to tap such definitions. Structural equation methods within the LISREL framework exist for making cross-population comparisons when indicators for concepts differ across groups (Allison 1985).

Viewed in broader perspective, our results raise larger questions concerning the role of social structure on race, cultural norms, and delinquency. That is, given that delinquency is largely determined by the learning of definitions of the legal code, what are the wider structural determinants of that learning process? Our ability to explain remarkably large amounts of variation in definitions with a small number of variables suggests that such a learning process is tightly structured. When examining a single cross-section of individuals, we find that the learning process is structured by elements of social organization such as age, neighborhoods, families, and peers. Moreover, the differential impact of these structures accounts, in large part, for racial disparities in delinquent behavior.

From both a scientific and policy standpoint, a more significant issue may be the historical emergence of social and economic structures that give rise to distinct racial patterns of social organization. Thus, the racial cleavages in normative definitions of delinquent behaviors may derive from a history of restricted opportunities, a sense of resignation, and ultimately, new ways of adapting to a bleak situation (Cloward and Ohlin 1960). For example, William Julius Wilson (1985) argues that increasing social dislocations among the urban underclass were a culmination of a number of demographic, economic, and cultural changes. Specifically, the increasing disparity in crime across race is a result of historic not contemporary discrimination, the unabated migration of Southern blacks to the centers of Northern cities, the drop in age structure among inner-city blacks and a general economic shift from a manufacturing to a service economy. In turn, these broad historical trends have led to different patterns of social organization among the urban underclass, which influence rates of delinquency. For example, we have shown that delinquency is in part

---

[11] We attempted to explore this inductively using the Richmond data. That is, with our confirmatory factor models of definitions, we examined the possibility that some indicators that are valid for nonblacks are invalid for blacks, and vice versa. By and large, we did not find such differences in validity across race; what was a strong indicator in one population was generally strong for the other. This is not surprising, of course, since the measures are global, and designed to apply across general populations.

spawned by broken homes, unsupervised family life, ineffective neighborhood organization, and, ultimately, differential association. If this historical explanation is correct, and the critical learning process is indeed interwoven in the fabric of such historical trends, it should be no surprise that simplistic policies of rehabilitation and deterrence have failed to stem the tide of rising rates of delinquency. Sweeping social and economic reforms may be necessary to reverse the strong currents of law violation (Wilson 1985).

In the absence of a substantial body of empirical research verifying these propositions, however, such theorizing is speculative. Nevertheless, such speculation is consistent with our principal findings that the influence of broken homes on delinquency is greater among blacks; that this influence is explained by the process of learning definitions of delinquency; and that, for both blacks and nonblacks, differential association theory is supported over social control theory.

References

Agnew, Robert. 1985. "Social Control Theory and Delinquency: A Longitudinal Test." *Criminology* 23:47–62.

Allison, Paul D. 1985. "Estimation of Linear Models with Incomplete Data." Revised version of a paper presented at the 1981 Annual Meetings of the American Sociological Association.

Austin, Roy L. 1978. "Race, Father-Absence, and Female Delinquency." *Criminology* 15:487–504.

Berger, Alan S. and William Simon. 1974. "Black Families and the Moynihan Report: A Research Evaluation." *Social Problems* 22:145–61.

Bielby, William T. 1986. "Arbitrary Metrics in Multiple Indicator Models of Latent Variables." *Sociological Methods and Research* 15:3–23.

Bielby, William T., Robert M. Hauser, and David L. Featherman. 1977. "Response Errors of Black and Nonblack Males in Models of the Intergenerational Transmission of Socioeconomic Status." *American Journal of Sociology* 82:1242–88.

Briar, Scott and Irving Piliavin. 1965. "Delinquency, Situational Inducements, and Commitment to Conformity." *Social Problems* 13:35–45.

Chilton, Roland and Gerald Markle. 1972. "Family Disruption, Delinquent Conduct, and the Effects of Sub-Classification." *American Sociological Review* 37:93–99.

Cloward, Richard A. and Lloyd E. Ohlin. 1960. *Delinquency and Opportunity*. New York: Free Press.

Elliott, Delbert S., David Huizinga, and Suzanne S. Ageton. 1985. *Explaining Delinquency and Drug Use*. Beverly Hills, CA: Sage.

Hindelang, Michael J. 1978. "Race and Involvement in Common Law Personal Crimes." *American Sociological Review* 43:93–109.

Hindelang, Michael J., Travis Hirschi, and Joseph G. Weis. 1979. "Correlates of Delinquency: The Illusion of a Discrepancy." *American Sociological Review* 44:994–1014.

———. 1981. *Measuring Delinquency*. Beverly Hills, CA: Sage.

Hirschi, Travis. 1969. *Causes of Delinquency*. Berkeley: Free Press.

———. 1983. "Crime and the Family." Pp. 53–68 in *Crime and Public Policy*, edited by J.Q. Wilson. San Francisco: ICS Press.

Jensen, Gary F. 1972. "Parents, Peers, and Delinquent Action: A Test of the Differential Association Perspective." *American Journal of Sociology* 78:562–75.

Johnson, Richard E. 1986. "Family Structure and Delinquency: General Patterns and Gender Differences." *Criminology* 24:65–80.

Joreskog, Karl G. and Dag Sorbom. 1984. *LISREL V: Analysis of Linear Structural Relationships by Maximum Likelihood and Least Squares Methods*. Chicago: National Educational Resources. Inc.

Kornhauser, Ruth R. 1978. *Social Sources of Delinquency*. Chicago: University of Chicago Press.

Liska, Allen E. and Mark D. Reed. 1985. "Ties to Conventional Institutions and Delinquency: Estimating Reciprocal Effects." *American Sociological Review* 50:547–60.

Matsueda, Ross L. 1982. "Testing Control Theory and Differential Association: A Causal Modeling Approach." *American Sociological Review* 47:489–504.

Matsueda, Ross L. and William T. Bielby. 1986. "Statistical Power in Covariance Structure Models." Pp. 120–58 in *Sociological Methodology 1986*, edited by N.B. Tuma. San Francisco: Jossey-Bass.

McLanahan, Sara. 1985. "Family Structure and the Reproduction of Poverty." *American Journal of Sociology* 90:873–901.

Minor, W. William. 1984. "Neutralization as a Hardening Process: Considerations in the Modeling of Change." *Social Forces* 62:995–1019.

Monahan, Thomas. 1957. "Family Status and the Delinquent Child: A Reappraisal and Some New Findings." *Social Forces* 35:250–58.

Moynihan, Daniel P. 1965. *The Negro Family: The Case for National Action*. Washington, DC: Office of Policy Planning and Research, U.S. Department of Labor.

Rankin, Joseph H. 1983. "The Family Context of Delinquency." *Social Problems* 30:466–79.

Rosen, Lawrence, M. Lalli, and Leonard Savitz. 1975. "City Life and Delinquency: The Family and Delinquency." Unpublished report submitted to the National Institute for Juvenile Justice and Delinquency Prevention, Law Enforcement Assistance Administration.

Shaw, Clifford R. and Henry D. McKay. 1969. *Juvenile Delinquency and Urban Areas*. Rev. ed. Chicago: University of Chicago Press.

Short, James F., Jr. and Fred L. Strodtbeck. 1965. *Group Process and Gang Delinquency*. Chicago: University of Chicago Press.

Sutherland, Edwin H. 1947. *Principles of Criminology*, 4th ed. Philadelphia: Lippincott.

Sutherland, Edwin H. and Donald R. Cressey. 1978. *Criminology*, 10th ed. Philadelphia: Lippincott.

Tennyson, R.A. 1967. "Family Structure and Delinquent Behavior." Pp. 57–69 in *Juvenile Gangs in Context*, edited by Malcolm W. Klein. Englewood Cliffs, NJ: Prentice-Hall.

Toby, Jackson. 1957. "The Differential Impact of Family Disorganization." *American Sociological Review* 22:505–12.

Wells, L. Edward and Joseph H. Rankin. 1986. "The Broken Homes Model of Delinquency: Analytic Issues." *Journal of Research in Crime and Delinquency* 23:68–93.

Williams, Richard and Elizabeth Thomson. 1986. "Normalization Issues in Latent Variable Modeling with Multiple Populations." *Sociological Methods and Research* 15:24–43.

Wilson, Alan B. 1965. *Richmond Youth Project* [MRDF]. Berkeley: Survey Research Center, University of California, Berkeley [Producer].

Wilson, James Q. and Richard J. Herrnstein. 1985. *Crime and Human Nature*. New York: Basic Books.

Wilson, William Julius. 1985. "Cycles of Deprivation and the Underclass Debate." *Social Service Review* 59:541–59.

Conclusion

Differential association and social learning theories place a premium on the individual being able to learn criminal behavior. Specifically, they proffer that individuals who have more contact with others involved in crime are likely to commit crime. These theories suggest that individuals who live in more diverse and underprivileged areas have a greater opportunity to be around individuals who have already been involved in crime.

These studies have shown some support for differential association theory's explanation of crime differences based on race. Specifically, these studies have shown differences in the way that peers operate in different racial groups. However, these studies do have limitations. For example, at the time of this writing, Akers's (1998) version of social learning theory that connects race to crime through the social learning process has not been tested in the empirical literature. This lack of testing does not allow for an examination of the race and crime link using this theory. Further, the article on differential association provides information only about associating with criminal peers. It does not provide information regarding the quality and amount of time spent with these peers. Further, these studies do not take into consideration the role of the community. Future research should take up these issues.

Discussion Questions

1. Using the social learning theory, describe and give examples of the major differences across races in the types of definitions that are favorable to crime?
2. As per social learning theory, where do racial influences come from?

3. Describe the key findings from Matsueda and Heimer's study? What recommendations would you provide from this study? How are they different from the recommendations that Matsueda and Heimer presented in their article?

References

Akers, R. L. (1985). *Deviant behavior: A social learning approach.* Belmont, CA: Wadsworth.

Akers, R. L. (1998). *Social learning and social structure: A general theory of crime and deviance.* Boston, MA: Northeastern University Press.

Burgess, R. L., & Akers, R. (1966). A differential association-reinforcement theory of criminal behavior. *Social Problems, 14,* 128–147.

Sutherland, E. H. (1947). *Principles of Criminology* 4th Ed. Philadelphia, PA: Lippincott.

Warr, M. (2002). *Companions in crime: The social aspects of criminal conduct.* New York, NY: Cambridge University Press.

CHAPTER 5

Social Strain Theory

Social strain theory suggests that the way a society is organized has implications for the distribution of occupational roles, opportunities, and the means to achieve goals. When one is blocked from achieving one's goals, it results in frustration and anger. Frustrated and angry individuals are likely to seek illegitimate means to achieve their goals.

Social strain theory assumes that individuals are born rational and have the capability to learn and associate with the goals that are valued in society. Further, the theory assumes that individuals not only are capable of learning the norms and skills that are required to achieve these goals but also have a tendency for conformity to social rules.

Based on this theory, several variants have been offered. In this chapter, Merton, Anderson, and Agnew's theories are discussed. These theories are chosen because of their differing bases: Merton presents a structural theory, Anderson a subcultural theory, and Agnew's individual-level theory.

Merton's (1938) theory of deviance places an emphasis on the structure of society. In particular, his theory suggests that society has a well-structured set of goals for its members, as well as well-structured means for achieving these goals. Thus, deviance becomes any form of behavior that does not follow these goals and avenues of achieving these goals.

Merton suggests that certain goals (e.g., financial success) and the specific means to achieve these goals (i.e., through hard work) are stressed in society. However, not everyone will have an opportunity, the work ethic, or the motivation to achieve the goal of financial success. This creates anomie.

Merton's theory has particular import for minorities. He sees minorities as being at a disadvantage in achieving success because of social inequality. Put another way, minorities are unable to reconcile their aspirations with the degree of success they achieve due to their social inequality. However, the anomie that this creates is not static but dynamic, which means as the social inequality changes, so does the state of anomie. For example, as an individual becomes more successful, he or she will not feel as helpless.

Merton identified five modes of adaptation to overcome the feeling of anomie and to achieve the aspired success, and they are as follows:

1. Conformity (i.e., the individual behaves as society wishes to achieve his or her aspirations)
2. Innovation (i.e., the individual behaves in a deviant manner to achieve his or her aspirations)
3. Ritualism (i.e., the individual does not aspire for any particular goal but maintains his or her view on the means of achieving a goal)
4. Retreatism (i.e., the individual rejects the goals and the means to achieve them by sinking into forms of self-medication [e.g., drugs and alcohol])
5. Rebellion (i.e., the individual rejects the existing goals and the means to achieve them and establishes a new society where aspirations can be met)

While Merton's theory emphasizes the development of deviance based on the entire social structure, Anderson's (2000) theory attempts to understand racial differences in crime by investigating the role of cultures within a culture (i.e., subcultures). Anderson's "code of the streets" theory is based on the view that respect is central to the individual within an inner city. To develop his theory, Anderson (2000) performed ethnographic research (i.e., research based on observations and interviews) on impoverished neighborhoods in inner cities to determine how individuals interpreted and adopted the "code of the streets" for survival. Anderson (2000) writes that "at the heart of the code is the issue of respect—loosely defined as being treated 'right,' or granted deference one deserves" (p. 82).

He describes two types of families—decent and street. These two types of families had very different ways of socializing their children. Decent families were more likely to adopt conventional society values and make an effort to instill these values in their children. According to Anderson (2000), these families were strict and attempted to teach their children to behave in moral ways that were respectful to authority. Overall, decent families were not bound by the code of the streets.

On the other hand, street families took a different perspective in socializing their children. They provided poor supervision for their children and had a low tolerance and poor coping strategies in handling their children's behavior. These families were bound by the code and utilized it to justify their children's behavior (Anderson, 2000). Thus, these families tended to be disorganized as their children learned very early that they had to take care of themselves. Taking care of themselves made the children become aware that the code is important, creating a cycle where the child had to demonstrate his or her "toughness" so that he or she may achieve the conventional upper-class success.

Agnew (1992, 2001) takes a different perspective of social strain theory. Rather than focusing on social structure or subcultures, Agnew (1992) places the emphasis on the individual. Agnew (1992) broadens "strain" to mean more than the discrepancy between blocked aspirations and goals to include multiple sources of strain. Thus, crime, deviance, and delinquency are adaptations to strain—whatever that strain may be.

Agnew identifies three types of strain. The first type of strain is the failure to achieve a positively valued goal. It includes the discrepancy between expectations and actual achievement, including those that are immediate, and the fairness or unjustness of the outcome. The second type of strain is the removal of positively valued stimuli. This is the removal of something that has great value to the individual. For instance, some can experience this sort of strain when a relationship ends or an individual looses his or her employment. The third type of strain is the presentation of noxious stimuli. This type of strain occurs when something is presented to an individual that he or she does not like. Specifically, this could be the presentation or the confrontation of the negative actions of others. For example, an individual may experience this sort of strain when he or she has been abused or victimized. One or a combination of these strains motivates an individual to react in a deviant manner, depending on the individual's emotional reaction.

The emotional reaction to these strains can vary from anger to depression. Agnew (1992) suggests that the anger allows the individual to blame "the system" or someone else. Once angry, the individual would choose one of many adaptations, the most likely being crime, deviance, or delinquency.

Some scholars have suggested that Merton's version of social strain has empirical support (Agnew, 2005). Others have shown empirical support for Anderson's view of subcultural social strain (Kubrin, 2005). Agnew (2005) also indicates empirical support for his strain theory. These studies have addressed the connection between race and crime to some extent.

They have postulated that racial minorities are more likely to experience social strain because they are likely to endure less opportunities to fulfill their American Dream (i.e., aspirations). Further, racial minorities are likely to encounter economic inequality that hinders their ability to achieve their aspirations through legitimate means. In addition, these individuals are likely to adopt the "code of the streets" to achieve the aspiration of respect and economic gain. Finally, because of these issues, racial minorities are also more likely to encounter failure to achieve their goals, presentation of a noxious stimuli, and removal of positively valued stimuli. In the following selection, Cernokovich, Giordano, and Rudolph illustrate these views.

Race, Crime, and the American Dream

Stephen A. Cernkovich
Peggy C. Giordano
Jennifer L. Rudolph

Although strain and social control theories assign a central role to the influence of the American dream on criminal behavior, little research has examined its impact on African Americans. Furthermore, while the criminology literature is replete with studies of the influence of aspirations and expectations on behavior, few of these have emphasized the economic goals so central to the core tenets of the American dream. In contrast, this study is based on a sample approximately half African American and measures the American dream in economic terms. The findings indicate that African Americans maintain a stronger commitment to the American dream than do Whites, but the nature of its influence on behavior offers little support for social control theory among either Whites or Blacks. Its effect is, however, consistent with strain theory, but only among Whites. The implications of the inapplicability of both strain and control theories to African Americans are discussed.

Two of the most dominant theories in the field of criminology—strain and social control—have for some 30 years taken opposing stances on the behavioral consequences of adherence to the American dream, with strain theory stressing its negative implications and social control theory emphasizing its decidedly positive impact. Consistent with these contrasting themes, few observers would question the power of the American dream both to frustrate and inspire the citizens of this country. While there are a variety of components to this dream, none competes with the promise of economic and material success. It is extolled in the family, from the pulpit, in our schools, via the media, and by politicians. Simply put, it is quite impossible to live in the United States and not be bombarded by images of materialism and economic achievement. That this reality has had both positive and negative consequences should be no surprise. The dream has inspired heroic individual success stories, but it also has expressed itself in nightmares and human misery. As society continues to grapple with the reality of inequality, the promise of the American dream is brought into sharp relief, and many have questioned whether it holds any sway over those who continue to face failure in its wake.

This research explores the extent to which African Americans, a group historically denied full access to the American dream, subscribe to the goals of economic and material success, relative to the importance attached to these goals by their White counterparts, and with what behavioral consequences. There certainly is ample evidence to suggest that many individuals recalibrate their definition of success in the face of failure, and the supposition by some observers is that African Americans have downgraded the importance of economic and material success on the basis of their inability to realize these goals historically. Indeed, some commentators believe that many African Americans have forsaken the American dream altogether, concluding that it applies to Whites only. On the other hand, others claim that the goal of economic success continues to captivate the imagination of African Americans and to motivate their behavior.

Surprisingly little research has focused directly on the comparative salience of various success goals among African Americans (see, however, Hochschild 1995 for an excellent review of the empirical literature that does exist; also see Nightingale 1993 for a historical account of the American dream among poor Black children). Instead, much of the research in this area has concentrated on social class differences in aspirations and expectations, implicitly assuming that class is a reasonable proxy for race. The result is that we actually know very little empirically about the salience and behavioral consequences of the American dream among African Americans.

Uncertainty about the influence of the American dream extends beyond the issue of race to the nature of the relationship between success goals and social position in general. In this regard, two quite opposed perspectives have staked a claim to the truth. One, championed most influentially by Merton (1938) and subsequent strain theorists in the field of criminology, holds that there is a universal set of goals toward which all Americans, regardless of background and position, strive. Chief among these is monetary success. The other position, represented most prominently by Hyman (1953), posits the existence of class-based goals and holds that many deprived Americans adapt to their circumstances by lowering their aspirations for success. Interestingly, both positions have been supported by research evidence: Some studies indicate that numerous lower-status individuals have aspirations that are as high as those of their middle-class counterparts, while others reveal that some deprived Americans do lower their aspirations as an adaptation to the frustration generated by their inability to compete in a stratified society (Agnew and Jones 1988:315–16).

In addition to these equivocal research findings, there are three other limitations to the work in this area. First, very little research in the field of criminology has focused specifically on economic goals, concentrating instead on educational or occupational aspirations (Agnew et al. 1996; Farnworth and Leiber 1989). To the extent that economic and material success represents the essence of the American dream and is central to the strain theory formulation, the existing research may actually tell us very little about the empirical status of either the dream or the theory. Second, little attention has been paid to the extent to which either of the above models applies specifically to African Americans. For example, although Agnew et al. (1996) have recently examined the influence of economic dissatisfaction and frustration on criminal behavior, their analysis was confined to White respondents. More generally, race is rarely treated as anything other than a control variable in the considerable body of criminological research in which aspirations and expectations assume central roles. Whatever the reasons for this "race gap" (see Matsueda and Heimer 1987 for a discussion of some of these), it represents a serious omission. Third, researchers typically have ignored another significant way in which deprived individuals might adapt to their circumstances: by actually raising expectations to quite inflated levels. As in the case with lowering aspirations, this brings aspirations and expectations into alignment and reduces frustration levels (Agnew and Jones 1988:316).

The notion of inflated goals is consistent with social control theory, a model in which high aspirations are seen as inhibiting deviant behavior because they represent a "stake in conformity" (Hirschi 1969). The control model, of course, poses a direct challenge to the strain interpretation, and considerable evidence does indicate that high aspirations function to inhibit rather than produce deviant behavior. Still, these data usually are generated from demographically undifferentiated or White male samples, rarely concentrating on African Americans and typically ignoring strictly economic aspirations (Farnworth and Leiber 1989).

In short, even though strain theory stresses the critical importance of economic goals and was intended from its inception to explain the deviant behavior of lower-status and underprivileged populations, we actually know very little about how it applies specifically to African Americans. Control theory, the dominant competing alternative to the strain perspective, also stresses the importance of aspirations but ignores African Americans by design, purporting to be a universal explanation of deviant behavior. The result is that while two of the most respected and thoroughly researched theories in the field of criminology assign a major role to economic aspirations, we do not know much about the economic goal orientation of African Americans or how this orientation affects their behavior.

Theoretical Background

Social control and strain theories have been two of the most influential explanatory models in the field of criminology. While strain theory has the longer history of the two, it had begun to lose some of its luster, particularly during the 1980s, in the face of negative research findings and as a result of the increasing popularity of the social learning and social control models. However, it has made a resurgence in recent years, thanks in large part to Agnew's (1992) introduction of his related General Strain Theory. For its part, social control theory has seen a continual increase in popularity since Hirschi's (1969) influential formulation (for earlier versions of control theory, see Nye 1958; Reckless 1961) and is attracting even more attention as a consequence of Gottfredson and Hirschi's (1990) introduction of their related General Theory of Crime.

We are interested in the strain and social control models in this research because both assign a central role to the influence of the American dream on behavior, although they posit different behavioral consequences for individuals with high aspirations. In general, strain theory proposes that high aspirations among those with limited opportunities generate pressures to deviate, while social control theory asserts that high aspirations ensure conforming behavior regardless of the level of available opportunities. Although control theory does not define aspirations in relation to the American dream per se, we believe that our conceptualization stressing material and economic success is consistent with the control theory perspective. That is, a critical focus of control theory is on the "motivation to strive for conventional goals" (Hirschi 1969:162). In direct contrast to the strain model, control theory avers that the delinquent is not motivated to achieve conventional goals; rather, the delinquent is a nonstriver, a nonaspirer: "The greater one's acceptance of conventional (or even quasi-conventional) success goals, the less likely one is to be delinquent. . . . It is not true that ambition leads to crime; on the contrary, ambition reduces the chances of crime" (Hirschi 1969:227). In addition, as Jensen (1995:154–55) has noted, Hirschi does not limit theoretically the types of aspirations that function to inhibit delinquency—even crass materialists are less prone to crime and delinquency than are low and nonaspirers. For control theory, ambition and high aspirations are central in producing conformity (Hirschi 1969:21). Because there is little question that material and economic success are dominant success goals in American society, we believe it is reasonable to index high aspirations—as defined by control theory—by the degree of commitment to the American dream as we have conceptualized it.

At the empirical level, considerable research has found the highest deviance rates among those with low aspirations, apparently supporting control theory. However, much of this research has operationalized success goals in educational and occupational terms, rather than as monetary success per se, a surprising orientation given the emphasis Merton and subsequent strain theorists placed on monetary goals (Agnew 1995:310). Educational and occupational aspirations obviously are related to economic success, but they are not at the heart of the American dream itself. In fact, Messner and Rosenfeld (1994:78) have pointed out that noneconomic goals and roles are actually devalued relative to economic success in American society. Education, for example, is not valued for its own sake but as a means to occupational attainment. Occupational attainment, in turn, is valued primarily because it is capable of producing economic rewards.

To the extent that researchers have ignored economic goals, they have failed to capture the essence of the American dream. To be sure, there are exceptions to this trend in the literature. For example, Farnworth and Leiber (1989) explicitly examined economic aspirations and found that failure to achieve monetary goals, especially in combination with low educational expectations, was a significant predictor of delinquency, while frustrated educational goals were relatively unimportant. This research stands out as much for its emphasis on economic goals as it does for its specific findings. Farnworth and Leiber's argument that the failure to properly operationalize strain theory may well account for its lack of empirical support historically is perhaps the most important contribution of their work.

Jensen (1995) has argued, however, that while Farnworth and Leiber (1989) show that the gap between aspirations and expectations is correlated with delinquency independent of the effects of aspirations, they failed to model the main effects of expectations in their analysis. This is critical because strain theory predicts an interaction between aspirations and expectations beyond the main effects of the two variables. As a result, the effects of strain and expectations are confounded in Farnworth and Leiber's research. In a reanalysis of their data—one in which strain and expectations are not confounded—Jensen finds that expectations produce the effect that Farnworth and Leiber mistakenly attributed to strain. That is, his reanalysis shows that the higher the aspirations, the greater the delinquency; similarly, the higher the expectations, the lower the probability of delinquency involvement. He finds no significant aspirations-by-expectations interaction and thus no need to incorporate the concept of strain into an explanation of delinquency (Jensen 1995:141–42, 146).

The significance of Farnworth and Leiber's (1989) and Jensen's (1995) findings notwithstanding, some criminologists have de-emphasized the results of such research because strain is operationalized via perceptual measures. Critics have argued that because strain theory is a structural model, only ecological measures can properly test the theory. However, this criticism fails to appreciate the distinction between microlevel and macrolevel strain theory (Agnew et al. 1996). The strain model clearly has applications at the individual level, and the history of research on the theory is replete with individual, perceptual measures of strain and blocked opportunity. Our purpose in this research is not to enter into this debate, much less resolve it. We acknowledge the dispute but remind the reader that our goal is to examine the behavioral consequences of commitment to the American dream among African Americans. We have chosen to do this via perceptual and behavioral measures because they best address the specific issues we are examining. This focus is consistent with the recent argument by Agnew et al. (1996:682–83) that researchers have virtually ignored the central variable in strain theory:

dissatisfaction/frustration with one's current monetary status. As an indicator of individual-level strain, Agnew believes that it is economic frustration or dissatisfaction, more so than any other variable, that distinguishes strain theory from alternative explanations. Defined in this fashion, strain necessarily must be measured at the individual level.

Related to the neglect of economic goals per se is the apparent inability of strain theory to explain why many objectively deprived individuals with high aspirations do not behave in the way the theory predicts (i.e., why they do not become frustrated and turn to deviance). The favored explanation has been that such individuals are able to avoid the frustration predicted by strain theory because they have lowered their aspirations; that is, they "settle for" lower levels of achievement and thus insulate themselves from the view that they are failures. An alternative mechanism of adaptation ignored by strain theorists but noted by Agnew and Jones (1988:316) is the raising of expectations to a level congruent with the promise of the American dream. This not only reduces frustration levels but also bolsters self-image since the expectation is that high achievement levels are indeed possible.

The notion of inflated aspirations and/or expectations is consistent with social control theory, which posits that high aspirations do not lead to deviance in the manner proposed by strain theory but actually insulate individuals from deviant involvement because they reflect a commitment to conformity. There is, in fact, considerable research supporting the control theory position (e.g., Hirschi 1969; Johnson 1979; Liska 1971). In addition, Agnew and Jones (1988:317) point to evidence in the status attainment literature indicating that inflated expectations are quite common. In regard to race, for example, this evidence shows that while Blacks have significantly lower levels of educational attainment than do Whites, they have similar levels of educational expectations. Such findings call into question the assumption that structural factors such as class and race overwhelm passive individuals who are unable to resist or adapt to their impact. Instead, these data show that many deprived individuals apparently

maintain aspiration levels that bear little relation to the objective conditions under which they live (Agnew and Jones 1988:332)—yet another indication of the spell the American dream casts.

This line of reasoning is consistent with Hochschild's (1995:72, 159–61) review of the research on the vitality of the American dream among African Americans. Her review reveals an interesting paradox: While belief in the American dream has declined sharply among the economically best-off African Americans over the past 30 years, it has retained its hold on the economically worst off. In fact, poor African Americans believe as much in the American dream today as they did some 30 years ago, even though Black poverty levels have become much more severe during this time span. Moreover, most of the poor Blacks who continue to adhere to the American dream express a great deal of confidence in schooling and hard work as the mechanisms for success. Hochschild (1995:218) claims that this incongruity between dream and reality persists because the internal contradictions of the American dream actually make it easier rather than harder for poor African Americans to believe in it. That is, the structural determinants of failure to achieve in American society—such as racial discrimination and the lack of jobs—are absent in the ideology's explanation of failure. Instead, individualistic explanations predominate. If the reasons for failure are viewed as individual in nature, then they can be overcome by individuals through dedication, hard work, and education.

Hochschild (1995:217) also believes that because lower-status Blacks experience poverty as a more severe day-to-day problem than racism, they have virtually no ideological alternatives to the American dream that offer a way out. Their belief that their odds of success are improved by following the promise of the dream is reinforced by the flexibility of what counts as success according to the rules of the dream. That is, the American dream permits relative levels of gratification as opposed to absolute success. In addition, Hochschild (1995:193) reminds us that the line between legitimate and illegitimate striving is often blurred in American society.

Consequently, some find it acceptable to turn to criminality when they are unable to realize the promise of the dream via legitimate avenues.

The basic argument that the American dream is alive and well among African Americans also finds support in MacLeod's (1987) ethnographic study of lower-class teenage boys. In contrast to the White boys (the "Hallway Hangers") he studied, MacLeod found that his Black respondents (the "Brothers") were much more optimistic about their futures, were more strongly attached to conventional morality and the American dream, and had "excessive ambitions" that were encouraged by parents and peers. While the Hallway Hangers had modest hopes for the future and viewed the opportunity structure as relatively closed, the Brothers saw it as open to all and were quite optimistic about their ability to compete. They took school seriously, followed its basic rules, and respected their teachers (MacLeod 1987:5, 42, 67–79, 96, 126). In other words, even though their objective life chances were quite unfavorable, the African American youths maintained a strong commitment to the American dream, and this orientation affected their outlook on life as well as their behavior in significant ways.

Although there was little evidence that it had paid dividends for earlier generations of African Americans, MacLeod (1987:129–30) theorizes that the Brothers were able to subscribe to the American dream because they could point to past racial discrimination, which in more recent times has abated, as the cause of their parents' and other Blacks' failure to realize the dream. For the same reason, the Brothers' parents could now actively encourage commitment to the dream for their children. The Hallway Hangers, on the other hand, rejected the promise of the American dream because to accept it would be to admit that their parents were either "lazy or stupid or both" since there was no racial discrimination on which to blame their failure. Similarly, the Hallway Hangers' parents did not encourage high achievement levels among their children because they thought it both unrealistic and foolish to do so. Commitment to the American dream clearly posed a much more serious threat

to the self-esteem of the White as compared to the Black youths in this study.

Such evidence makes it clear that there is sufficient reason to believe that the American dream continues to generate high levels of commitment among African Americans. However, studies such as MacLeod's (1987) are both rare and limited. In addition, MacLeod admits that the Brothers may not be representative of young Blacks in the United States; in fact, they may be quite atypical. Consequently, despite the contribution of such studies, we know relatively little about the extent to which African Americans are committed to the American dream, how important economic goals are relative to other goals, and what behavioral consequences that commitment to the American dream has for African Americans.

With this background in mind, the purpose of this research is to examine the behavioral impact of commitment to the American dream among a sample of young adults. Specifically, we are interested in the level and the effect of economic aspirations. Although there need be no necessary relationship between the level and the effect of success goals (i.e., differential levels of commitment to economic goals do not necessarily result in differential behavioral outcomes), there certainly is sufficient theoretical justification to expect an association. That is, strain theory predicts that high aspirations among the objectively deprived increase the likelihood of negative behavioral outcomes such as crime and deviance, while control theory proposes that high aspirations ensure conformity, regardless of the level of economic deprivation.

Beyond evaluating which of these two alternative theoretical perspectives most accurately captures the empirical reality of economic success goal orientation, our research is guided by a desire to understand more about the aspirations of African Americans and how these compare to those of their White counterparts. Although control and strain theories have been dominant theoretical models in the study of crime, delinquency, and deviant behavior, neither has spawned a systematic study of the role of race. This is because neither model directly addresses race theoretically: control theory because its key predictors are proposed to be invariant across racial boundaries (i.e., race "doesn't matter") and strain theory because it is a class-based model that deals with race only by implication (i.e., race differences are generally assumed to parallel class differences). Contrary to this orientation, we focus explicitly on race.

Research Design

Sample

Agnew (1995) has noted that much of the research that fails to support classic strain theory is based on samples of high school students, ignoring both adults and the hard-core urban poor. He speculates that the basic strain model may, in fact, be more applicable to adults, "to whom the pursuit of money is a more serious matter, and to the hard core poor, who face the greatest barriers to goal achievement" (Agnew 1995:310-11). Our sample generally meets the criteria proposed by Agnew: It is composed of young adults just embarking on their quest of the American dream, includes many hardcore urban poor, and is approximately half African American, a group substantially overrepresented among the economically deprived.

Two related data sources are the basis for this study: (1) a sample of individuals living in private households and (2) a sample of previously institutionalized offenders. Respondents in both of these samples were interviewed initially in 1982 when they were adolescents and subsequently in 1992 (the household sample) and in 1995 (the previously institutional respondents) as young adults.[1] With the exception of our prior delinquency measure, all variables included in this research are measured at the time 2 interview period.

Household sample. The 1982 household study was based on a sample of 942 youth ages 12 to 19 living in private households in the Toledo, Ohio, metropolitan area. A multistage modified probability sampling procedure was employed in which area segments were selected with known probability. The most recent census

data available at the time (U.S. Bureau of the Census 1980) were used to stratify the sample by racial composition and average housing value. Within area segments, eligible household respondents were selected to fill specified gender and race quotas; no specific age quotas were allocated, although the ages of respondents were tracked as the interviews were conducted to ensure adequate representation of all age groups. The respondents were equally divided among males and females and Blacks and Whites.

An effort was made in 1992 to locate and reinterview all of the original 942 household respondents. Respondents who had moved significant distances from the region completed mailed questionnaires. Most respondents, however, lived in geographically proximate areas and were interviewed personally. The overall completion rate for the second wave of interviews was 77 percent of the original sample (adjusting the base rate for 10 confirmed deaths); of these, 82 percent completed personal interviews. Of the 721 respondents interviewed at time 2, 45 percent were male and 47 percent were White. Of the non-Whites, most (95 percent) were African American. The respondents ranged in age from 22 to 29 years, with a mean of 25.31 years at the time of the reinterview. The average household income of the respondents was $21,100. Of the household respondents, 30 percent were unemployed at the time of the reinterview.

Institutional sample. The initial institutional data were derived from 254 personal interviews conducted in 1982, using the same interview schedule as for the household respondents. The respondents were drawn from the populations of three male juvenile institutions in the state of Ohio and the entire population of the only female juvenile institution in the state. Of the institutional respondents, 50 percent were female. Of the institutionalized respondents, 65 percent were White; the remaining non-Whites were predominantly Black (32 percent of the institutional sample).

In 1995, 210 of the initial 254 institutional respondents were reinterviewed. This represents an 83 percent reinterview rate (85 percent when the sample is adjusted for deceased respondents).

The second wave of data was collected via face-to-face interviews (91 percent) as well as through a mailed version of the interview schedule. Of the reinterviewed respondents, 48 percent were male, and 63 percent were White. Of the non-White respondents, 84 percent were African American. The respondents ranged in age from 29 to 34 years, with a mean of 29.30 years. The average household income of the institutional respondents was $14,900. Of the respondents, 39 percent were unemployed at the time of the second interview.

Combined sample. We combined the household and institutional samples for the present analysis to represent the full range of criminal offending levels; in particular, we wanted to ensure that the analytic sample included offenders at the high-frequency/high-seriousness end of the crime and delinquency continua. We do not believe that general population samples, such as our household-based one and other typical self-report surveys, represent serious chronic offenders in sufficient number for meaningful analysis. Although it is important to be cognizant of processing biases in the justice system, institutional samples are a logical source of chronic offenders. Our data show that the institutional offenders are, by their own admission, much more frequent and serious offenders than even the most hard-core offenders from the household sample (for a more complete discussion of the delinquency involvement differences between these two samples and of the issues involved in sampling for serious chronic offenders, see Cernkovich, Giordano, and Pugh 1985).

Due to our interest in African Americans in this research and because of the small number of other minorities included in our samples, the present analysis is limited to Black and White respondents from the household ($n = 684$) and institutional ($n = 197$) samples. This restriction resulted in a combined analytic sample of 881 respondents. Males comprised 45 percent of the combined sample, while 54 percent of the respondents were White. The average household income of the combined sample was $19,800. Of the respondents, 32 percent were unemployed at the time of the reinterview. Table 1 presents a more detailed description of the demographic characteristics of the household, institutional, and combined samples.

Logistic regression modeling of response/nonresponse indicated that follow-up respondents were slightly more likely to be White and female, although there were no significant social class or age differences between the two groups. Analysis of responses derived from the questionnaires in contrast to the personal interviews revealed few significant differences; however, those who completed the mailed version were somewhat more likely to be White and to report higher social status scores. Because of the possibility of overrepresenting the more conforming individuals found in the original samples, several sources of information (e.g., records of military service, driver license registration lists, criminal offender databases, relatives and neighbors of the respondent) for relocating and reinterviewing difficult-to-find respondents were used and successfully implemented. That these procedures were successful is reflected in a relocation rate for the previously institutionalized respondents (85 percent), which was higher than that for the household respondents (77 percent). Further analysis revealed no differences in prior delinquency involvement among those who participated in the reinterview and those who did not. In short, we are confident that those youth who were the most conforming in 1982 were not overrepresented among the reinterviewed respondents.

A potentially more serious problem has to do with differential measurement error by race. Hindelang, Hirschi, and Weis (1981) have presented evidence that Black males' self-reports of delinquency involvement are less valid than the reports of other groups: Black males underreport involvement at every level of delinquency, especially at the high end of the continuum. African American males may provide inaccurate estimates on a variety of other measures as well. If this is the case and if misreporting is more common among serious offenders, our parameter estimates could be affected, especially if our

TABLE 1 Demographic Characteristics of Samples (percentage distribution)

Variable (coding)	Household Sample	Institutional Sample	Combined Sample
Gender			
Male (0)	45	48	45
Female (1)	55	52	55
Race			
White (0)	47	63	54
Black (1)	50	31	46
Education			
Less than high school (1)	16	70	28
High school graduate (2)	43	20	38
Some college (3)	29	9	25
College graduate (4)	8	1	7
Postcollege (5)	3	—	2
Occupational status			
Executive, administrative, managerial (7)	4	—	3
Professional specialties (6)	9	2	8
Administrative support, clerical (5)	15	10	14
Sales, technical, military (4)	18	8	16
Protective services, production (3)	10	16	11
Private household, machine operators (2)	17	21	18
Nonhousehold service, laborers (1)	27	42	30
Employment status			
Employed (1)	70	61	68
Unemployed (0)	30	39	32
Household income			
Less than $7,000 (1)	12	27	15
$7,000–$9,999 (2)	8	15	10
$10,000–$13,999 (3)	8	11	9
$14,000–$17,999 (4)	9	10	9
$18,000–$20,999 (5)	6	5	6
$21,000–$24,999 (6)	9	7	8
$25,000–$29,999 (7)	10	4	9
$30,000–$34,999 (8)	10	6	9
$35,000–$39,999 (9)	9	7	8
$40,000–$49,999 (10)	7	4	6
$50,000 or more (11)	12	4	10

indicators are better predictors of serious as opposed to minor delinquency (or vice versa). While this has important implications for our analysis, it would be a mistake to conclude that such measurement error invalidates the data provided by the Black males in our sample. There are several good reasons to believe that it does not.

First, Hindelang et al. (1981) conclude that while differential validity by race means that self-reports are poor social indicators of the absolute volume of crime and delinquency among Black males, such data can still be quite useful in etiological research. Etiological research is less interested in the absolute frequency of delinquency than with how individual or group rankings on delinquency are associated with individual or group rankings on various independent variables of interest (Hindelang et al. 1981:215–16). The latter is clearly the focus of our research. Second, Hindelang et al. note that while the differential validity problem makes comparison across groups potentially misleading, analysis within groups is not compromised. This means that we can have confidence in the relative explanatory power of our independent variables within race subgroups. A third mitigating factor is our reliance on face-to-face interviews in the collection of these data—the method Hindelang et al. found to produce the least-biased self-reports among Black males (Hindelang et al. 1981:178). Finally, our research has incorporated the most basic implication of the Hindelang et al. findings: stratification by race in both sampling and data analysis.

In short, we believe our research design and analytic approach minimize any bias of differential self-reporting by race. While we have no illusions that we have eliminated this problem entirely, we believe that it is preferable to proceed with research on African Americans cognizant of such problems than to take the more radical approach of throwing the data out because the respondents may be less than completely candid. Although the differential validity issue means that comparisons across race groups must be made with caution, we believe we can have considerable confidence in our within-group analyses. Confidence in these data is bolstered by our previous research on the relationship between delinquency and family, as well as school and peer relations (Cernkovich and Giordano 1987, 1992; Giordano, Cernkovich, and Pugh 1986), suggesting that if Black males are misreporting, they are not doing so in consistent and predictable directions. That is, the several family, peer, school, and crime and delinquency scales we have created evoke among Black males the full range of responses, in both a positive and a negative direction and in ways that do not suggest social desirability or response set biases.

A related problem is the potential of differential validity and reliability of our measures across sample type. Although there have been numerous studies examining the measurement properties of scales created from the self-reports of respondents similar to those in our household sample, we actually know very little about this issue in regard to serious and persistent offenders (see, e.g., Hagan et al. 1997). Although not the focus of this research, our data are quite encouraging on this matter in that the reliabilities of our scales are generally comparable for the institutional and household respondents. In short, we do not believe that differential reliability is a problem in these data. Simply because our scale reliabilities are acceptable does not mean, of course, that there is not a problem of differential validity across sample type. However, as was the case regarding race differences in validity, we believe that the likelihood of this sort of bias has been minimized by our data collection and analytic procedures, our focus on theory testing, and our within-sample analyses.

Additional data not used in the current analysis but gathered as part of this research also support the conclusion that differential validity across race and sample type is not a significant problem. First, formal arrest history data collected from police agencies throughout the state are strongly correlated with respondents' self-reports of their offending and arrest careers; this is true across all groups of offenders, including African Americans and those previously institutionalized. Second, in-depth narrative data derived from semi-structured interviews conducted after completion of the structured survey indicate that our interviewers established very high levels of rapport with the respondents. This is evidenced by their voluntary disclosure of quite sensitive and discrediting types of information, bolstering our confidence in the veracity of the information provided in all portions of the interview. In short, these two supplementary sources of respondent information further increase our confidence in the general validity of the data.

MEASURES   *Success goal orientation: the American dream.* The Life Role Salience Scales provide a useful index of success goal orientation because they measure the "personal importance or value attributed to participation in a particular role and . . . the intended level of commitment of personal time and energy resources to enactment of a role" (Amatea et al. 1986:831). The roles included in the scale—parental, marital, occupational, and home care—are generally considered to be the major stabilizing influences in the transition from adolescence to adulthood. One of the advantages of the items included in our interview schedule is that they allow a common set of responses across all respondents, regardless of whether they are currently engaged in these roles. In addition, the items reference not only the perceived desirability of a given role (i.e., "My life would seem empty if I never had children") but also the strength of a respondent's commitment to that role ("I expect to devote whatever time and energy it takes to move up in my job/career"). The life salience items included in our interview schedule were pretested, and the scales were evaluated for potential gender, race, and social class bias. With this in mind, we deleted several "home care" items and added items concerning commitment to religion, as well as to monetary goals.

We factor analyzed 13 life salience items and used two of the five resulting subscales: material salience and career salience (the other three subscales were not relevant to this research). Response categories for the two scales range from 1 to 5, with high scores indicating high salience levels. The Material Salience Scale (alpha = .766) is composed of three items: "Having lots of money is one of my major goals in life," "I will sacrifice a lot of other things to have a lot of money," and "I intend to do whatever it takes to have some of the really expensive things in life." The Career Salience Scale (alpha = .768) is made up of two items: "I expect to make as many sacrifices as are necessary in order to advance in my work/career," and "I expect to devote whatever time and energy it takes to move up in my job/career field." We believe that the items comprising these scales operationalize success goals in realistic and concrete terms, rather than in the ideal or utopian terms that have been characteristic of the research in this area historically.[2]

Economic satisfaction. Agnew et al. (1996:682–83) have argued that very little of the research testing strain theory has properly operationalized the strain construct. That is, most of this research has focused on occupational and educational aspirations, occupational and educational exceptions, and often on the disjunction between aspirations and expectations. Agnew et al. (1996) believe that this traditional focus has been misdirected, and they propose instead that the central variable in strain theory is dissatisfaction with one's current economic situation—a variable rooted in the concrete reality of the moment, rather than in some future or ideal reality suggested by the concepts of aspirations and expectations. Consistent with this argument, the focus in this research is on the respondent's assessment of his or her current economic situation. The interview schedule included a global life satisfaction item ("How satisfied these days are you with your life as a whole?") followed by 20 more specific items indexing satisfaction in relation to a variety of personal arenas, including health, employment, finances, physical appearance, personal and family relations, housing, and spiritual needs. The structure of these items is similar to that developed for Campbell and Converse's (1980) Quality of Life Study. Because of our interest in economic aspirations, we combined (with the aid of a factor analysis of the 21 life satisfaction items) 6 of the items into a scale measuring how satisfied respondents were with their economic situation: "How satisfied are you these days with your employment (or job prospects)? Your financial situation? Your personal achievements? Your educational achievements? Your economic prospects for the future? Your material possessions?" Scale scores ranged from 1 through 4, with high scores indicating high levels of economic satisfaction. The alpha reliability coefficient for the scale is .761.

Social class. Following House (1981), Jarjoura and Triplett (1997), and Title and Meier (1990), we operationalized several individual components of social class rather than relying on a composite measure. This approach is based on the logic that if social class predicts crime and delinquency because lower-status individuals are more economically deprived than their higher-status counterparts, for example, then it makes more sense to measure deprivation directly rather than to use a composite measure of class that may obscure the effects of deprivation (Tittle and Meier 1990:294). That is, rather than combine the effects of deprivation along with those of education and income, for example, in a composite measure of social class, this approach permits a consideration of the independent effects of each (Jarjoura and Triplett 1997:767; also see Farnworth et al. 1994). This research incorporates several separate socioeconomic variables: education, occupational status, household income, and employment status.

Educational level. Educational level of the respondents ranges from 4 years or more of college (coded 5) to less than a high school education (coded 1). The mean educational level of the sample was 3.825 with a standard deviation of 0.995.

Occupational status. This is intended to be a very general prestige ranking. The occupations range from executives, administrators, and managers (coded 7) to service workers and laborers (coded 1). The mean occupational status was 4.976 with a standard deviation of 1.823.

Household income. This is rank ordered across 11 categories, ranging from less then $7,000 annually (coded 1) to $50,000 and above annually (coded 11). The mean income of the respondents was 5.611 with a standard deviation of 3.340.

Employment status. Employment status was determined via a single item: "Are you employed now?" Of the respondents, 32 percent were unemployed at the time of the second interview. Responses were dummy coded, with 1 representing those who were employed at the time of the second interview.

It is important to note that our use of several individual indicators of social class creates potential collinearity problems. However, correlational data . . . indicate that while education, occupation, income, and employment status are significantly correlated with one another in the

house-hold, institutional, and combined samples, none of these associations is of sufficient magnitude to present collinearity problems. In addition, education, occupation, and income were all centered at their means for the analyses that follow, reducing substantially any multicollinearity present in the data (Aiken and West 1991:12–15, 35–38). Indeed, in the numerous regression models that we estimated, almost all of the variance inflation factors were under 2.00, and none exceeded 4.00, well under the threshold that is customarily accepted as indicative of collinearity problems.

Criminal involvement was measured at the time 2 interview by a modified version of Elliott and Ageton's (1980) Self-Report Delinquency Scale. This scale indexes the respondent's reported level of involvement in property and personal crimes, as well as drug and alcohol use, during the past year. Items were deleted that would have been inappropriate for an adult sample (i.e., status offenses). Each offense item was assigned a ratio score seriousness weight derived from the National Survey of Crime Severity (Wolfgang et al. 1985:46–50; also see Cernkovich and Giordano 1992), ranging from 1.42 for drug use to 25.85 for rape. Because of strain theory's historical focus on income-generating and other acquisition-oriented offenses, the dependent variable in this study is a specific offense subscale derived from the more general crime scale—income-generating crime involvement (alpha = .855). The total income-generating crime involvement score for a respondent is the mean of the sum of the products of each item's frequency and its seriousness weight. Prior delinquency involvement (alpha = .917), an independent variable in the analyses that follow, was measured at time 1 as the self-reported involvement in a variety of status, property, and violent offenses. The scale items were weighted and calculated in the manner described above. . . .

Sample. Because of the possibility that the influence of the variables we are examining in this research may differ for the household and previously institutionalized respondents, thereby confounding any results based on the combined sample, we will include in the regression analyses that follow a variable that distinguishes between the two samples. This variable is dummy coded, with the household sample as the omitted category.

Interaction terms. Although strain and social control theories are distinct conceptual models, they actually share many variables in their explanations of crime and delinquency. What differentiates the two theories is the prediction each makes regarding the effects of these shared variables. For example, both theories attach a great deal of importance to economic aspirations as a cause of crime. However, while strain theory proposes that high economic aspirations combined with limited opportunities are likely to be productive of crime, control theory avers that high aspirations, regardless of the level of objective opportunity to realize these aspirations, will result in conformity. Thus, to assess the relative merits of control and strain theories, our modeling must incorporate interaction terms that represent the conditional relationships proposed by strain theory. To this end, we created 10 product terms involving each of our two measures of commitment to the American dream (material salience and career salience) and five indicators of economic attainment (economic satisfaction, education, occupational status, income, and employment status). With the exception of employment status (which is a dummy variable), all of the variables involved in the product terms were centered (i.e., expressed as deviation scores so that their means are zero) to minimize collinearity problems and to permit a more meaningful and straightforward interpretation of any interaction effects (Aiken and West 1991:9, 12–15, 35–38).

Because most of the variables included in our analysis—material salience, career salience, economic satisfaction, occupation, education, income, and employment status—are indicators of both strain and control theories, we will consider control theory to be supported if our findings show that high levels of material and career salience are associated with conforming behavior, net of the other variables in the model. In other words, social control theory proposes that commitment to the American dream should be a strong predictor of crime: Those with high levels of commitment are those who are, by definition, strongly bonded to the society and its basic values. Consequently, they should be insulated from any significant involvement in crime. If control theory is correct, high levels of material salience and career salience should inhibit crime; income level, education, occupational status, degree of economic satisfaction, and employment status should not matter. Strain theory, on the other hand, predicts a more conditional relationship: Those respondents with a strong attachment to the American dream, combined with low levels of education, occupation (or who are unemployed), income, and economic satisfaction should be more likely to engage in crime because of the frustration and anger such a disjunction between aspirations and actual attainment produces. Finally, both strain and control theories will be supported if income, education, occupation, unemployment, and economic dissatisfaction are predictive of income-producing crime (i.e., these variables are indicators of social bonding as well as individual strain).

Analysis and Findings

Table 2 presents mean scores by race[3] for the life salience, socioeconomic, and criminal involvement variables, for the combined sample, and for the household and institutional samples separately. The combined sample data reveal significant race differences for all but one of the examined variables. Whites report significantly higher levels of prior delinquency, while African Americans report higher mean scores on material and career salience, education, and income-generating crime. Blacks have lower incomes than Whites and are more likely to be unemployed.

These data indicate that the Black respondents maintain a very strong commitment to the American dream when it is conceptualized in career and material salience terms. The magnitude of the *F*-statistics are impressive and indicate that Blacks are much more strongly committed to economic success goals than are their White counterparts and report that they are prepared to work harder and sacrifice more to realize them.[4] This willingness to work harder may be viewed as

TABLE 2 Mean Scores of Life Salience, Social Bonding, Economic, and Criminal Involvement Variables, by Sample Type

	Combined Sample (N = 881)			Household (n = 684)			Institutional (n = 197)		
	White	Black	F	White	Black	F	White	Black	F
Material salience	2.71	3.03	33.18***	2.66	3.01	33.92***	2.85	3.13	4.40*
Career salience	3.54	3.94	58.14***	3.50	3.94	56.54***	3.65	3.90	4.99*
Economic satisfaction	2.22	2.14	3.56	2.24	2.18	1.70	2.16	1.93	5.97***
Education	2.12	2.28	5.52*	2.36	2.46	1.80	1.48	1.35	1.36
Occupation	3.11	2.94	1.65	3.37	3.08	4.10*	2.39	2.22	0.51
Income	6.05	5.26	11.61***	6.55	5.62	13.48***	4.70	3.39	7.18**
Employment status	0.74	0.63	10.68***	0.75	0.67	5.63**	0.70	0.44	11.57***
Income-generating crime	6.99	8.29	14.48***	6.52	7.22	9.54**	8.25	13.95	20.01*
Prior delinquency	39.42	24.93	9.04**	8.98	9.54	0.11	120.78	106.29	0.75

$* p < .05. ** p < .01. *** p < .001.$

a necessity by African Americans, as 81 percent of the Black respondents, compared to only 34 percent of the Whites, agreed or strongly agreed with the following statement presented near the end of the interview: "In order to get ahead, minorities almost always have to work harder than members of the White majority." This attitude helps explain why such a strong commitment to economic success can exist side by side with low incomes and high levels of unemployment.

Many of the race differences noted in the combined sample persist in the household and institutional subgroups identified in Table 2, suggesting a powerful race effect, particularly in regard to the relative salience of economic goals. While the magnitude of the F-statistics is smaller for the institutional respondents, this is not unexpected given the small sample size. Nonetheless, it is significant that race differences exist in both samples for material and career salience, income, employment status, and income-generating crime. The only inconsistencies across samples

involve economic satisfaction and occupation: Economic satisfaction levels are significantly lower for Blacks than for Whites in the institutional but not the household sample, while occupation differences are significantly lower among African Americans than Whites in the household but not the institutional sample. These exceptions notwithstanding, it is clear that the Black respondents in our sample are more likely than their White counterparts to endorse the basic tenets of the American dream, and this is true in both the household and institutional samples.

The findings in Table 2 are consistent with MacLeod's (1987) ethnographic research in which he found that Black youths, despite their unfavorable economic circumstances, were more optimistic than their White counterparts about their futures and ability to compete, were more strongly committed to the American dream, and generally had very high levels of self-esteem and ambition. We find hints of the same pattern in our data: Even though the young Black adults in our study report low incomes, are more likely to be unemployed than are Whites, and (among the institutional respondents) report lower levels of economic satisfaction, they continue to maintain a very strong commitment to the American dream. This suggests that money and material possessions can be terribly important to those who do not have them and lack access to conventional opportunities for obtaining them. This may be especially the case among Blacks, who are generally devalued in American society because of their race and who often are denied access to the broader criteria of prestige available to Whites. In this sort of environment, a material/monetary yardstick becomes a critical and very tangible symbol of having "made it." It is also likely that many African Americans define "lots of money" and career advancement differently than do Whites, and this may also account for some of the race differences in our data. However, since we measured the relative strength of one's goal commitment rather than the precise amount of money or type of career desired, this explanation must remain speculative in nature.

In general, the data in Table 2 are consistent with the strain theory perspective on success goal orientation and crime. That is, African Americans are more materialistic and career oriented than their White counterparts, but they are more likely to be unemployed, to have low incomes when they are employed, and (among the institutional respondents) to report lower levels of economic satisfaction than Whites. In addition, they report higher levels of income-generating crime than do Whites. While we cannot be certain of the temporal ordering of these variables, these relationships are informative. Far from lowering their aspirations or abandoning their pursuit entirely, the Black respondents in our sample clearly maintain a strong commitment to the American dream, even in the face of low levels of socioeconomic attainment. Although these data are consistent with strain theory, they do not directly address the relationships between the American dream, attainment levels, and criminal involvement.

Table 3 presents the results of analyses in which income-generating offense involvement

TABLE 3   Regression Coefficients for Income-Generating Offense Involvement, for Combined Sample and Race Subgroups

	Combined Sample $(N = 881)$[a]		Blacks $(n = 407)$[b]		Whites $(n = 474)$[c]	
	Beta	b	Beta	b	Beta	b
Sample	.102	1.213*	.167	2.867*	.047	.345
Prior delinquency	.264	7.495*	.339	.036*	.258	.011*
Gender	−.055	−.544	−.069	−.877	−.059	−.388
Race	.148	1.464*				
Material salience	.026	.158	.001	.010	.052	.223
Career salience	.059	.371	.070	.630	.107	.430*
Economic satisfaction	−.083	−.720*	−.077	−.796	−.101	−.629*
Education	−.033	−.166	−.009	−.054	−.036	−.121
Occupation	−.026	−.070	−.037	−.126	−.012	−.022
Income	.037	.055	.003	.005	.093	.096
Employment status	−.068	−.727*	−.040	−.519	−.106	−.800*

[a] $R^2 = .180$.

[b] $R^2 = .253$.

[c] $R^2 = .160$.

* $p < .05$.

was regressed on the independent variables described above, for the combined sample and for Blacks and Whites separately. All of the independent variables were entered into the equations as a single block. In general, the data in Table 3 show that prior delinquency, the dummy variable distinguishing between the institutional and household samples, economic satisfaction, and employment status are the most consistent predictors of income-generating crime across the three groups. Among respondents in the combined sample, prior delinquency (Beta = .264) is the single best predictor: Those who were delinquent as adolescents are the most likely to report current involvement in crime. In addition, Blacks, those who were institutionalized as adolescents, those who are dissatisfied with their current economic situation, and the unemployed are the most likely to be involved in income-generating crime.

The data in Table 3 show that our model does a somewhat better job of accounting for the offense involvement of Blacks in comparison to Whites (R^2 = .253 and .160, respectively). However, prior delinquency and the sample variable are the only significant correlates of offending among Blacks; that is, once these two offense-based measures are controlled, the other variables included in the model do not contribute significantly to the explained variance.[5] Among Whites, prior delinquency is the best predictor of income-generating crime (Beta = .258), but career salience, dissatisfaction with one's current economic situation, and unemployment are significant correlates as well. While these results are generally consistent with strain theory, the influence of unemployment and economic dissatisfaction can be explained from a control theory perspective as well since these variables are indicators of weak conventional bonding.

These findings notwithstanding, the data in Table 3 may be of greatest interest for what they do not show than for what they reveal. That is, our two basic measures of the American dream—material salience and career salience—are not significant predictors of offending among Blacks, and only career salience is related to

White offending but in a direction opposite to that proposed by control theory. In fact, the economic salience variables are not related to criminal involvement in the manner proposed by social control theory among any of the groups represented in Table 3; that is, high levels of material and career salience are not associated with low levels of criminal involvement net of the other variables included in the model. Thus, our data to this point do not appear to offer very strong support for either social control or strain theory. Before we conclude that this is the case, however, we must examine the conditional relationships that are so critical to strain theory—those that evaluate the effect on criminal involvement of adherence to the American dream at various levels of socioeconomic attainment.

The reader will recall that strain theory proposes a conditional relationship between adherence to the American dream and anticipated/actual socioeconomic attainment: Those individuals with a strong commitment to the American dream, combined with low levels of education, occupation (or who are unemployed), income, and economic satisfaction, will be more likely to engage in crime than those not experiencing a disjunction between their aspirations and actual attainments. To examine these conditional relationships, we created 10 product terms involving our two measures of commitment to the American dream (material salience and career salience) and five indicators of attainment (economic satisfaction, education, occupational status, income, and employment status). With the exception of employment status (a dummy variable), all of the variables involved in the product terms were centered at their means. Centering reduces substantially any multicollinearity present in the data, and it allows for a meaningful interpretation of the main effects of the variables making up the product term[6] (Aiken and West 1991: 12–15, 35–38).

Table 4 presents the coefficients for those interaction terms that are statistically significant when entered into the main effects models reported in Table 3. Because our intent is to evaluate the empirical veracity of each conditional relationship proposed by strain theory, each

TABLE 4   Interaction Terms for Income-Generating Offense Involvement

	Combined Sample (N = 881)			Whites (n = 474)		
	Beta	**b**	**R²**	**Beta**	**b**	**R²**
Material Salience × Satisfaction				−.113	−.899	.173
Material salience				.059	.251	
Satisfaction				−.088	−.551	
Material Salience × Education	−.075	−.428	.185	−.122	−.504	.174
Material salience	.029	.172		.048	.205	
Education	−.039	−.195		−.065	−.218	
Material Salience × Occupation	−.074	−.249	.185	−.121	−.292	.174
Material salience	.018	.113		.039	.169	
Occupation	−.025	−.066		−.010	−.017	
Material Salience × Income				−.093	−.128	.168
Material salience				.053	.228	
Income				.089	.091	
Material Salience × Employment Status	−.124	−.904	.184	−.274	−1.332	.176
Material salience	.128	.769*		.293	1.257*	
Unemployment	−.068	−.724*		−.124	−.932*	
Career Salience × Satisfaction	−.085	−.875	.187	−.129	−.976	.176
Career salience	.074	.463*		.124	.500*	
Satisfaction	−.076	−.662*		−.092	−.570*	
Career Salience × Education	−.091	−.544	.188	−.138	−.535	.179
Career salience	.068	.427*		.117	.474*	
Education	−.041	−.203		−.049	−.162	
Career Salience × Occupation	−.078	−.252	.186	−.106	−.222	.171
Career salience	.069	.429*		.111	.448*	
Occupation	−.023	−.062		−.011	−.019	
Career Salience × Income	−.067	−.122	.184			
Career salience	.076	.473*				
Income	.040	.060				
Career Salience × Employment Status	−.142	−1.051	.185	−.413	−1.937	.202
Career salience	.177	1.110*		.446	1.802*	
Unemployment	−.071	−.754*		−.130	−.979*	

Note: Only the coefficients for those product terms that result in statistically significant increases in the explained variance—as measured by the incremental R^2 when the product term is added to the main effects model presented in Table 3—are shown. The R^2s reported above represent the total explained variance accounted for in income-generating crime when the interaction term is included in the full model. The main effects of the two variables that constitute each product term are shown for interpretative purposes. Even though the coefficients for the remaining variables included in the models vary somewhat from those reported in Table 3, this variation is statistically and substantively unimportant, and the coefficients are not reported here to conserve space.

* Main effect statistically significant.

product term was entered into the equation singly and tested for its explanatory contribution. At the outset, it is important to note that none of the product terms is a significant correlate of income-producing crime among the African Americans in our sample. In short, once prior delinquency and an institutional past are factored into the equation, none of the other variables included in our model matters much, including the interaction terms. This is not to say that strain or social control theory may not be useful in explaining the prior delinquent and criminal involvement of these respondents, only that they do not contribute much to our understanding of their involvement in income-producing crime as young adults. An identification of other factors that may account for the criminal involvement of African Americans is beyond the scope of this research; we only know from our data that the strain and social control variables we have examined provide little insight into their criminality. This is not the case, however, when the model is tested among Whites.

While Table 4 presents the product term data for the combined sample as well as for Whites, we will confine our discussion to the effects of these interactions among Whites. These data show that all but one of the interaction terms (Career Salience × Income) are significant correlates of offending among the Whites in our sample. Although material salience has a significant main effect on criminality in only one instance (the equation in which it interacts with unemployment), career salience has a significant main effect on criminality in all of the equations represented in Table 4. The reader should be aware of this distinction when interpreting the meaning of the effects of these variables. In the case of the product terms involving career salience, it is appropriate to conclude in all instances that the main effects of career salience on criminal involvement are statistically significant, and these effects also vary significantly by level of economic satisfaction, education, occupational status, and employment status. In the case of the material salience interactions, however, the main effects are not statistically significant (except in the equation

modeling Material Salience × Unemployment). Consequently, it is not appropriate to conclude that material salience has a significant main effect on income-producing crime, only that there is a statistically significant difference in its effect at varying levels of economic satisfaction, education, occupation, and income.

To facilitate the interpretation of these product terms, we calculated the effects of material salience and career salience at the mean and at one standard deviation above and one standard deviation below the mean of each of the attainment variables (Aiken and West 1991: 12-15). These data are presented in Table 5. The data in Tables 4 and 5 are strongly supportive of the strain theory hypothesis of a conditional relationship between commitment to the American dream and criminal involvement. That is, the precise effect of material salience and career salience on criminal involvement depends on the level of economic attainment. Furthermore, the direction of these effects is as proposed by strain theory: At low levels of economic satisfaction, education, occupational status, and income and among those who are unemployed, high levels of material salience and career salience are productive of involvement in income-producing crime. At high levels of attainment, on the other hand, commitment to the American dream is associated with low levels of involvement in crime.

Two examples illustrate these conditional relationships. The data in Table 4 show that the regression coefficient for the interaction between material salience and economic satisfaction is −.899, indicating that the impact of material salience on income-producing crime varies inversely with the level of economic satisfaction. The data in Table 5 show that at high levels of economic satisfaction, the effect of materialism on crime is moderately negative (−.224), indicating that among those who are economically satisfied, the higher the level of material salience, the lower the level of involvement in crime. On the other hand, at low levels of economic satisfaction, the effect of materialism is strongly positive (.726): High levels of material salience increase the likelihood of criminal involvement among those who are economically dissatisfied. At mean

TABLE 5 Effects of Material Salience and Career Salience at Selected Levels of Economic Satisfaction, Education, Occupation, Income, and Employment Status

	Combined Sample ($N = 881$)	Whites ($n = 474$)
Effect of material salience at		
Satisfaction mean + 1 SD		−.224
Satisfaction mean		.251
Satisfaction mean − 1 SD		.726
Effect of material salience at		
Education mean + 1 SD	−.254	−.294
Education mean	.172	.205
Education mean − 1 SD	.598	.704
Effect of material salience at		
Occupation mean + 1 SD	−.341	−.363
Occupation mean	.113	.169
Occupation mean − 1 SD	.567	.701
Effect of material salience at		
Income mean + 1 SD		−.184
Income mean		.228
Income mean − 1 SD		.640
Effect of material salience when		
Unemployed	.769	1.257
Employed	−.135	−.075
Effect of career salience at		
Satisfaction mean + 1 SD	−.029	−.015
Satisfaction mean	.463	.500
Satisfaction mean − 1 SD	.955	1.015
Effect of career salience at		
Education mean + 1 SD	−.114	−.056
Education mean	.427	.474
Education mean − 1 SD	.968	1.004
Effect of career salience at		
Occupation mean + 1 SD	−.030	.044
Occupation mean	.429	.448
Occupation mean − 1 SD	.888	.852
Effect of career salience at		
Income mean + 1 SD	.066	
Income mean	.473	
Income mean − 1 SD	.880	
Effect of career salience when		
Unemployed	1.110	1.802
Employed	.059	−.135

levels of satisfaction, the effect of material salience is also positive but of significantly less magnitude (.251).[7] Similarly, the impact of career salience on criminal involvement is conditioned by level of education. At the educational mean of the Whites in our sample, high levels of career salience are associated with high levels of income-producing crime (.474). This relationship is in the same direction but significantly stronger among those with low levels of education (1.004) and in the opposite direction and quite weak (−.056) among those with high levels of education.

The pattern of associations apparent in these two illustrations is characteristic of all of the relationships reported in Tables 4 and 5. That is, the effect of both material salience and career salience on criminal involvement is consistently positive among those with low levels of attainment and uniformly negative among those with high levels of attainment. In short, these data are strongly supportive of the strain theory argument that the effect of commitment to the American dream is conditioned by socioeconomic attainment levels. This is the case, however, only for the Whites in our sample.

Although our findings that economic variables better explain the criminality of Whites than of African Americans are counterintuitive to our theoretical expectations, we certainly are not the first to report such results. For example, a number of studies have found that while poverty and other economic indicators are major determinants of homicide among Whites, they have relatively weak effects among Blacks (Messner and Rosenfeld 1999; also see Messner and Golden 1992; Peterson and Krivo 1993; Smith 1992; Smith, Devine, and Sheley 1992). In an attempt to account for why our economic measures are significant predictors among the Whites but not among the African Americans in our sample, we examined the effect of several interaction terms involving prior delinquency and our salience and socioeconomic variables. We also modeled several product terms involving sample type (household or institutional) and the salience and socioeconomic variables. The logic underlying these analyses assumes that a strong economic orientation and/or the experience of economic strain is most likely to lead to adult criminality among those with a history of involvement in antisocial behavior. In short, high levels of economic salience and/or the presence of strain may provide the final push or allow for a seamless entry into adult criminality among those with a history of antisocial behavior but may not be sufficient to do so among those without this previous high level of involvement. Following this logic, it may only be among African Americans with a prior history of antisocial involvement that our economic variables are predictive of adult criminality.

To examine this possibility, we conducted several interaction analyses, focusing on respondents with high and low levels of prior delinquency involvement, as well as on those who had and had not been previously institutionalized. While these data (not shown) reveal several significant interaction effects among both Whites and African Americans, none of these account for the general inapplicability of our model to African Americans. For example, the two interaction terms for prior delinquency and sample type with our strain measure (economic satisfaction) are significant predictors only among Whites: Economic dissatisfaction is most strongly associated with adult criminality among those with high prior delinquency scores and among those who were previously institutionalized. There is no significant interaction between our strain measure and prior delinquency/sample type for African Americans.

While there are several product terms that are associated with adult criminality among both Blacks and Whites, these do not substantially improve the fit of our model to African Americans. For example, the effect of high levels of career salience is to increase the likelihood of adult criminality among Blacks and Whites with high prior delinquency scores and to decrease it among those with low prior delinquency scores. Similarly, high levels of career salience were more likely to lead to high rates of criminality among the institutional than the household respondents. This was true for both White and Black respondents. Unemployment also increases the likelihood of adult criminality, but while this effect is greatest among Whites with high prior delinquency scores, it is greatest among Blacks with low prior delinquency scores. The effect of unemployment on crime also was conditioned by sample type, although this effect was in contrasting directions for Whites and Blacks. For Whites, unemployment was most likely to lead to increased criminality among the household respondents, while for African Americans, it was among the previously institutionalized respondents that unemployment was most strongly related to adult criminality.

While these interaction effects are interesting, it is important to underscore that these results are generally consistent with those from our overall analysis: The product terms are more likely to be significant correlates of adult criminality among Whites than among African Americans, and when these terms are entered into the equation, the resulting models continue to be relatively uninformative regarding the criminality of African Americans.

Summary and Implications

We began this research with the goal of exploring the extent to which African Americans subscribe to the promise of the American dream—economic and material success—and the implications of this for criminal behavior. Although two of the most well-respected theories in criminology—strain and social control—assign a central role to the influence of the American dream on criminal and deviant behavior, surprisingly little research has examined its impact on African Americans. In addition, while the criminology literature is replete with studies of the influence of aspirations and expectations on criminal and deviant behavior, few of these have emphasized the economic goals that are so central to the core tenets of the American dream. In contrast, this study was based on a sample approximately half African American in racial composition and measured the American dream in strictly economic terms.

Our data indicate that African Americans maintain a very strong commitment to the American dream. Blacks report higher levels of commitment to economic success goals than do their White counterparts and indicate that they are prepared to work harder and sacrifice more to realize them. Even though the young Black adults in our study report low incomes and are more likely to be unemployed than are Whites, they continue to maintain a very strong commitment to the American dream. Such a commitment in the face of economic adversity may be

due to the role of economic and material success as symbols of success—they function as tangible indicators for many African Americans that, despite the many disadvantages to which they are subjected, they have in fact "made it."

Our regression analyses show that the main effects model, including prior behavior, material and career salience, and several economic and demographic variables, does a somewhat better job of accounting for the income generating offense involvement of Blacks in comparison to Whites. Once prior delinquency and having been institutionalized as a juvenile are controlled, however, the other variables included in the model do not contribute significantly to the explanation of criminality among African Americans. For Whites, on the other hand, career salience, dissatisfaction with one's current economic situation, and unemployment are significant correlates of criminal involvement, although prior delinquency is the single best predictor. While these results are generally supportive of strain theory, the influence of unemployment and economic dissatisfaction is consistent with the social control model as well.

Because economic aspirations assume such a central role in both social control and strain theories, we were surprised that our two basic measures of the American dream—material salience and career salience—were not related to offending among Blacks. Although career salience was related to White offense involvement, it was in the direction opposite to that proposed by control theory. Thus, the findings regarding the impact of the American dream on behavior offer little support for social control theory among either Whites or Blacks: High levels of material and career salience are not associated with low levels of criminal involvement. This was surprising because of our expectation that social control theory would be particularly relevant in accounting for criminal behavior during young adulthood. This is the time of life during which most of our respondents have married, started families, and are busily pursuing jobs and careers. The American dream is no longer an abstract phenomenon but has taken on a very concrete reality. If control theory is correct, we would expect those who maintain a strong commitment to the American dream at this point in their lives to be quite conforming in their behavior. Yet our data show either no relationship between commitment to the American dream and criminal behavior (among African Americans), or high levels of career salience increase rather than decrease the probability of involvement in income-producing crime (among Whites). In short, there is little evidence in our data that the indicators of social control theory we have examined help account for the involvement of young adults in criminal behavior. This does not mean, of course, that elements of control theory that we did not explore in this research—such as family bonding—are unrelated to criminal involvement. Indeed, prior research has indicated that such variables are important correlates of crime (see, e.g., Cernkovich and Giordano 1987; Sampson and Laub 1993). Still, our findings concerning one aspect of social control theory—the relationship between economic aspirations and criminal involvement—are not supportive of the theory.

Does strain theory fare any better, particularly in regard to African Americans? To evaluate the explanatory merit of strain theory, we examined the conditional relationships that are central to this model—those that model the effect of commitment to the American dream on criminal involvement at various levels of economic attainment. This analysis revealed that none of the product terms was a significant correlate of income-producing crime among African Americans. On the other hand, all but one of the interaction terms were significant predictors among Whites: At low levels of economic satisfaction, education, occupational status, and income and among those who are unemployed, high levels of material salience and career salience are productive of involvement in income-producing crime. At high levels of attainment, on the other hand, commitment to the American dream is associated with low levels of criminal involvement.

These findings are consistent with the strain theory position that the effect of commitment to the American dream is conditioned by anticipated and/or actual attainment of economic goals. At the same time, these data challenge an important component of social control theory. That is, control theory proposes that commitment to the American dream inhibits crime under all circumstances because such commitment reflects a "stake in conformity." For social control theory, actual attainment levels are not an important consideration—they do not influence the impact of high aspirations on behavior. However, our data indicate that attainment levels do matter. Among those with high levels of attainment, commitment to the American dream inhibits crime. On the other hand, among those with low levels of attainment, a continuing commitment to the American dream is actually productive of criminal involvement. This is contrary to the control theory position but easily accounted for by the strain model. Compared to previous research, we suspect that we successfully modeled strain effects not simply as a result of our focus on monetary goals but because our goal measures were operationalized in very concrete terms and because we examined the disjunction between these goals and actual achievements.

This focus on concrete economic and material goals also suggests an explanation for the lack of support for social control theory in our data. That is, commitment to the economic goals of the American dream may be a significant exception to the normal social controls resulting from a conventional normative orientation. While commitment to values and norms such as honesty, hard work, and delayed gratification can be expected to inhibit antisocial behavior, commitment to material and economic success—the hallmarks of the American dream—may often necessitate and justify deviant behavior. In this way, commitment to the American dream may actually impede the effective operation of other social controls. This interpretation suggests an area of complementarity between control and strain theories, wherein commitment to the American dream actually facilitates deviant behavior. Alternatively, our respondents may have exaggerated the degree of their commitment to the American dream as a way of justifying their antisocial behavior. This is most likely to be the case among the Whites in our sample since it is among them that commitment to the American dream is associated with high levels of criminal involvement. Just as some individuals inflate their aspirations to excuse misbehavior. Thus, while high aspirations may insulate individuals from deviant involvement among those who are truly committed to the American dream, such aspirations may facilitate antisocial behavior among those who purposively exaggerate their commitment to the dream to provide a convenient excuse for misbehavior. If this indeed is the case, it suggests a modification of control theory along the lines of Sykes and Matza's (1957) techniques of neutralization. Our data are not inconsistent with the concept of appeal to higher loyalties in that respondents may be reasoning that "the dream made me do it" or "the dream required that I do it." While these interpretations are speculative in nature, they are not inconsistent with our data and suggest the need for social control theory to more explicitly address the role of material and economic goals. The status of such goals is currently quite ambiguous in control theory, and it is unclear whether commitment to economic and material success produces the same consequences as commitment to conventional noneconomic goals.

Our findings also underscore the need to better understand why the strain theory variables we examined were significant correlates of crime among the Whites in our sample but not among the African Americans. One explanation for the inapplicability of our model to young Black adults is the possibility that the African Americans in our sample, especially those who were previously institutionalized, did not respond with total candor during the reinterview. It is not unreasonable to expect that those respondents with a history of legal trouble might be reluctant to report certain behaviors, particularly those that are violations of probation or parole guidelines. We noted above the steps that were taken in the collection of these data to minimize this sort of bias, but ultimately we cannot determine the extent to which such a bias might have affected our findings. We doubt that it had a significant impact, but we cannot say with certainty that the effect was nil.

Alternatively, the differential findings by race may be due in part to the possibility that Whites are more likely than African Americans to feel frustrated when they are unable to realize the promises of the American dream. That is, Whites may not anticipate or expect failure to the same extent as African Americans, and such failure, when it does occur among Whites, may generate high levels of anger and frustration and result in criminal behavior in some instances. In short, even though African Americans experience greater levels of objective deprivation, Whites may experience greater levels of subjective or relative deprivation. Because African Americans have been subjected to a long history of racial and economic discrimination, economic failure, while never welcomed, is not entirely unexpected. Indeed, African Americans have developed a repertoire of survival strategies to cope with a hostile environment that often fails to deliver on its promises (see, e.g., Bowman 1989; Gary 1981; Hill 1971). In short, Blacks may have adopted a very practical interpretation of the American dream: They recognize that despite its promises and their efforts to compete by its rules, there is a good possibility of failure. This explanation is consistent with the segmented labor market theory (Bluestone and Harrison 1982; Doeringer and Piore 1971; Gordon, Edwards, and Reich 1982; Sullivan, 1989) view that there are two avenues of economic achievement in American society. The primary labor market is characterized by steady work and good wages, while the secondary market consists of "low-wage jobs, welfare, employment and training programs, informal economic activities and crime [that] must be alternated and combined because none of these economic activities alone can provide a steady living" (Sullivan 1989:11). Thus, although African Americans may aspire to the promises of the American dream, they are realistic enough to understand that their access to the primary market is limited at best. Instead, their opportunities often lie in the secondary market, and this necessitates a mix of low-wage jobs, welfare, and crime. To the extent that they have made this adaptation, we would not expect to find among African Americans a relationship between our strain measures and criminal behavior. The combination of low-wage jobs, welfare, and crime acts as a buffer against the frustrations and strain that might otherwise exist if they had to rely on the primary labor market alone.

Such explanations notwithstanding, the general inapplicability of both social control and strain theories to the African Americans in our sample is one of the most important findings of our research. We certainly did not anticipate this, and if our results are supported by subsequent research, particularly that which taps dimensions of strain and control theories not examined here, they should encourage researchers to examine more explicitly the manner in which major theories of crime and delinquency apply to African Americans and other minorities. African Americans are overrepresented in crime and delinquency statistics, and much of the racial tension in American society is related to the actual and perceived racial distribution of crime. Yet African Americans continue to be underrepresented as research participants in criminological research. Additional research on Blacks and other minority groups is essential if we are to better understand how our theories apply across racial groups and the implications this has for social policy. Our findings suggest that it may be erroneous to conclude that research based on White or demographically undifferentiated samples apply to African Americans in precisely the same fashion. Various theories may not be applicable to African Americans at all, may apply in dramatically different ways, or there may be more subtle variations across race groups that need to be identified. To explore these possibilities, researchers must move beyond treating race as a simple control variable and begin sampling African Americans and other minorities in sufficient numbers to permit comprehensive evaluations of the major theories of crime and delinquency.

Notes

[1] While this is not an equal probability of selection sample, it was drawn to represent race and gender groups in sufficient numbers for meaningful analysis and to include a wide range of offending levels, from nonoffenders to serious chronic offenders. The reader is cautioned against generalizing beyond the data presented here.

It is important to note that the reinterview periods are different for the two subsamples (1992 and 1995). We believe that any bias introduced by this will likely be conservative, resulting in institutional respondents who are less criminal than they would have been had they been interviewed in 1992. Simply put, they have had three additional years to "mature out" of crime. On the other hand, it could be argued that these respondents have had additional time and opportunity to establish themselves in income-generating criminal careers; in this case, their reported criminal involvement in 1995 would be greater than that reported had they been reinterviewed in 1992. Regardless of which of these two opposing arguments is correct, the institutional respondents are considerably more delinquent/criminal than the household respondents, and consistent with our rationale for interviewing them for this research in the first place, their inclusion permits us to represent a wide range of offending levels in our sample.

[2] In conceptualizing success goals for this research, we have purposely avoided defining them strictly as aspirations or expectations. The literature in criminology on the distinction between expectations and aspirations is quite extensive (e.g., Agnew 1983; Farnworth and Leiber 1989; Hirschi 1969; Jensen 1995), and there is considerable debate as to which is most important and whether a discrepancy measure based on the two is necessary. While we recognize the problems inherent in not making a distinction between aspirations and expectations, we are convinced by the theoretical rationale underlying the concept of life salience, as well as the empirical reliability of our scales, that we are measuring success goals in a sensible, realistic, and concrete way.

[3] It might reasonably be argued that treating race as a variable independent of social class implies a subcultural as opposed to a strain theory line of reasoning. While our empirical focus on race differences in commitment to

the American dream has necessarily resulted in some sacrifice of theoretical purity, we believe this in no way compromises our analysis or the implications of our results for strain and social control theories.

[4] The reader will recall that the career and material salience scales included such items as the following: "I will sacrifice a lot of other things to have a lot of money," "I expect to make as many sacrifices as are necessary in order to advance in my work/career," and "I expect to devote whatever time and energy it takes to move up in my job/career field."

[5] Although the sample variable is a significant correlate of criminal involvement in the combined sample and among African Americans, we have not presented the results of separate analyses for the two sample groupings. Because there are only 65 Blacks in the institutional sample, we would have little confidence in the stability of the resulting regression coefficients. Consequently, we have used the variable distinguishing between the two samples as a control variable in the regression analyses.

[6] Even though there is considerable debate as to whether it is appropriate to interpret main effects when an interaction term is included in a regression model, centering permits a meaningful interpretation of the main effect because it creates a variable with a mean of zero. For example, if x and z are centered variables and $x \cdot z$ is a product term included in the equation, the main effect of x on the dependent variable y can be interpreted as the effect of x on y at the mean of z (i.e., when $z = 0$). In short, "centering produces a value of zero on a continuous scale that is typically meaningful" (Aiken and West 1991:37).

[7] By its very nature, this interaction term also permits an examination of the effect of economic satisfaction on criminal involvement as a function of level of material salience. However, because our interest is in the conditional effect of commitment to the American dream as specified by strain theory, we have chosen to limit our interpretation of the product terms to the manner in which the attainment variables condition the impact of material salience and career salience.

References

Agnew, Robert. 1983. "Social Class and Success Goals: An Examination of Relative and Absolute Aspirations." *The Sociological Quarterly* 24:435–52.

———. 1992. "Foundation for a General Strain Theory of Crime and Delinquency." *Criminology* 30:47–87.

———. 1995. "Strain and Subcultural Theories of Criminality." Pp. 305–27 in *Criminology: A Contemporary Handbook*, 2nd ed., edited by Joseph F. Sheley. Belmont, CA: Wadsworth.

Agnew, Robert, Francis T. Cullen, Velmer S. Burton, Jr., T. David Evans, and R. Gregory Dunaway. 1996. "A New Test of Classic Strain Theory." *Justice Quarterly* 13:681–704.

Agnew, Robert, and Diane H. Jones. 1988. "An Examination of Inflated Educational Expectations." *The Sociological Quarterly* 29:315–37.

Aiken, Leona S., and Stephen G. West. 1991. *Multiple Regression: Testing and Interpreting Interactions*. Newbury Park, CA: Sage.

Amatea, S., E. G. Cross, J. E. Clark, and C. L. Bobby. 1986. "Assessing the Work and Family Role Expectations of Career Oriented Men and Women: Life Role Salience Scales." *Journal of Marriage and the Family* 48:831–38.

Bluestone, Barry, and Bennett Harrison. 1982. *The Deindustrialization of America: Plant Closings, Community Abandonment, and the Dismantling of Basic Industry.* New York: Basic Books.

Bowman, Phillip J. 1989. "Research Perspectives on Black Men: Role Strain and Adaptation across the Adult Life Cycle." Pp. 117–50 in *Black Adult Development and Aging*, edited by Reginald L. Jones. Berkeley, CA: Cobb and Henry.

Campbell, A., and P.E. Converse. 1980. *The Quality of American Life, 1978.* Ann Arbor, MI: Inter-University Consortium for Political and Social Research.

Cernkovich, Stephen A., and Peggy C. Giordano. 1987. "Family Relationships and Delinquency." *Criminology* 25:401–27.

———.1992. "School Bonding, Race, and Delinquency." *Criminology* 30:261–91.

Cernkovich, Stephen A., Peggy C. Giordano, and M. D. Pugh. 1985. "Chronic Offenders: The Missing Cases in Self-Report Delinquency Research." *Journal of Criminal Law and Criminology* 76:705–32.

Doeringer, Peter B., and Michael J. Piore. 1971. *Internal Labor Markets and Manpower Analysis*. Lexington, MA: Heath.

Elliott, Delbert, and Suzanne Ageton. 1980. "Reconciling Race and Class Differences in Self-Reported and Official Estimates of Delinquency." *American Sociological Review* 45:95–110.

Farnworth, Margaret, and Michael Leiber. 1989. "Strain Theory Revisited: Economic Goals, Educational Means, and Delinquency." *American Sociological Review* 54:263–74.

Farnworth, Margaret, Terrance Thornberry, Marvin Krohn, and Alan Lizotte. 1994. "Measurement in the Study of Class and Delinquency: Integrating Theory and Research." *Journal of Research in Crime and Delinquency* 31:32–61.

Gary, L. E. 1981. *Black Men*. Beverly Hills, CA: Sage.

Giordano, Peggy C., Stephen A. Cernkovich, and M. D. Pugh. 1986. "Friendships and Delinquency." *American Journal of Sociology* 91:1170–1202.

Gordon, David M., Richard Edwards, and Michael Reich. 1982. *Segmented Work, Divided Workers: The Historical Transformation of Labor in the United States*. Cambridge, UK: Cambridge University Press.

Gottfredson, Michael R., and Travis Hirschi. 1990. *A General Theory of Crime*. Stanford, CA: Stanford University Press.

Hagan, John, Bill McCarthy, Patricia Parker, and Jo-Ann Climenhage. 1997. *Mean Streets: Youth Crime and Homelessness*. New York: Cambridge University Press.

Hill, R. 1971. *The Strengths of Black Families*. New York: Emerson Hall.

Hindelang, Michael R., Travis Hirschi, and Joseph G. Weis. 1981. *Measuring Delinquency*. Beverly Hills, CA: Sage.

Hirschi, Travis. 1969. *Causes of Delinquency*. Berkeley: University of California Press.

Hochschild, Jennifer L. 1995. *Facing Up to the American Dream: Race, Class, and the Soul of the Nation*. Princeton, NJ: Princeton University Press.

House, J. S. 1981. "Social Structure and Personality." Pp. 525–61 in *Social Psychology: Sociological Perspectives*, edited by M. Rosenberg and R. H. Turner. New York: Basic Books.

Hyman, Herbert H. 1953. "The Value System of Different Classes: A Social Psychological Contribution to the Analysis of Stratification." Pp. 488–99 in *Class, Status, and Power*, edited by Rinehard Bendix and Seymour Martin Lipset. New York: Free Press.

Jarjoura, J. Roger, and Ruth A. Triplett. 1997. "Delinquency and Class: A Test of the Proximity Principle." *Justice Quarterly* 14:763–92.

Jensen, Gary F. 1995. "Salvaging Structure through Strain: A Theoretical and Empirical Critique." Pp. 139–58 in *The Legacy of Anomie Theory*, edited by Freda Adler and William S. Laufer. New Brunswick, NJ: Transaction Publications.

Johnson, Robert. 1979. *Juvenile Delinquency and Its Origins*. New York: Cambridge University Press.

Liska, Alan. 1971. "Aspirations, Expectations, and Delinquency: Stress and Additive Models." *Sociological Quarterly* 12:99–107.

MacLeod, Jay. 1987. *Ain't No Makin' It*. Boulder, CO: Westview.

Matsueda, Ross L., and Karen Heimer. 1987. "Race, Family Structure, and Delinquency: A Test of Differential Association and Social Control Theories." *American Sociological Review* 52:826–40.

Merton, Robert K. 1938. "Social Structure and Anomie." *American Sociological Review* 3:672–82.

Messner, Steven F., and Reid M. Golden. 1992. "Racial Inequality and Racially Disaggregated Homicide Rates: An Assessment of Alternative Theoretical Explanations." *Criminology* 30:421–47.

Messner, Steven F., and Richard Rosenfeld. 1994. *Crime and the American Dream*. Belmont, CA: Wadsworth.

———. 1999. "Social Structure and Homicide: Theory and Research." Pp. 27–41 in *Homicide: A Sourcebook of Social Research,* edited by M. Dwayne Smith and Margaret A. Zahn. Thousand Oaks, CA: Sage.

Nightingale, Carl Husemoller. 1993. *On the Edge: A History of Poor Black Children and Their American Dreams*. New York: Basic Books.

Nye, F. Ivan. 1958. *Family Relationships and Delinquent Behavior*. New York: John Wiley.

Peterson, Ruth D., and L. J. Krivo. 1993. "Racial Segregation and Black Urban Homicide." *Social Forces* 71:1001–26.

Reckless, Walter. 1961. "A New Theory of Delinquency and Crime." *Federal Probation* 25: 42–46.

Sampson, R., and J. Laub. 1993. *Crime in the Making: Pathways and Turning Points through Life*. Cambridge, MA: Harvard University Press.

Smith, M. D. 1992. "Variation in Correlates of Race-Specific Urban Homicide Rates." *Journal of Contemporary Criminal Justice* 8:137–49.

Smith, M. D., J. A. Devine, and J. F. Sheley. 1992. "Crime and Unemployment: Effects across Age and Race Categories." *Sociological Perspectives* 35:551–72.

Sullivan, Mercer L. 1989. *Getting Paid: Youth Crime and Work in the Inner City*. Ithaca, NY: Cornell University Press.

Sykes, Gresham, and David Matza. 1957. "Techniques of Neutralization: A Theory of Delinquency." *American Sociological Review* 22 (December): 664–70.

Tittle, Charles R., and Robert F. Meier. 1990. "Specifying the SES/Delinquency Relationship." *Criminology* 28:271–99.

U.S. Bureau of the Census. 1980. *Alphabetical Index of Industries and Occupations, 1980 Census of Population*. Washington, DC: Government Printing Office.

Wolfgang, Marvin E., Robert M. Figlio, Paul E. Tracy, and Simon L. Singer. 1985. *The National Survey of Crime Severity*. Washington, DC: Bureau of Justice Statistics.

Conclusion

The reading presented in this chapter provides qualified support for social strain theories. In particular, it shows that social structure, subcultures, and individual's encountering stressful situations have important implications for race and crime. However, this study has its limitations. From meta-analyses we find that, for instance, articles on social structure do not provide longitudinal insight into the changes in the degree of strain and their effects on frustration. Further, subculture studies are unable to provide specific information concerning the connection between race and the two types of families mentioned. Finally, individual-level studies on strain theory are unable to determine the fluid nature of emotions and how they can influence the decision to perform criminal acts.

Discussion Questions

1. How do the features of goal aspirations differ across the races? Do you agree with Merton's view that aspirations lead to increased crime rates and criminality?

2. Describe the differences between families based on Anderson's "code of the streets"? What racial implications do the different types of families have for crime rates and criminality?

3. How do individuals of different races feel strain differentially that might push them to crime?

4. From any one of the strain perspectives, what recommendations might be made to reduce crime rates and criminality?

References

Agnew, R. (1992). Foundation for general strain theory of crime and delinquency. *Criminology, 30*, 47–87.

Agnew, R. (2001). Building on the foundation of general strain theory: Specifying the types of strain most likely to lead to crime and delinquency. *Journal of Research in Crime and Delinquency, 38*, 319–361.

Agnew, R. (2005). *Why do criminals offend? A General Theory of Crime and Delinquency*. Los Angeles, CA: Roxbury.

Anderson, E. (2000). *Code of the street: Decency, violence, and the moral life of the inner city*. New York, NY: W.W. Norton & Company.

Merton, R. K. (1938). Social structure and anomie. *American Sociological Review, 3*, 672–682.

Kubrin, C. E. (2005). Gangstas, Thugs, and Hustlas: Identity and the code of the street in rap music. *Social Problems, 52*, 360–378.

CHAPTER 6

Conflict Theory and Racial Threat Theory

In criminology, many take the perspective that social structure has implications for how laws are made and how groups are viewed as criminals. Conflict and racial threat theories are used to understand this perspective. This chapter presents an overview of both theories and provides the specific propositions that these theories have to understand race and crime.

According to conflict theory, capitalism is the basis of the inequality that determines the structure of society. Two groups exist. The first group is in power and they are the owners of property and the means of production. The second group does not own property or the means of production. The differences between these two groups create unequal monetary and power distributions. These inequalities create the conditions for criminal behavior.

Conflict theorists see humans as social beings who have a connection with others. This connection is shaped by their social structural context. Further, this theory suggests that individuals will join others of similar status to form groups of like-minded individuals.

Conflict theory views the law as a set of rules developed and enforced by those who own property and the means of production. It posits that these rules are developed so that the powerful can maintain their holdings in politics, economics, and society. The content of these rules and acceptable forms of behavior are determined by the powerful. Therefore, those who are not empowered to make the laws are subservient to the powerful.

In general, criminals are rationally responding to their social position and they threaten the powerful. That is, there is not a major difference between the criminals and noncriminals. However, noncriminals are able to better manipulate the criminal justice system and provide for themselves in a pseudo-legal manner. Two theoretical perspectives view crime as being influenced by the development and use of social control—Turk's (1966, 1969) conflict theory and Blalock's (1967) racial threat perspective.

According to Turk's (1966, 1969) version of conflict theory, individuals who are in subordinate positions in society are subject to the laws, values, and standards of individuals in authority. The behavior of those in subordinate positions will be deemed criminal if they do not learn to become deferential to those in authority.

Turk argues that a substantial amount of learning about the difference between the superior and inferior classes takes place in this sort of society. The superior class will be those who are in authority, and those who are subject to the laws, values, and standards set by the superior classes are inferior. Also, the norms of deference and domination are learned in this process. Domination norms are learned by both the superior and the inferior classes. However, the extent to which these norms are learned varies based on an individual's age, gender, and race. In Turk's view, not everyone learns these norms. Those who do not learn these norms are "norm resisters," and they are relatively unsophisticated in the methods that the powerful use to manipulate them through society. For Turk (1966, 1969), crimes are the behaviors of individuals who have not been able to grasp that they need to confront those individuals who are authority figures.

Turk (1966, 1969) identified three conditions that would make the conflict between authorities and subjects over values and norms more likely. The first is when cultural values and social actions of the authorities are in close agreement with those of the subjects. The second is when the authorities and subjects are organized. The third is when the authorities or subjects are less sophisticated.

Turk (1966, 1969) went on to outline three conditions that would result in the criminalization of subjects. The first is when law enforcement and the judicial branch of government agree on the seriousness of an offense. The second is when there is a substantial difference between those who enforce the law and those who do not enforce the law. The third is when there is an unrealistic expectation of change such that resistance is unimportant.

Over time, the relationship between the authority figures and the subjects becomes less coercive. This takes place as newer generations are socialized to the existing set of laws and rules. Thus, the relationship between the authority figures and the subjects becomes more automatic because less deference is likely.

Blalock's (1967) version of racial threat has enjoyed substantial success in the sociological, economic, political, and criminological literatures. This premise focuses on racial differences in society as they pertain to power and economic development. For Blalock (1967), as the size of a racial minority group begins to increase—economically and politically—it will directly threaten the majority group in these positions. The threat from the racial minority group will create a fear that initiates a response from the majority group. Blalock (1967) argued that this threat can be imaginary and not real. The response from the majority group is generally to increase the social controls on the racial minority group to reduce their growth in economics and politics. For Blalock (1967), social controls refer to the use of the criminal justice system. The increased level of social controls creates conflict between the two racial groups.

Overall, the threat to the majority group can take many forms. However, the two predominate forms are economic and political. Economically, the majority group sees the increase in the size of the racial minority group as resulting in competition for jobs, positions, and economic resources. So the majority group will develop social controls to relieve the racial economic threat.

Politically, as racial minorities grow in number, their opportunity for political participation also grows, which threatens the power base of whites. This has the effect of reducing opportunities for whites to repress through legislation. Therefore, the majority group uses social controls to reduce instances of racial minority political threat.

As a whole, conflict theory has relatively little empirical support. The difficulty is in the ability of researchers to operationalize the central components of the theory. Specific forms of conflict theory have been operationalized and are able to be used in empirical analyses. These have been shown to have empirical support, but the majority of the support has been for propositions about class differences and not about racial differences. Unlike conflict theory, racial threat theory has been shown to have moderate support in the empirical literature.

Although designed to explain class differences, conflict theory can also be applied to explain the race differences in crime. Specifically, political movements have been used to target or criminalize behaviors of the poor or any other group that behaves in this way. McCall and Parker illustrate these points in the selection provided here.

A Dynamic Model of Racial Competition, Racial Inequality, and Interracial Violence

Patricia L. McCall, *North Carolina State University*
Karen F. Parker, *University of Florida*

Race relations and stratification literatures offer explicit expectations concerning interracial conflict. Causal arguments derived from these perspectives are examined in this study to explore their ability to explain interracial violence above and beyond criminological perspectives of economic deprivation and racial inequality. The vast majority of previous aggregate-level studies on violence are cross-sectional, ignoring the importance of a dynamic model that incorporates the influence of changing structural conditions in urban areas on interracial violence. We explore theories that incorporate dynamic explanations for the influence of structural factors related to crime as well as racial conflict and employ a methodological approach that models the change in structural conditions for rare events such as interracial homicide. We find that changes between 1980 and 1990 in urban Black and Hispanic population composition, racial competition and racial inequality differentially explain the variation in White and Black interracial homicide offending.

Introduction

Since researchers began disaggregating homicides in order to examine race specific offending, unique contributions have been made to understanding the influence of social and economic forces on homicide behavior of subgroups in the population (Harer and Steffensmeier 1992; Krivo and Peterson 2000; Messner and Golden 1992; Parker and McCall 1997, 1999; Peterson and Krivo 1993; Shihadeh and Flynn 1996; Shihadeh and Maume 1997; Williams and Flewelling 1988). The field also has benefitted in recent decades from the wedding of race relations and stratification literature with criminological theories in pursuing explanations for the widely disparate violent offending rates between Whites and Blacks (Krivo and Peterson 2000; Messner and Golden 1992; Messner and South 1986; Parker and McCall 1997; Peterson and Krivo 1993; Sampson 1987). Others have linked racial conflict to interracial homicide (Jacobs and Wood 1999; Parker and McCall 1999) and provide evidence that local opportunity structure, racial inequality, and political competition differentially influence White-on-Black versus Black-on-White homicide offending.

Central to these race relations and stratification literatures is the notion that changes in minority population composition (Blalock 1967) and economic forces (Massey and Eggers 1990; Wilson 1987, 1991) are catalysts for interracial conflict and concentrated disadvantage. An examination of race relations theories, such as Blalock's minority-threat thesis, requires a dynamic model or analysis over time. Yet most aggregate-level studies that incorporate this literature into studies of race-specific violence are cross-sectional (Krivo and Peterson 2000; Parker and McCall 1999; Peterson and Krivo 1993). Our current study provides an examination of the influence that change in racial competition and racial inequality has on interracial violence. We propose that incorporating change into the research model is needed in exploring the dynamics that are central to some of these theories and in evaluating their application to the study of interracial violence. Thus, the present study examines the dynamic nature of the relationships between racial competition, racial inequality and interracial homicide between 1980 and 1990 in large U.S. cities using Poisson regression estimation techniques. These theories should find support during these periods which witnessed change in the social and economic forces underlying these causal arguments. We begin by briefly outlining the key concepts from the race-relations and stratification literatures that inform our study of interracial violence.

Threat and Conflict between Racial Groups

Traditionally economic deprivation and racial inequality arguments have been used to explain race-specific violence (Harer and Steffensmeier 1992; Messner and Golden 1992; Messner and South 1992; Parker and McCall 1997). More recently race relations arguments have been introduced along with criminological perspectives in addressing race-specific criminal offending (Jacobs and Wood 1999, Parker and McCall 1999). Our research builds on the efforts of others by emphasizing the importance of shifts or change in economic resources and urban conditions identified in these literatures.

Blalock's (1967) theory of minority-group relations—also referred to as his "minority threat" thesis—claims that as the relative size of the minority group increases, members of the majority group perceive a growing threat to their positions and will take steps to reduce the competition. Blalock argues that the competition between interracial groups assumes two forms—competition over economic resources, and power threats. Most extant research examining Blalock's thesis relies on the concentration of Blacks in the population to measure minority threat.

Racial Composition

Blalock (1967) postulates that racial threat is positively related to the amount of minority concentration in a population with a decreasing slope. That is, as the concentration of minorities increases in a location, so too will the threat Blacks pose to Whites; and as this concentration of Blacks reaches some threshold, the threat of competition will diminish. Importantly, Blalock's theory emphasizes the *dynamic* forces associated with an increase or change in the minority group (Black) population.

Economic and Labor Force Competition

Racial competition perspectives suggest that conflicts between racial groups are a result of minorities being positioned disproportionately among the lower classes and typically relegated to unskilled or semiskilled occupations. As Whites attempt to maintain their economic positions in the labor market, minorities are disproportionately found among lower paid positions with little hope for advancement (Bonacich 1976). Racial conflict ensues because Blacks pose an economic threat to low-skilled White workers as they compete for lower-level jobs (Blalock 1967; Blauner 1982; Lieberson 1980). Attempts to exclude Blacks from participating in the labor market and competing against Whites for jobs can take the form of violence by Whites against Blacks (Huff-Corzine, Corzine, and Moore 1991; Olzak 1990; Parker and McCall 1999; Tolnay, Beck, and Massey 1992). Therefore, Whites' hostilities toward Blacks are a function of the (real or perceived) threat of competition Blacks pose as their numbers increase. Moreover, these theories describe a dynamic process, in that the change in economic opportunities is the key to linking racial competition to White interracial violence.

Labor force competition is posited to be related to Black interracial violence because labor force competition between Whites and Blacks is likely to be manifested in racial inequality—the aggravations and hostilities engendered by their history of subordination and discrimination by Whites (Bobo and Gilliam 1990; Bobo and Hutchings 1996). Because minorities are disproportionately represented among the lower class and the unemployed, discrimination experienced within these economic spheres engenders strain, frustration, and animosity. Relatively few studies have incorporated these arguments to explain interracial homicide (for exceptions, see Jacobs and Wood 1999; Messner and Golden 1992; Parker and McCall 1997, 1999).

Political Competition

In early U.S. history, Blacks had no power or status in the political arena. More recently, Blacks' relative powerlessness has improved as growing numbers of Blacks win elections for municipal and national political offices. As Jacobs and Wood (1999) argue, these political victories for Blacks alter racial tensions and decrease interracial violence. Not only does Black political presence diminish racial strife and decrease incidents of Black racial violence against Whites, Blacks' growing political strength may be perceived by Whites as another form of threat that increases resentment on the part of Whites, and, thereby, increases the chances for White-on-Black interracial violence (Jacobs and Wood 1999). Thus, it can be argued that political competition will threaten Whites' dominant position and engender hostility among Whites as Blacks improve their economic and political status. Because Whites have long dominated the political domain, changes in political competition are not likely to influence Black-on-White violence.

Hypotheses

While the structural conditions reviewed above have been incorporated in previous studies of interracial homicide, by and large, the change in these structural conditions has not. Based on the theoretical arguments described above, we test the following relationships. First, according to Blalock, an increase in the percentage of the Black population elevates rates of White violence. This measure has been used widely in the race relations literature for the purpose of testing the power threat thesis (Olzak, Shanahan, and McEneaney 1996; Tolnay and Beck 1992; Tolnay, Beck, and Massey 1989). Consistent with this literature, we pose that growing Black population composition (or an increase in the Black population from 1980 to 1990) will increase the likelihood of White interracial homicide.

Second, racial competition theorists posit that as Whites lose out to, or perceive themselves as threatened by, Blacks in the labor force, Whites will become (more) hostile toward Blacks, thereby increasing the likelihood for conflict between members of these two groups. Therefore, with regard to our examination of the changing forces occurring between 1980 and 1990, we hypothesize that cities with increasing labor force competition (declining labor market security for Whites) will experience increasing White interracial homicides.

Labor force competition faced by Blacks and the injustice Blacks endure through discriminatory hiring practices breeds resentment and animosity toward Whites. While researchers suggest improved conditions for Blacks may decrease Black interracial competition and interracial conflict (Jacobs and Wood 1999), we propose that as competition between these two groups increases between 1980 and 1990, Black interracial homicide should increase. In summary, the parameter coefficients for the variables measuring this concept are posited to be negative in the White and positive in the Black interracial homicide models. The data and strategy we employ to analyze these proposed relationships are described in the following sections.

Data and Methods

U.S. cities with populations of 100,000 and over in 1980 constitute our sample of cases included in the analyses. The selection of cities during this time period allows for greater comparability with existing research. Wilson (1987, 1991) as well as Massey and Eggers (1990) focus on the changing structure of central cities in recent decades and demonstrate how poor and minority populations have been stranded in urban areas where local opportunities for employment have diminished along with deindustrialization—the exodus of major industries into suburban and rural areas. The resulting social isolation and poverty concentration have dealt a harsh hand—one that is accompanied with dwindling hope and even fewer opportunities for escape from poverty. Inclusion of this time period allows us to estimate the impact of various structural indicators on interracial homicide events during a decade of significant change (Shihadeh and Ousey 1996, 1998). Because our conceptual model emphasizes change between 1980 and 1990, measures for key concepts were collected for the two decennial points. The full data set based on the 1980 largest cities is restricted to 168 cases. To minimize the impact of year-to-year fluctuations for the rare events of interracial homicide, interracial offending counts are based on a five-year average of homicide data for the years, 1978 to 1982 and 1987 to 1991—years circa 1980 and 1990 for which data were available at the time of data collection. Missing data on some variables further reduced our sample to 146 cases for the two time points.[1]

The Comparative Homicide Files (CHF), which are derived from the FBI's Supplemental Homicide Reports, provide data for our measure of interracial homicide.[2] These data are widely employed in race-specific analyses of homicide (Allen and Buckner 1997; Harer and Steffensmeier 1992; Jacobs and Wood 1999; Krivo and Peterson 1996, 2000; Messner and Golden 1992; Ousey 1999; Parker and McCall 1997, 1999; Peterson and Krivo 1993; Sampson 1987; Shihadeh and Flynn 1996; Shihadeh and Maume 1997; Shihadeh and Steffensmeier 1994; Williams and Flewelling 1988). U.S. Bureau of the Census population statistics are sources for our social and economic indicators and represent those widely employed in studies of homicide offending.

Dependent Variables

This study focuses on 1980 and 1990 murders and nonnegligent manslaughters with a single offender and single victim, which is consistent with previous research investigating race-specific offending (Krivo and Peterson, 2000; Messner and Golden 1992; Parker and McCall 1997, 1999; Williams and Flewelling 1988). Although instances of multiple-offender homicides are omitted from this analysis, this method avoids ambiguous classifications of incidents with multiple victims and offenders of different racial groups. Until further information is available on the nature of those homicides omitted by this data, it is difficult to assess the implications of these omissions on the findings of the present study.[3] The interracial (White-on-Black and Black-on-White) homicide counts for each race-specific offending group are computed as the average number of homicides involving an offender and victim of opposite races around the two decennial time points, 1980 and 1990. For example, the White interracial homicide count is the total number of homicides involving a White offender with a Black victim. Rather than interracial homicide rates, we use interracial homicide counts which are more appropriate for Poisson-based regression models, which are preferable in analyzing data with the distributional properties of such rare events (Osgood 2000).

Explanatory and Control Variables

The concepts comprising our causal models include racial composition, racial competition (political, labor market, and economic), racial inequality, economic disadvantage, and racial segregation. The reader should bear in mind the theories driving this analysis imply that changes in the relative well-being of Whites vis-à-vis Blacks are the catalyst for conflict between members of these two groups. Therefore, it is the contextual dynamics of urban centers about which we are concerned and our discussion of the relationships of these social and economic factors on interracial homicide is an examination of how the changes in U.S. cities during this period influenced interracial homicide offending.

We begin by operationalizing racial composition which is measured by calculating the percent of the total urban population that is Black. This measure of Black population composition is posited to be positively related to White interracial homicide.

There are separate concepts derived from competition theory—in particular, those pertaining to racial competition. Political competition is measured as whether or not the city has a Black mayor (Bobo and Gilliam 1990; Bobo and Hutchings 1996; Jacobs and Wood 1999). The rationale for employing this measure is that Whites are likely to feel that their political power is diminished and that their majority position is threatened when a Black mayor is elected (Bobo and Gilliam 1990; Bobo and Hutchings 1996).

We operationalize labor force competition as the ratio of the percentage of Blacks not employed in the labor force to the percentage of Whites not employed in the labor force. This ratio reflects the need or competition for jobs by race-specific populations. Thus, lower values of this measure capture greater labor force competition faced by Whites relative to Blacks while higher values represent greater labor force competition for Blacks. Following Krivo, Peterson, Rizzo, and Reynolds (1998) and Parker and McCall (1999), the percent of persons not employed is used because it includes those persons who are not actively seeking employment relative to the official definition of unemployment which excludes these individuals. The percent not employed for each racial group is computed by dividing the number of employed by the number of persons 16 years of age and over, multiplying by 100, and then subtracting the result from 100.

Economic competition is operationalized as the ratio of White to Black median family income—one that has been traditionally used to measure the economic aspect of racial inequality. Larger values of the ratio represent a better economic situation for Whites relative to Blacks.

Previous research exploring race-specific homicide offending and racial inequality have found economic disadvantage (Krivo and Peterson 1996, 2000) and racial segregation (Massey and Eggers 1990; Messner and Golden 1992) to be contributing factors. These concepts are employed as explanatory variables and are measured, respectively, as the percentage of the population living below the poverty level for each race-specific population and the index of dissimilarity which is based on the racial composition of urban census tracts and depends on the relative size of the two groups.[4]

Population size and Hispanic population composition also are employed as control measures in this study. Population size is measured by the race-specific resident population residing in these central cities and is included as an exposure measure (elaborated below). Another aspect of population composition, the percentage of the population which is Hispanic, is introduced as a control for police error when identifying and recording victims and offenders as Whites or Blacks rather than correctly identifying them as Hispanics in police reports (Parker and McCall 1999). Regional differences are captured with three dummy measures for the South, West, and Midwest regions—the Northeast region omitted as the reference category.

Finally, because the model investigates the influence of changing social and economic conditions on interracial homicide offending, each of these measures (except the regional indicators) also are entered as the change between 1980 $(t-1)$ and 1990 (t)—with the change (delta) calculated as: $D = (t - (t - 1))$.

Analytic Procedures

Poisson regression is employed because the dependent variables are based on discrete counts of rare events (i.e., the number of interracial homicides), have skewed distributions and include cases (cities) with zero counts. Poisson gives unbiased, consistent, and efficient estimates for these types of dependent variables and is preferred over ordinary least squares (OLS) regression when one is not able to meet the assumptions for OLS— such as, the assumptions of homogeneity of error variance and normal error distributions (see Osgood 2000:22–3).[5] The statistical software we employ provides the capacity to correct for the city's race-specific population (of offenders) as an exposure variable by constraining its coefficient to equal one (STATA, version 7). This method converts the counts of interracial homicide into the equivalent of a rate for each city (Maddala 1983; Osgood 2000).

There is no clear consensus regarding the best way to model change in sociological research (Firebaugh and Beck 1994; Hausman, Hall, and Griliches 1984; Kessler and Greenberg 1981). To test the element of change underlying the theoretical approaches outlined above, we follow the model specification employed by Greenberg and West (2001:635) which includes difference measures for the independent variables.[6] The model specification takes the following form: $y_t = a + b_1 y_{t-1} + b_2 x_{t-1} + b_3(x_t - x_{t-1}) + \ldots + e_t$, where **t** represents 1990 and **t − 1** represents 1980, x_{t-1} represents the 1980 independent variables, and $x_t - x_{t-1}$ represents the change between 1980 and 1990 for the independent variables.

Table 1 provides descriptive information for our city-level variables measured in 1980 and

TABLE 1   **Means, Standard Deviations (in parentheses), and Percent Change for Characteristics of Cities in 1980 and 1990**

	1980	1990	Percent change (%)
Black interracial	6.63	6.71	1.21
homicide (counts)	(18.00)	(20.91)	
White interracial	2.98	3.66	22.82
homicide (counts)	(9.30)	(15.69)	
Percent Black population	20.26	22.26	9.87
	(16.85)	(18.01)	
Proportion of cities	.07	.14	100.00
with Black mayor	(.25)	(.34)	
Ratio of not employed	1.11	1.16	4.50
Blacks to Whites	(.14)	(.18)	
Ratio of median family	1.58	1.73	9.49
Income of Whites to Blacks	(.26)	(.37)	
Percent Blacks in poverty	26.68	28.12	5.40
	(6.94)	(8.18)	
Percent Whites in poverty	10.16	10.83	6.59
	(3.35)	(3.86)	
Racial segregation	71.89	53.77	−25.20
	(10.95)	(16.91)	
Population size	363.95	386.59	6.22
(in thousandths)	(690.18)	(719.23)	
Percent Hispanic population	8.41	11.21	33.29
	(10.93)	(13.44)	
South		.34	
		(.47)	
West		.32	
		(.47)	
Northeast		.16	
		(.36)	
Midwest		.19	
		(.40)	

1990. Changes between 1980 and 1990 are presented in the third column which reveals increasing mean numbers of Black and White interracial homicides committed during this period for these U.S. cities and increasing (positive) means for all explanatory measures except for racial segregation—likely declining as a result of gentrification of segments of these urban centers.

The bivariate correlations reveal evidence of collinearity or problems associated with the partialing fallacy. Techniques for identifying the extent of this problem are undertaken in estimating the regression models to determine whether these high correlations have a substantive influence on the findings.[7] The overall support for the theories examined in this analysis are largely unchanged when estimating alternate models.[8] Bivariate scatterplots revealed no curvilinear relationships between the dependent and independent variables; therefore, there is no need for variable transformations.

Findings

Table 2 presents the parameter coefficients estimated from the Poisson regression analyses. Models 1 and 3 represent the results for Black and White interracial homicide offending, respectively, that omit the change measures and are provided only as a baseline for comparison with the Models

TABLE 2 Poisson Regression Coefficients (and Z-Scores) for Change in 1990 Black and White Interracial Homicides, *N* = 146

	Black Interracial		White Interracial	
	(1)	(2)	(3)	(4)
Interracial homicides 1980	0.003**	0.004**	0.012**	0.012**
	(3.16)	(2.58)	(5.73)	(4.06)
Percent Black population	−.008*	−.006⁺	0.037**	0.034**
(Racial composition)	(−2.23)	(−1.28)	(6.99)	(5.43)
Black mayor	0.125	0.061	0.212	−.021
(Political competition)	(1.00)	(0.43)	(1.13)	(−.10)
Ratio of not employed B/W	−.707	.004	−.618	0.536
(Labor force competition)	(−1.22)	(0.01)	(−.87)	(0.57)
Ratio of income of W/B	.995**	0.924**	−.030	−.144
(Racial income inequality)	(3.68)	(2.74)	(−.07)	(−.29)
Race-specific poverty	−.030**	−.022⁺	−.029	−.001
(Poverty concentration)	(−3.15)	(−1.76)	(−1.14)	(−.05)
Racial residential segregation	−.009*	−.015*	0.010+	0.007
(Interracial contact)	(−1.76)	(−2.24)	(1.51)	(0.76)
Percent Hispanic population	0.022**	0.018**	0.023**	0.011
	(4.83)	(2.71)	(3.41)	(1.11)
South	−.021	−.102	−.437*	−.087
	(−0.14)	(−.53)	(−2.15)	(−.34)
West	0.436**	0.335*	−.058	0.078
	(2.89)	(2.08)	(−.28)	(0.34)
Midwest	.220	.085	0.521*	−.432
	(1.41)	(0.44)	(−2.28)	(−1.55)

(continued)

TABLE 2 Continued

	Black Interracial		White Interracial	
	(1)	**(2)**	**(3)**	**(4)**
D-Percent Black mpopulation	—	0.022	—	0.100**
		(1.01)	—	(3.17)
D-Black mayor	—	0.100	—	−.007
		(0.61)		(−.03)
D-Ratio of not employed Blacks to Whites	—	1.006*	—	1.846**
		(1.66)		(2.42)
D-Ratio of income of Whites to Blacks	—	−.020	—	−.230
		(−.07)		(−.63)
D-Race-specific poverty	—	0.007	—	−.035
		(0.46)		(−1.03)
D-Racial residential segregation	—	−.008	—	0.013
		(−.91)		(1.19)
D-Percent Hispanic population	—	0.033*	—	0.088**
		(2.02)		(3.74)
Constant	−9.18**	−9.90**	−12.15**	−13.58**
Log-likelihood	−263.99**	−258.90**	−209.59**	−196.35**
Pseudo R-square	.354	.367	.466	.500

Notes: $**p < .01$, $*p < .05$, $^+p < .10$ (one-tailed). "D" = change measure (1980–1990).

of interest, 2 and 4, that include the change measures indicated with "D" (symbolizing "delta") preceding the variable name that represents the change between 1980 and 1990. We focus our review of the results on the change measures in Models 2 and 4 that are statistically significant. The implications of these results will be elaborated in the discussion section.

The primary support for the influence of change on interracial violence is found for Blalock's minority threat thesis—the coefficient for the change in percent Black population is positive and statistically significant in the White interracial homicide model. In addition, one of the three measures for racial competition, labor force competition, is statistically significant in the White interracial model although the relationship is positive and, therefore, not consistent with theoretical prediction. Competition theory states that increasing racial competition would be asso-

ciated with interracial conflict. The labor force competition measure (ratio of not-employed Blacks to not-employed Whites) indicates that White-on-Black homicides were higher in 1990 in cities where Blacks faired worse relative to Whites in the labor force between 1980 and 1990. This finding is contrary to the theoretical prediction because Black's declining labor force participation relative to Whites' would not pose any threat of job security for Whites. On the other hand, in the Black interracial homicide model, the coefficient for this labor force competition variable is statistically significant and positively related to Black-on-White homicides. This supports the hypothesis that increasing competition between the races in the labor force between 1980 and 1990 and resulting frustrations engendered among Blacks were associated with higher Black-on-White homicides with our sample of cities for 1990.

Turning to our control measure for Hispanic population composition, change in the percent Hispanic population is statistically significant and positive in both of the interracial homicide models. This implies that cities with growing proportions of Hispanics in the population between 1980 and 1990 had larger numbers of interracial homicides involving Black as well as White offenders in 1990. Recall that this control measure is included primarily to account for police misrecording the race of the offender in police reports. Among the regional effects, the West has a significant, positive influence only in the Black interracial homicide model—that is, cities in the west have higher numbers of Black interracial homicides than cities in the Northeastern part of the United States (the reference category for region). We now elaborate these findings in relation to their theoretical underpinnings.

Discussion and Conclusions

The purpose of this research is to model and test the dynamic nature of the arguments underlying major race relations theories to determine the extent to which these theories account for interracial violent behavior. Based on race relations literature, we hypothesized that mounting racial economic, labor force, and political competition would spur White interracial homicide offending whereas Black interracial homicide would be associated with increasing labor force competition and racial inequality. By and large, our findings show mixed support for the importance of change implicit in these competition arguments in the White interracial homicide model. We begin our discussion of our findings with the classic indicator of racial competition—growing Black population.

We find support for Blalock's minority threat thesis that members of the majority group perceive a growing minority population as a threat to their dominant social position. Consistent with Jacobs and Wood's (1999) cross-sectional analysis of interracial homicide and with many extant race relations analyses that employ percentage Black population as a measure of minority threat (Olzak and Shanahan 1996; Olzak, Shanahan and McEneaney 1996; Tolnay and Beck 1992; Tolnay, Beck, and Massey 1989), our analysis provides evidence that the increasing Black population between 1980 and 1990 is related to White interracial homicide. Blau's (1977) macrostructural perspective provides another explanation for these findings. As Blau argues, in cities where there are higher proportions of the urban population comprised of Blacks, there will be an increase in the likelihood of interracial interaction and, in turn, a greater likelihood of interracial violence. As Blau noted in his macrostructural theory, the opportunity for interracial contact is required for meaningful interracial association. Therefore, the population composition of a community sets the stage for the likelihood of these contacts. More importantly, the nature as well as the extent of interracial contact are sculpted by the social and economic conditions in which interracial contact occurs (Messner and Golden 1992; Messner and South 1992; Sampson 1987; South and Messner 1986). Therefore, the statistical significance of the percent Black population may be explained by Blalock's minority threat thesis, Blau's macrostructural (opportunity) perspective, or both.

Competition theorists argue that it is the threat of competition for jobs, power, and positions (whether such threats are real or imagined), whereby Blacks pose a political or economic threat to Whites that leads to an inherent conflict between them (Blauner 1982; Lieberson 1980). Change in labor force competition (the ratio of the percent not-employed Blacks to not-employed Whites) affects White interracial homicide, but the effect has a positive coefficient which is contrary to the hypothesis derived from racial competition theory. Although racial competition theory is not supported with our indicators of economic, political competition, or labor force competition as predicted in the White interracial homicide model, one could argue that growing proportions of minorities in the population would pose a sense of threat to the majority population regardless of whether there was an actual economic or political threat as reflected in the empirical indicators employed in this study. A study of labor market influences during a period of more severe economic downturn and job losses such as that between 1970 and 1980 may reveal evidence of such effects, but supplemental homicide data were not available until the mid-1970s.

Whereas the influence of changes in labor force competition is opposite to theoretical prediction in the White interracial homicide model, this competition measure has a positive, statistically significant influence on Black interracial homicide and provides support for this argument. These results indicate that cities with diminishing labor force opportunities for Blacks relative to Whites' opportunities between 1980 and 1990, experienced higher numbers of Black interracial homicides in 1990. The influence of this aspect of racial competition is an indicator of structural discrimination, and evidence that Whites' labor force gains at the expense of Blacks' continue to disrupt to race relations. As noted earlier, when this model was estimated using a three-year average for Black-on-White homicides for the period circa 1990 (1989–1991 three-year average versus 1987–1991 five-year average), these findings were not substantiated. Therefore, these findings are not robust across the two models.

The other statistically significant coefficient among the change measures in the White interracial and Black interracial homicide models is that for the percent of Hispanics in the population. One could argue that the significant influence of the growing Hispanic population may represent a logical extension of Blalock's threat thesis. Growing Hispanic populations could pose the same type of threats to Whites and Blacks as Hispanics move into an area and compete with them in the labor force and in the political arena. Because the Hispanic population composition was not introduced as an indicator for our theoretical arguments and hypotheses, we will leave this finding to simply reflect that for which it was introduced—a correction for police recording practices. Other researchers interested in the

study of minority population composition and the influence of minority population dynamics on interracial interaction may want to consider this potential source of interracial conflict in future research.

In conclusion, Blalock's minority threat thesis is supported in the White-on-Black homicide model and support emerges for the importance of labor force competition in the Black-on-White homicide model. We find evidence that racial competition theory vis-à-vis a growing Black population best explains higher numbers of White interracial homicide offending in large U.S. cities in 1990, whereas changes in labor market opportunities account for higher Black-on-White homicides in 1990.

As we take stock of our findings and examine the broader implications of these results, we warn the reader against committing the ecological fallacy. These findings do not necessarily demonstrate that certain social and economic factors or changes in these factors are forces that influence a member of one racial group to commit homicide against persons of other races. We argue, though, that certain social and economic forces create contexts which engender stress, frustration, and hostility among some societal members more so than others. In turn, these interracial hostilities have the potential to result in interpersonal conflict that may have a lethal outcome. The race of the homicide "victim" may not necessarily represent the source of the frustration or hostility, and it is not possible to distinguish the aggressor from the assaulted in these interracial homicide statistics. The fact that the instigator of the conflict may become the "victim" of homicide may account for the anomalous support for the positive effect of the change in labor force competition in the White interracial homicide model. Nevertheless, these analyses shed light on and further refine the theoretical arguments which address race relations in the United States.

The results of these analyses of change do not diminish the importance of the enduring influence of power differentials between Whites and Blacks on interracial conflict. Prior research has demonstrated how economic and political rivalries are related to interracial conflict (Myers 1990; Olzak 1990; Tolnay, Beck, and Massey 1989) and interracial homicide (Jacobs and Wood 1999). Nevertheless, the extent to which change in various aspects of racial competition over time is related to interracial violence is not well established. Our study of the dynamics between 1980 and 1990 provide additional support for this association. Future research that examines periods with more dramatic rates of economic downturn and political power shifts may provide evidence substantiating the dynamic nature of these associations. Our research demonstrates the importance of measuring change and examining the influence that change in population composition and racial competition has on interracial conflict. These findings emphasize how social and economic dynamics contribute to our understanding of interracial violence over and above extant efforts that examine relationships between racial threat, competition, and interracial violence in the cross-sectional literature. Thus, while theoretical arguments have been developed in the past 25 years to account for racial disparities by investigating racially disaggregated homicide events, there is still much work to be done in this area.

Endnotes

The authors thank John MacDonald, David Jacobs, Rodney Engen, William R. Smith, David Greenberg, and anonymous reviewers for their assistance and comments.

[1] Our use of different years circa the decennial time point (that is, 1978–1982 versus 1987–1991) simply had to do with the years for which data were available when we initially constructed our data set. At that time, the data for 1992 were not available and because we were collecting data for estimates of the decennial time point (using five rather than three years to take into account the rare nature of interracial homicides). We contend that the choice of years provides only an approximation for these homicide events. The models were estimated using more standard-

ized four-year average homicide measures (1978–1981 and 1988–1991) and we found that there was one substantive difference in the findings regarding the influence of change on interracial homicide: change in labor force competition measure in the Black interracial homicide model was no longer statistically significant.

In addition, the fact that interracial homicide is a rare event raises the question of the reliability of aggregate-level estimates—especially in cities with small populations of Blacks. Other studies of race-specific offending have restricted the cases included in analyses to those with at least five percent of Blacks in the city (Krivo and Peterson, 2000; Messner and Golden 1992; Parker and McCall 1997, 1999; Peterson and Krivo 1993; Sampson 1987). Because we employ one of the Poisson family of regression techniques (which were developed for estimating rare events) and because our focus is on the dynamics related to the impact of varying sizes of minority populations, we do not restrict our sample to those with a minimum percentage of Blacks. In addition to missing data, the sample was reduced also because homicide data are not available for cities in Florida circa 1990. Although the data circa 1990 do not represent the standard five years—from 1988 through 1992—these are the years for which data were available at the time of our data collection. Nevertheless, these five-year averages should provide sufficient estimates for this decennial time period.

[2] The Comparative Homicide File (CHF) was created by Williams and Flewelling who compiled this information from the Homicide Supplemental Reports. We acknowledge alternative procedures are also available to deal with missing data (see Messner, Deane, and Beaulieu 2002). However, our read of that literature which analyzes and compares alternative methods (i.e., Messner et al. 2002; Pampel and Williams 2000) leads us to the conclusion that there is no evidence supporting one method over the other. See also Messner and Golden (1992) and Williams and

Flewelling (1988) for further detailed descriptions of these data.

[3] Another important data issue in this study is the problem of missing data on offenders' race. Approximately one-fourth of the recorded homicides in the CHF report the race of the offender as unknown. Furthermore, the potential for measurement bias is created as the racial patterning of nonmissing events (Messner and South 1992). The imputation algorithm developed by Williams and Flewelling (1988) was employed to address this problem. This algorithm is used to "extrapolate the characteristics of the known cases to those with missing information. Essentially the procedure involves the estimation of the race of the offender (where unknown) on the basis of the type of incident under investigation and the observed racial patterning of that type of incident when the offender's race is known for a given city" (1988: 426).

[4] The index of dissimilarity is one of many measures of segregation being proposed for use in criminological research (see Shihadeh and Flynn 1996; Shihadeh and Maume 1997). We employ the index of dissimilarity to capture the distribution of population subgroups across census tracts and the relative size of the two groups (Massey and Denton 1988)—the relative size being one of the key factors underlying competition theses.

[5] The basic Poisson regression equation is comparable to the practice of using the logarithmic transformation of the aggregate crime rate dependent variable in Ordinary Least Squares (OLS) regression which is used in most extant homicide research. Employing Poisson regression avoids many estimation problems (e.g., heterogeneity) associated with OLS analyses of crime rates. Chi-square goodness of fit test statistics indicate Poisson rather than negative binomial is the appropriate estimation technique for these models (STATA, version 7). See Osgood (2000:24) for an excellent discussion of related methodological issues.

[6] We depart from Greenberg and West's model specification by regressing the interracial homicides in 1990 rather than the difference between the numbers of homicides in 1990 and 1980 that was central to Greenberg and West's hypotheses, on the explanatory variables.

[7] Other models we estimated included measures of percent of the Black population squared in attempts to model Blalock's thesis of a positive influence of percent Black population with a decreasing slope—that is, we anticipated a reduction in White interracial homicide as the Black population reaches a point of concentration in these cities. This measure was correlated above .9 with the 1980 interracial homicide measure and could not be estimated without producing collinearity problems. Variance Inflation Factors (VIF) were not available in the software program for Poisson; however, VIFs derived from OLS regressions estimated for these models (while using the log transformed dependent variables) revealed VIF values between 11 and 13 for the percent Black squared measure. Nevertheless, we found no major substantive difference in the findings among the change measures in our models when the quadratic term was included. In addition, the murder rate was initially introduced as a control as did Jacobs and Wood (1999) but VIFs above 5 and 6 also indicated estimation problems.

[8] Evidence of potential partialling problems was explored by estimating separate equations by omitting variables with bivariate correlations above .5. This revealed problems with the percentage Black population measure in the White interracial homicide model. Omitting this variable resulted in the following additional statistically significant variables in the indicated direction: Black mayor 1980 (+), racial labor market competition (+), south (+), change 1980–1990 Black mayor (+, $p < .09$, one-tailed), and change 1980–1990 race segregation (+)—all differences, by and large, supporting the hypotheses. Results from the alternative model showed no major substantive changes in statistical significance of the coefficients. . . .

References

Allen, Terry and Glen Buckner. 1997. "A Graphical Approach to Analyzing Relationships between Offenders and Victims Using Supplementary Homicide Reports." *Homicide Studies: An Interdisciplinary and International Journal* 1(2):129–40.

Blalock, Hubert M. 1967. "Status Inconsistency, Social Mobility, Status Integration and Structural Effects." *American Sociological Review* 32(October):790–801.

Blau, Peter M. 1977. *Inequality and Heterogeneity: A Primitive Theory of Social Structure.* New York: Free Press.

Blauner, Robert. 1982. *Racial Oppression in America.* New York: Harper & Row.

Bobo, Lawrence and Franklin D. Gilliam. 1990. "Race, Sociopolitical Participation, and Black Empowerment." *American Political Science Review* 84:377–93.

Bobo, Lawrence and Vincent Hutchings. 1996. "Perceptions of Racial Group Competition: Extending Blumer's Theory of Group Position in a Multiracial Social Context." *American Sociological Review* 61:951–72.

Bonacich, Edna. 1976. "Advanced Capitalism and Black/White Relations in the United States: A Spilt Labor Market Interpretation." *American Sociological Review* 37:547–59.

Firebaugh, Glenn and Frank D. Beck. 1994. "Does Economic Growth Benefit the Masses?" *American Sociological Review* 59(5):631–53.

Greenberg, David F. and Valerie West. 2001. "State Prison Populations and Their Growth, 1971–1991." *Criminology* 39(3):615–53.

Harer, Miles D. and Darrell Steffensmeier. 1992. "The Differing Effects of Economic Inequality on Black and White Rates of Violence." *Social Forces* 70:1035–54.

Hausman, Jerry, Bronwyn H. Hall, and Zvi Griliches. 1984. "Econometric Models for Count Data with an Application to the Patents—R & D Relationship." *Econometrica* 52(4):909–38.

Huff-Corzine, Lin, Jay Corzine, and David C. Moore. 1991. "Deadly Connections: Culture, Poverty, and the Direction of Lethal Violence." *Social Forces* 69:715–32.

Jacobs, David and Katherine Wood. 1999. "Interracial Conflict and Interracial Homicide: Do Political and Economic Rivalries Explain White Killings of Blacks or Black Killings of Whites?" *American Journal of Sociology* 105(1):157–90.

Kessler, Ronald C. and Dvid F. Greenberg. 1981. *Linear Panel Analysis: Models of Quantitative Change.* New York: Academic Press.

Krivo, Lauren and Ruth D. Peterson. 2000. "The Structural Context of Homicide: Accounting for Racial Differences in Process." *American Sociological Review* 65(4):547–59.

———. 1996. "Extremely Disadvantaged Neighbor-hoods and Urban Crime." *Social Forces* 75:619–48.

Krivo, Lauren, Ruth D. Peterson, Helen Rizzo, and John R. Reynolds. 1998. "Race, Segregation, and the Concentration of Disadvantage: 1980–1990." *Social Problems* 45(1):61–79.

Lieberson, Stanley. 1980. *A Piece of the Pie: Blacks and White Immigrants, 1880–1930.* Berkeley: University of California Press.

Maddala, George S. 1983. *Limited-Dependent and Qualitative Variables in Econometrics.* Cambridge, UK: Cambridge University Press.

Massey, Douglas and Nancy Denton. 1988. "The Dimensions of Residential Segregation." *Social Forces* 67(2):281–305.

Massey, Douglas and Mitchell L. Eggers. 1990. "The Ecology of Inequality: Minorities and the Concentration of Poverty, 1970–1980." *American Journal of Sociology* 95(5):1153–88.

Messner, Steven F. and Reid M. Golden. 1992. "Racial Inequality and Racially Disaggregated Homicide Rates: An Assessment of Alternative Theoretical Explanations." *Criminology* 30(3):421–47.

Messner, Steven F. and Scott South. 1992. "Interracial Homicide: A Macrostructural-Opportunity Perspective." *Sociological Forum* 7(3):517–36.

———. 1986. "Economic Deprivation, Opportunity Structure, and Robbery Victimization." *Social Forces* 64(4):975–91.

Messner, Steven F., Glenn Deane, and Mark Beaulieu. 2002. "A Log-Multiplicative Association Model for Allocating Homicides with Unknown Victim-Offender Relationships." *Criminology* 40(2):457–79.

Myers, M. 1990. "Black Threat and Incarceration in Postbellum Georgia." *Social Forces* 69(2): 373–93.

Olzak, Susan. 1990. "The Political Context of Competition: Lynching and Urban Racial Violence." *Social Forces* 69:395–421.

Olzak, Susan and Suzanne Shanahan. 1996. "Deprivation and Race Riots: An Extension of Spilerman's Analysis." *Social Forces* 74(3): 931–61.

Olzak, Susan, Suzanne Shanahan, and Elizabeth H. McEneaney. 1996. "Poverty, Segregation, and Race Riots: 1960 to 1993." *American Sociological Review* 58:590–613.

Osgood, D. Wayne. 2000. "Poisson-Based Regression Analysis of Aggregate Crime Rates." *Journal of Quantitative Criminology* 16(1):21–43.

Ousey, Graham C. 1999. "Homicide, Structural Factors, and the Racial Invariance Assumption." *Criminology* 37:405–26.

Pampel, Fred C. and Kirk R. Williams. 2000. "Intimacy and Homicide: Compensating for Missing Data in the SHR." *Criminology* 38:661–80.

Parker, Karen F. and Patricia L. McCall. 1999. "Structural Conditions and Racial Homicide Patterns: A Look at the Multiple Disadvantages in Urban Areas." *Criminology* 37(3):447–77.

——. 1997. "Adding Another Piece to the Inequality-Homicide Puzzle: The Impact of Structural Inequality on Racially Disaggregated Homicide Rates." *Homicide Studies: An Interdisciplinary and International Journal* 1:35–60.

Peterson, Ruth D. and Lauren J. Krivo. 1993. "Racial Segregation and Black Urban Homicide" *Social Forces* 71:1001–26.

Sampson, Robert J. 1987. "Urban Black Violence: The Effect of Male Joblessness and Family Disruption." *American Journal of Sociology* 93:348–82.

Shihadeh, Edward S. and Nicole Flynn. 1996. "Segregation and Crime: The Effects of Black Social Isolation on the Rates of Black Urban Violence." *Social Forces* 74:1325–52.

Shihadeh, Edward S. and Michael O. Maume. 1997. "Segregation and Crime: The Relationship between Black Centralization and Urban Black Homicide." *Homicide Studies: An Interdisciplinary and International Journal* 1:254–80.

Shihadeh, Edward S. and Graham C. Ousey. 1998. "Industrial Restructuring and Violence: The Link between Entry-Level Jobs, Economic Deprivation, and Black and White Homicide." *Social Forces* 77(1):185–206.

——. 1996. "Metropolitan Expansion and Black Social Dislocation: The Link between Suburbanization and Center-City Crime." *Social Forces* 75(2):649–66.

Shihadeh, Edward S. and Darrell Steffensmeier. 1994. "Economic Inequality, Family Disruption, and Urban Black Violence: Cities as Units of Stratification and Social Control." *Social Forces* 73:729–51.

South, Scott J. and Steven F. Messner. 1986. "Structural Determinants of Intergroup Association: Interracial Marriage and Crime." *American Journal of Sociology* 91(6): 1409–30.

Tolnay, Stewart E., E. M. Beck, and James L. Massey. 1989. "Black Lynchings: The Power Threat Hypothesis Revisited." *Social Forces* 67(3):605–23.

Tolnay, Stewart E., and E. M. Beck. 1992. "Racial Violence and Black Migration in the American South, 1910 to 1930." *American Sociological Review* 57(1):103–16.

Tolnay, Stewart E., E. M. Beck, and James L. Massey. 1992. "Black Competition and White Vengeance: Legal Execution of Blacks as Social Control in the Cotton South, 1890–1929." *Social Forces* 73:627–44.

Williams, Kirk and Robert L. Flewelling. 1988. "The Social Production of Homicide: A Comparative Study of Disaggregated Rates in American Cities." *American Sociological Review* 53: 421–31.

Wilson, William Julius. 1991. "Studying Inner-City Social Dislocations: The Challenge of Public Agenda Research: 1990 Presidential Address." *American Sociology Review* 56:1–14.

———. 1987. *The Truly Disadvantaged: The Inner City, The Underclass, and Public Policy.* Chicago: University Chicago Press.

Conclusion

This chapter examines conflict theory. The theory maintains that power and influence are not equally distributed among members in a society. Individuals with power will hold key positions that determine the direction of justice administration. Racial threat theory suggests that as racial minority groups grow, they will threaten the economic and political positions of whites. Thus, whites will develop means to institute more social control to reduce the growth of the racial minority group.

While these theories have some support in the empirical literature, the studies regarding them are not without their limitations. The conflict theory literature should go beyond examining the influence of the police and examine other parts of the criminal justice system as well. The literature on racial threat theory needs to focus more on the role of Latinos. Future research should take these aspects into consideration.

Discussion Questions

1. According to conflict theory, what are the different forms of authority–subject relationships? In particular, how do these different forms of relationship influence race relations, crime rates, and criminality?

2. How would racial threat theory influence policy development to reduce instances of criminality and the racial differences in crime rates?

References

Blalock, H. (1967). *Toward a theory of minority-group relations*. New York, NY: John Wiley.

Turk, A. (1966). Conflict and criminality. *American Sociological Review, 55*, 454–461.

Turk, A. (1969). *Criminality and legal order.* Chicago, IL: Rand McNally.

CHAPTER 7

Social Bonding and Self-Control Theories

Criminologists recognize that most of the society does not commit crime. Control theories are interested in why individuals do not commit crime. This chapter examines two control theories: social bonding and self-control theories

In 1969, Hirschi formally presented his version of social control theory, which is now known as social bonding theory. Rather than answering the question "Why do people commit crime?" social bonding theory is designed to answer the question "Why don't people commit crime?" The theory is a development on previous control theories by Reiss, Reckless, and Toby. It proposes that individuals who have strong bonds or connections with society are likely not to commit crime. Thus, the bonds serve as a form of insulation from criminal behavior, and therefore, criminal behavior is likely when the bonds are worn or broken.

Hirschi outlined four specific bonds that are important to insulate individuals from criminal behavior. The first bond is attachment. Attachment is the emotional connection to others (e.g., family or friends) or to some other entity (e.g., school or church) because of which he or she is less likely to commit crime. The second bond is commitment. Hirschi purported that an individual who is committed to a conventional activity (e.g., education or career) is more likely to think through the implications that can arise from criminal activity. The third bond is involvement. Involvement is when an individual is active in conventional activities and is therefore less likely to commit criminal acts because he or she does not have the time to perpetrate such acts. The fourth bond is belief. Belief is an understanding that a common values system exists in society. Hirschi argued that weakening or breaking one or more of the bonds will increase the susceptibility for criminal behavior. That is, an individual who is not bonded to society is likely to be attracted to criminal activity because he or she has less to lose.

The first empirical examination of this theory comes from Hirschi. His original study shows that racial differences occur in criminal offending. While acknowledging sociological differences among the races (e.g., opportunity structure, stake in conformity, lower-class culture, and difficulties in family life), Hirschi's research does not account for the racial differences in criminal offending. Specifically, Hirschi's interpretation indicates that the racial differences may be attributed more to police presence.

Although earlier research using this theory to explain racial differences in crime produced mixed results, recent research using this theory has been able to account for the differences among African Americans and whites with respect to crime rates. Additional research has been able to show that social bonding is able to account for similar disparities when considering Hispanic and Asian populations. Thus, the theory is an important one in understanding the racial disparities in criminal behavior.

Because of the simplicity of its central components, social bonding theory is one of the most-studied theories in criminology. Hirschi teamed with Michael Gottfredson to present a revision to social bonding theory, which has been used to provide some understanding of the racial differences in criminal behavior.

Gottfredson and Hirschi base their control theory on rational choice, self-control, parenting, and opportunity. To begin, Gottfredson and Hirschi (1990) built on the rational choice perspective—that is, they assumed that individuals would weigh the potential advantages of an act against the potential disadvantages. Consistent with the classical school of thought in criminology, they argued that individuals would seek and choose pleasurable acts and avoid painful acts.

One potential pleasurable act is crime. Crime is an act of force or fraud that an individual pursues for his or her own interest. Crime has several attributes: "short-lived, immediately gratifying, easy, simple, and exciting" (Gottfredson & Hirschi, 1990, p. 14). Crimes are believed to be attractive to individuals who have a tendency to be "impulsive, insensitive, physical (as opposed to verbal), risk-taking, short-sighted, and nonverbal" (Gottfredson & Hirschi, 1990, p. 90). These tendencies influence how individuals view the potential pleasure of an act. In particular, Gottfredson and Hirschi argued:

> The dimensions of self-control are . . . factors affecting calculation of the consequences of one's acts. The impulsive or short-sighted person fails to consider the negative or painful consequences of his acts; the insensitive person has fewer negative consequences to consider; the less intelligent person also has fewer negative consequences to consider (he has less to lose). (1990, p. 95)

This suggests that individuals with low self-control are likely to consider only the potential benefits of their actions for themselves and to not consider the implications of their acts for others or any long-term consequences for themselves. Thus, low self-control refers to the tendency to not avoid acts whose long-term costs exceed their momentary advantages.

Gottfredson and Hirschi (1990) argue that low self-control is the likely result of poor or ineffective parenting practices. According to them, parents were to perform four interdependent acts:

1. The parenting practices were contingent on the parents' developing an emotional bond with their child.
2. In the presence of an emotional bond, parents were more likely to monitor their child's behavior to gather behavioral information.
3. Next, parents were to evaluate the behavioral information to determine if the behavior was delinquent.
4. If the behavior was delinquent, then parents were to use noncorporal punishment to discipline their behavior.

However, if these parenting practices did not take place effectively and early in life—before 8 years of age—then the child was likely to develop low self-control, making him or her more susceptible to criminal activity.

Gottfredson and Hirschi (1990) specifically theorized about race and criminal behavior by comparing strain theory and their version of self-control. Importantly, their theory does not explain the differences for only certain minority groups but for all minority groups. They argued that strain theorists tend to overstate the connection between race and criminal behavior because they see strain as governing the behavior. Gottfredson and Hirschi state that opportunities and the ease with which a crime can be committed tend to govern the differences between race and criminal behavior. Therefore, they believed that self-control would account for all the differences in criminal offending.

The empirical research on Gottfredson and Hirschi's self-control theory is mounting. To date, a meta-analysis shows self-control has a moderate link with criminal behavior (Pratt & Cullen, 2000). Early research that examined the connection between race and criminal behavior tested the differences only between African Americans and whites, and this research presented mixed results. Some scholars have examined this connection using other populations, including Asians and Native Americans. These studies show that self-control plays a role in understanding the disparities among the different populations with regard to criminal behavior. In the selection provided in this chapter, Vazsonyi and Crosswhite illustrate the promise of social bonding and self-control theories in understanding the connection between race and crime.

A Test of Gottfredson and Hirschi's General Theory of Crime In African American Adolescents

Alexander T. Vazsonyi
Jennifer M. Crosswhite

Considerable empirical support exists for The General Theory of Crime. However, little work has been completed on members of minority populations in the United States. The current investigation examined whether low self-control predicted deviance in a sample of African American adolescents (n = 661; 55.1 percent female; mean age = 15.7 years). Confirmatory Factor Analyses provided evidence that the low self-control measure was a valid and reliable multidimensional scale in this sample, for both males and females. In addition, low self-control explained between 8.4 percent and 13.0 percent of the variance in male deviance measures and between 4.0 percent and 8.4 percent in female deviance. Follow-up z-tests by sex indicated few differences in the relationships between low self-control and deviance. In addition, comparative analyses by race between African American and Caucasian adolescent males provided evidence of similarity in the importance of self-control. Findings support the cross-cultural validity of the General Theory of Crime, particularly for male adolescents and to a lesser extent for female youth.

The current investigation addressed two principal gaps in the empirical literature on *The General Theory of Crime*. First, Gottfredson and Hirschi

(1990) hypothesized that low self-control explains deviance in males, females, different racial and ethnic groups, and cross-nationally. Empirical investigations to date have included mostly Caucasian participants from the United States (Pratt and Cullen 2000; cf., Longshore, Turner, and Stein 1996, for a study on ethnically diverse convicted drug users); few studies have focused on African American adolescents or adults from the general population (cf., Hay 2001). Thus, it remains unanswered whether low self-control can be reliably measured in African American populations employing existing low self-control scales (e.g., Grasmick et al. 1993); in addition, the question of the dimensionality of low self-control remains open.

A second apparently unresolved issue in the literature is whether low self-control predicts deviance similarly or differently in males and females. Previous work based largely on Caucasian adolescents and adults as well as youth from different countries has found that low self-control was predictive of deviant behaviors in both males and females (e.g., Burton et al. 1998; LaGrange and Silverman, 1999; Vazsonyi et al. 2001). However, few previous efforts that have compared the importance of self-control in male and female deviance have used direct comparative difference tests. The current investigation attempted to address these two important gaps in the literature by studying a community sample of rural African American youth, by completing direct comparisons of the importance of low self-control in deviance by sex, and by making direct comparisons between African American and Caucasian adolescents. In the following sections, we review theoretical issues and relevant empirical studies. In addition, we first critically discuss two debated topics in this literature, namely the dimensionality of self-control and the related issue of disaggregation of the self-control construct.

Dimensionality and Disaggregation of the Self-Control Construct

Gottfredson and Hirschi (1990) conceptualized low self-control as a construct with six distinct dimensions (i.e., impulsivity, simple tasks, risk seeking, physical activities, self-centeredness, and temper); however, whereas some empirical evidence has indicated that low self-control is multidimensional (i.e., based on exploratory or confirmatory analyses, multiple factors or indicators measure the low self-control latent trait; Arneklev, Grasmick, and Bursik 1999; Grasmick et al. 1993; Longshore et al. 1996; Longshore, Stein, and Turner 1998; Vazsonyi et al. 2001), other evidence has suggested that it is unidimensional (Piquero and Rosay 1998). Part of the issue is that there may be differences in the interpretation of Gottfredson and Hirschi's original thesis (for a discussion, see e.g., Arneklev et al. 1999) and in the use of terminology. In fact, Gottfredson and Hirschi (1990) suggest that multiple, different traits seem to circumscribe the general tendency or latent construct of low self-control—a tendency that is best described by six different elements (or traits). More specifically,

> In sum, people who lack self-control will tend to be impulsive, insensitive, physical (as opposed to mental), risk-taking, short-sighted, and nonverbal, and they will tend therefore to engage in criminal and analogous acts. Since these traits can be identified prior to the age of responsibility for crime, since there is a considerable tendency for these traits to come together in the same person, and since these traits tend to persist through life, it seems reasonable to consider them as comprising a stable construct useful in the explanation of crime. (pp. 90-91)

Consider the following as an additional illustration—much like intelligence is described as a persistent human quality that defines how human beings process information, few would argue with the fact that intelligence is best described through a large number of underlying elements or traits, all of which operationalize different aspects of intelligence. Consequently, most modern intelligence tests, such as Wechsler's child or adult inventories, include assessments of 12 to 14 distinct dimensions of intelligence, that in summary assess a person's intellectual aptitude. These distinct dimensions "come together in the same person" and define intelligence; yet, focusing on or even omitting 3 or 4 dimensions provides an incomplete picture of a person's intelligence. The same argument can be made for low self-control.

According to the General Theory, the self-control construct includes multiple dimensions; therefore, psychometrically speaking, it is multidimensional. Yet, conceptually, all six elements come together in the same person (or as Pratt and Cullen [2000] described, "they see these elements as forming a unitary, underlying propensity" [p. 932])—in effect, these different elements are highly correlated as are the different subtests of an intelligence test. Finally, and perhaps most important, the majority of empirical tests that have thoroughly examined the dimensionality question based on confirmatory factor analytic techniques support the original multidimensional operationalization and measurement of low self-control as proposed by Gottfredson and Hirschi (1990; Arneklev et al. 1999; Longshore et al. 1996; Vazsonyi et al. 2001; cf. Piquero and Rosay 1998).

A second related and salient issue regarding the dimensionality of self-control is whether the self-control construct should be disaggregated in comparative empirical investigations (see e.g., Wood, Pfefferbaum, and Arneklev 1993). Considering Gottfredson and Hirschi's original intention of specifying the multiple dimensions of the self-control construct, it seems unlikely that they were trying to promote compartmentalization of the importance of the different aspects of low self-control. Each subscale is important and describes one unique aspect of the self-control construct—a probabilistic construct useful in the prediction of crime. The following explanation of the theory by Hirschi and Gottfredson (2001) provides additional insights:

> Theories explain facts by stating general propositions from which specific facts may be derived. For example, in Newton's theory, apples fall to earth *because* every particle of matter in the universe is attracted by every other particle. The larger the particle, the stronger the attraction. We often condense this explanation into one word, *gravity*, but the truth and value of the explanation are not reduced by this practice. By the same logic, in self-control theory, people commit criminal acts because they fail to consider their long-term consequences. This explanation, too, may be condensed into a single concept, (low) self-control, but its truth and value are not reduced by this practice. (P.91)

Again, a similar analogy applies from work on intelligence. Just because the object assembly task (one of a dozen subtests of the Wechsler Adult Intelligence Scale) measures spatial abilities, and therefore better predicts a person's ability and speed to manipulate three-dimensional objects than the verbal comprehension task, this does not mean that undue emphasis should be placed on only the object assembly task in understanding and predicting intelligence. In fact, both object assembly and verbal comprehension are very important indicators of intelligence. Physical activity, risk taking, and impulsiveness are all important indicators of low self-control, even if different subscales predict various amounts of variance in different deviant outcomes (see e.g., Arneklev et al. 1999; Longshore et al. 1996; Vazsonyi et al. 2001). Therefore, it seems that examining the importance of the entire self-control construct (including all dimensions), "a single concept," in comparative tests would be theoretically and conceptually justified.

African American Adolescents

Although consistent support has been found for *The General Theory*, research participants have mostly been Caucasian. In the few studies that have included participants from other races, the sample size was relatively small, and therefore no separate analyses were possible by racial group (e.g., Burton et al. 1998, 1999; Gibbs and Giever 1995; Gibbs, Giever, and Martin 1998) or analyses were simply not completed by race (e.g., Arneklev et al. 1993; Vazsonyi et al. 2001).[1]

According to the General Theory, low self-control should predict deviant or criminal behaviors in all cultural, racial, and national groups. In fact, Gottfredson and Hirschi (1990) note that "cultural variability is not important in the causation of crime, that we should look for constancy rather than variability in the definition and causes of crime, and that a single theory can encompass the reality of cross-cultural differences in crime rates" (p. 175).

This rather controversial position is in direct contrast to most conventional explanations of crime and deviance that at times focus on the very cultural or racial group membership as the source of etiological differences, something Gottfredson and Hirschi have termed *cultural models or views of criminality*. The authors also point out, however, that none of the assumptions of this cultural view of criminality find empirical support. Most important, they suggest that

> the cultural view misconstrues the nature of the criminal act. There is nothing in crime that requires the transmission of values or the support of other people. There is nothing in crime that requires the transmission of skills, or techniques, or knowledge from other people. On the contrary, it is the nature of crime that it can be invented instantly, on the spot, by almost anyone, and its own reward is its justification. (Gottfredson and Hirschi 1990:151)

Thus, according to the General Theory, racial group membership does not inherently contain much causal significance. In fact, Gottfredson and Hirschi argue that the focus of efforts directed at studying different racial and ethnic groups should be to some extent on socialization similarities and differences, but principally, the focus should be on self-control. They note that "differences in self-control probably far outweight differences in supervision in accounting for racial and ethnic variations" (p. 153).

This proposition by the General Theory becomes an empirical question because it implies that the variability in self-control accounts for variability in measures of crime and deviance across different racial groups, in a similar manner. It does not speak to or imply the relative levels of self-control in different groups, as these may differ dramatically. In other words, even if members of group A have been socialized to comparatively high levels of self-control vis-à-vis members of group B, this does not mean that the mechanism or causal process between low self-control and deviance differs by group membership. In fact, the magnitude of the relationship between low self-control and measures of deviance may be the same. Therefore, one important empirical question is whether the causal process proposed by the General Theory can be empirically substantiated.

Some support for this idea, and at the very least, for the prediction by low self-control of deviance has been found across different countries outside the United States, across different national groups, namely in Canada, Hungary, the Netherlands, and Switzerland (e.g., Junger and Tremblay 1999; Junger, West, and Timman 2001; LaGrange and Silverman 1999; LeBlanc 1993; Vazsonyi et al. 2001). However, few studies have examined predictions of the General Theory in different racial groups in the United States (cf., Hay 2001; Longshore 1998; Longshore et al. 1996; Longshore and Turner 1998). Work by Longshore and colleagues has provided evidence that there is empirical support for the theory based on data from African American youth and adult offenders part of the Treatment Alternatives to Street Crime (TASC) program. More specifically, their work has documented how low self-control is predictive of both crimes of force and fraud. Hay (2001) also found general support of the low self-control-deviance (predatory delinquency and substance use) relationship based on an ethnically diverse sample; however, the study did not directly examine similarities or differences in these relationships by racial groups. Therefore, despite some initial evidence supporting basic tenets of the General Theory in minority populations in these latter studies, very little work has been completed on nonmajority adolescents or adults.

Male and Female Adolescents

Gottfredson and Hirschi (1990) make an analogous argument about sex differences in the explanation of crime as about racial or cultural differences. Both official data as well as self-report data provide evidence that males are disproportionately more likely to engage in deviant behaviors, to commit crimes, especially more serious forms of norm-violating conduct. They find that the differences in levels of crime committed by males and females are stable across time and place, and that neither opportunity structures nor different *levels* of socialization (e.g., parental monitoring) experienced by males versus females can address "the gender gap" in offending. In addition, the very variables that are causally antecedent to the socialization of self-control and to the prediction of norm-violating behaviors, such as parental attachment or supervision, are related to deviance in the same manner for males and for females. In other words, despite the fact that on average females may be more closely monitored (*levels*) than males or that males report lower levels of self-control than females, these very predictors appear to be the same ones for both males and females, and they appear to be related in a similar fashion in both groups.

Empirical studies attempting to examine this issue have provided evidence that supported predictions by the General Theory. A small number of studies have tested both the psychometric properties and dimensionality of self-control in males and females as well as the predictive relationships between measures of self-control and deviance. Specifically, using a multidimensional, 5-factor model, Longshore and colleagues (1996) found support for the factor structure in males based on Confirmatory Factor Analyses (CFAs), but they did not find support for their final model in females. However, multiple-group comparisons indicated that although the final model did not fit the female sample part of their investigation, the difference in factor structures between males and females was not statistically significant. In a last step, based on regression analyses, predictive models were largely similar for males and females. Piquero and Rosay

(1998) also tested the factor structure of their unidimensional final model on male and female participants using a constrained model (of invariance); their findings indicated invariance across the two groups. Subsequent regression analyses were only completed on the total sample with age, gender, and ethnicity entered as controls; therefore, their study did not specifically evaluate similarities or differences in the predictive relationships between self-control and measures of deviance. Vazsonyi and colleagues (2001) also tested their final multidimensional, 6-factor model on male and female adolescents from four countries. Their findings indicated good model fit for both groups. Furthermore, follow-up regression analyses with age and country entered as controls suggested that the relationships between low self-control and a variety of deviance measures were largely similar.

Finally, Arneklev and colleagues (1999) also used CFAs to confirm the multidimensional structure (6 dimensions) of self-control and found consistent support for it, both based on a college sample as well as an adult sample. In addition, consistent with Gottfredson and Hirschi's (1990) idea of a "latent construct," the authors also tested a second order CFA that conceptualized self-control as a second order latent trait. In our opinion, this is perhaps the closest approximation to the theoretical specification of self-control. Findings from CFAs and from invariance tests between the two samples strongly supported predictions by the General Theory. Vazsonyi and colleagues (2001) also tested this multidimensional, second-order conceptualization of the self-control construct and found support for the model based on their cross-national sample of adolescents.

A few other studies simply examined potential similarities and differences in the self-control-deviance relationship. For example, LaGrange and Silverman (1999) tested the importance of low self-control in offending frequencies in male and female adolescents. Using a regression framework to test the unique explanatory power of sex, they concluded that it maintained a very modest, but significant effect in the prediction of some of the deviance measures. Subsequently, the authors also tested prediction models separately by sex due to this initial finding; however, no direct comparisons of regression coefficients were completed based on these latter analyses (for similar empirical tests, see Burton et al. 1998; Gibbs and Griever 1995; Keane, Maxim, and Teevan 1993; Tibbetts 1997; Wood, Pfefferbaum, and Arneklev 1993). Most of these studies that tested the gender gap found mixed evidence on the importance of low self-control for deviance above and beyond gender, and thus have concluded that findings provided only partial support for the theory. As a result, some of these studies have introduced alternative or competing explanations to apparent differences in the relationship between self-control and deviance between male and female samples. For instance, Burton and colleagues (1998) found that associating with criminal friends seemed to be important for females only, thereby partially accounting for the observed difference. On the other hand, follow-up analyses in the same study where self-control predicted crime-analogous behaviors indicated few differences between males and females. It is worth noting again, however, that few studies have used stringent differences tests (e.g., Paternoster et al. 1998) to further examine this question. In addition, and perhaps most important for this issue, the only comprehensive meta-analysis on the self-control-deviance relationship by Pratt and Cullen (2000) found no significant differences in the effects of low self-control on deviance by sex.

The Current Investigation

In conclusion, few studies have tested the utility of the predictions made by General Theory for minority adolescents or adults; furthermore, inconclusive evidence exists on how the theory informs our understanding of the gender gap, and whether the proposition by the General Theory about its importance (or lack thereof) finds empirical support. Therefore, in the current study, we were interested in testing the measurement of low self-control in a sample of African American youth, in examining the relationship between low self-control and a

variety of deviance measures ranging from trivial misconduct to serious assault, in assessing both measurement and etiological questions in both males and females, and in completing a stringent comparison of the importance of low self-control in African American and Caucasian adolescents based on identical measurement.

The following research questions were examined in the investigation:

1. Is the Grasmick et al. (1993) measure of low self-control valid and reliable in a sample of African American adolescents?
2. Is the factor structure of the low self-control measure uni- or multidimensional in this sample?
3. Is the relationship between low self-control and different measures of deviance similar or different in African American males versus females?
4. Is the relationship between low self-control and different measures of deviance similar or different by race (African American versus Caucasian youth)?

Method

Sample

Data were collected from a rural, low socioeconomic status (SES) public school that included grades 7 through 12. The study was approved by the superintendent, principal, and a university institutional review board. The school, which is located in a small town in rural Alabama, included $N = 814$ male and female students. A letter explaining the importance of the study, a support letter from the administration, and an informed consent letter were sent home with students for their parents to sign. In addition, the participants were asked to sign a Minor Assent form before completing the questionnaire. Only questionnaires completed 25 percent or more were included in the current analyses. Data were analyzed from $n = 661$ African American participants (males, $n = 297$; females $n = 364$) ranging from 12.3 to 20.7 years old (males, $M = 15.6$ years old, $SD = 1.8$; females, $M = 15.7$ years old, $SD = 1.7$). Table 1 provides

TABLE 1 Descriptive Statistics on Family Income and Family Structure for Total Sample and by Sex

	Total Sample		Males		Females	
	n	Percentage	*n*	Percentage	*n*	Percentage
Family income						
$20,000 or less	177	35.0	76	32.9	101	36.9
$20,000 to 35,000	138	27.3	65	28.1	73	26.6
$35,000 to 60,000	112	22.2	54	23.4	58	21.2
$60,000 to 100,000	48	9.5	18	7.8	30	10.9
More than $100,000	30	5.9	18	7.8	12	4.4
Family structure						
Biological parents	169	27.7	81	30.2	88	25.7
Biological mother only	248	40.7	106	39.6	142	41.5
Biological father only	22	3.6	15	5.6	7	2.0
Biological mother and stepfather	99	16.2	34	12.7	65	19.0
Biological father and stepmother	8	1.3	3	1.1	5	1.5
Biological parents and significant other	13	2.1	5	1.9	8	2.3
Other	51	8.4	24	9.0	27	7.9

Note: Of the 661 participants, only 505 (231 males, 274 females) participants indicated their family income and 610 (268 males, 342 females) their family structure.

descriptive information on family income and family structure for the participants. According to the Alabama Department of Education (2001), 90.6 percent of the students attending this school during the 2000 to 2001 school year were eligible for free or reduced meals.

For comparison purposes, data were also collected from Caucasian youth using the same data collection protocol and identical measures. These adolescents attended a high school in a small city in the same general vicinity as the primary sample located in the southeastern region of the United States (Vazsonyi et al. 2001). Although the schools were similar in general vicinity, one was rural and the other one was from a small city. In addition, whereas African American youth were poor, Caucasian youth were of average or above-average SES. Data were collected from $n = 626$ Caucasian students (males, $n = 315$; females

$n = 311$) in grades 9 through 12 (age $M=16.3$, $SD = 1.1$; males, $M = 16.4$ years old, $SD = 1.2$; females, $M = 16.3$ years old, $SD = 1.1$; . . .).

Procedure

Data were collected on two days (e.g., the first half of the survey on the first day and the second half of the survey on the second day) during the first hour of the school day. Researchers were available to answer questions during the completion of the surveys.

Measures

Participants completed a questionnaire that included demographic and background variables (e.g., age, sex), the Grasmick et al. (1993) low self-control measure, and the Vazsonyi et al. (2001) deviance measure.

Sex. Sex of the participants was determined by a single item: "What is your sex?" (1) male or (2) female.

Age. Participant age was computed by the date of birth supplied by the school administration.

Racial background. Racial background of the participants was assessed by a single item where participants answered if they were (1) African American, (2) Asian American, (3) Caucasian, (4) Hispanic, (5) Native American, or (6) Pacific Islander.

Family income. Family income of the participants was determined by a single item where the participants rated their approximate total annual family income: (1) $20,000 or less, (2) $20,000 to $35,000, (3) $35,000 to $60,000, (4) $60,000 to $100,000, or (5) $100,000 or more.

Family structure. Family structure of the participants was determined by a single item where the participants indicated their type of family structure: (1) biological parents, (2) biological mother only, (3) biological father only, (4) biological mother and stepfather, (5) biological father and stepmother, (6) biological parent and significant other, and (7) other (e.g., grandmother, grandparents, or aunt). Family structure was dummy coded for subsequent analyses.

Low self-control. The Grasmick et al. (1993) self-control measure consists of 24 items and 6 dimensions (impulsivity, simple tasks, risk seeking, physical activities, self-centeredness, and temper). Items were worded in the same manner as in the original measure. However, instead of the 4-point Likert scale, the measure was used with a 5-point Likert scale ranging from (1) *strongly disagree* to (5) *strongly agree* (Vazsonyi et al. 2001). In addition, instead of the 24-item scale, a revised 22-item scale was used (Vazsonyi et al. 2001). Past research has demonstrated that the measure was reliable ($\alpha = .81$; Grasmick et al. 1993). In the current study, the 22-item scale was also reliable for the total sample ($\alpha = .92$) and by sex (males, $\alpha = .93$, females, $\alpha = .92$; see Table 2). Reliability analyses also indicated that the scale was internally consistent for Caucasian youth (total sample: $\alpha = .90$; males, $\alpha = .91$; females $\alpha = .89$).

Deviance. The Normative Deviance Scale (NDS; Vazsonyi et al. 2001, 2002) consisted of 55 items organized in 7 subscales, namely vandalism, alcohol use, drug use, school misconduct, general deviance, theft, and assault. Lifetime deviance items were rated on a 5-point Likert scale: (1) *never*, (2) *one time*, (3) *two to three times*, (4) *four to six times*, and (5) *more than six times*. Past

TABLE 2 Reliability Analysis on Low Self-Control and Deviance Measures for Total Sample and by Sex

	Total Sample		Males		Females	
	n	α	*n*	α	*n*	α
Low self-control	377	.92	148	.93	229	.92
Deviance						
Vandalism	489	.94	200	.93	289	.95
Alcohol use	490	.91	207	.89	283	.91
Drug use	463	.94	188	.93	275	.94
School misconduct	470	.92	192	.92	278	.91
General deviance	454	.96	179	.96	275	.96
Theft	468	.96	192	.95	276	.96
Assault	466	.92	192	.92	274	.91
Total deviance	378	.99	144	.99	234	.98

Note: Because of pairwise deletions, sample sizes varied by analysis.

research has shown that the total deviance scale was reliable (α = .95); it has also shown that individual subscales were reliable (alpha range: .76 to .89; Vazsonyi et al. 2001, 2002). A total NDS measure was computed by averaging all items. Higher scores reflected higher levels of deviance. The current study also demonstrated that the total deviance scale was reliable for the total sample (α = .99) and by sex (males, α = .99, females, α = .98; see Table 2). individual subscales were also reliable for the total sample; alphas ranged from .91 to .96 for the total sample, from .89 to .96 for males, and from .91 to .96 for females (see Table 2). Subscales were also internally consistent for Caucasian youth (alphas ranged from .84 to .92 for the total sample, from .83 to .93 for males, and from .78 to .90 for females).

Plan of Analysis

First, descriptive statistics were computed on background variables. Second, CFAs were completed on the 22-item self-control measure (Vazsonyi et al. 2001). CFAs addressed the dimensionality question of the self-control measure; they were also completed by sex. Model fit was evaluated using the χ^2 fit statistic, the Comparative Fit Index (CFI), and the Root Mean Square Error of Approximation (RMSEA). When determining model fit, an acceptable fit for the CFI is between .9 and 1.0 (Crowley and Fan 1997); for the RMSEA, an excellent fit is below .5, a moderate fit between .5 and .8, and an acceptable fit between .8 and 1.0 (Browne and Cudeck 1993). In a next step, to examine the relationship between self-control and deviance, hierarchical regression analyses were conducted by sex. These analyses included regressions in which low self-control predicted total deviance as well as seven different deviance measures (vandalism, alcohol use, drug use, school misconduct, general deviance, theft, and assault). In all of these analyses, age, family income, and family structure (and in some cases sex) were entered as control variables. Finally, z-tests (Paternoster et al. 1998) were completed to compare regression coefficients—whether the low self-control-deviance relationship differed by sex and by race.

Results

Confirmatory Factor Analysis

To test the validity of the low self-control measure and whether self-control was a uni- or multidimensional latent construct, CFAs were completed on the low self-control measure as a one-factor model and as a six-factor model. Because there were missing data,[2] AMOS (4.0) was used to impute full information maximum likelihood (FIML) estimates in CFAs. This method of handling missing data is considered the most reliable because it is associated with the least amount of bias in parameter estimates (Enders 2001); it is also considered the current state of the art procedure on handling missing data. Each CFA model initially consisted of 22-items without cross-loadings or correlated errors terms.

Results from the one-factor solution indicated that the data fit the model moderately well (χ^2 = 1010.85, df = 209, CFI = .96, RMSEA = .08); however, the six-factor model improved fit (χ^2 = 866.58, df = 194, CFI = .97, RMSEA = .07). A chi-square difference test indicated that the difference (χ^2 = 144.28) was statistically significant (p < .01; $df\ change$ = 15; critical value: 30.58). Furthermore, the RMSEA decreased from a level considered to be just acceptable fit (>.08) to moderate fit. Thus, the second model provided a statistically significant improvement in model fit to the data, although the difference was rather small. Next, as previously found by Vazsonyi et al. (2001), two correlated error terms (between items 3 and 4 and items 5 and 7) were added in a final model. Results indicated that this further improved model fit (χ^2 = 799.63, df = 192, CFI = .97, RMSEA = .07); again, the chi-square difference test was statistically significant (χ^2 difference = 66.95; $df\ change$ = 2; critical value: 9.21; p < .01). Finally, CFAs were also completed by sex. For this purpose, the final model was used. These analyses indicated model fit was acceptable for males (χ^2 = 594.50, df = 192, CFI = .96, RMSEA = .08) and for females (χ^2 = 526.03, df = 192, CFI = .97, RMSEA = .07).

Partial Correlations

Next, partial correlations were computed by sex between low self-control and each NDS subscale (vandalism, alcohol use, drug use, school misconduct, general deviance, theft, and assault). These correlations were computed controlling for age, family structure, and family income (see Table 3). For males, associations ranged from $r = .32$ (school misconduct) to $r = .41$ (total deviance), whereas for females, they ranged from $r = .23$ (general deviance) to $r = .32$ (alcohol use). However, for females, the relationships between low self-control and theft and between low self-control and assault were not statistically significant.

Hierarchical Regression Analysis

A series of hierarchical regression analyses was completed to further investigate the relationship between low self-control and deviance. Initially, descriptive statistics including skewness were examined for low self-control and deviance (see Table 4). Results indicated that most deviance measures were skewed (> 1.0) for females, but that none of the deviance measures were highly skewed (< 2.0). Tabachnick and Fidell (1996) suggest that transformation is unnecessary

when all variables of interest are skewed to the same moderate extent. For example, when all variables are skewed > 1.0 but < 2.0, then transforming the data provides minimal improvements. Second, they also suggest that if skew is minor in large samples, transforming the data will not affect the results. In fact, Vazsonyi et al. (2001) found that results with untransformed skewed outcome data were robust in multiple regression analyses. In other words, the transformation of skewed variables resulted in trivial changes in explanatory power (the main goal of these analyses) in comparison to results from untransformed data. Therefore, the data were not transformed for the current analyses.

Regression analyses were completed on total deviance and each deviance subscale (vandalism, alcohol use, drug use, school misconduct, general deviance, theft, and assault) by sex controlling for age, family income, and family structure (entered order).[3] Results indicated that family structure was not a significant predictor of total deviance or deviance subscales. Therefore, regressions were completed without family structure as a control variable. Results indicated that age explained 0 percent of the variance in total deviance and between 0 percent and .1 percent in each deviance subscale for males. However,

TABLE 3   Third-Order Partial Correlations for Low Self-Control and Deviance Measures Controlling for Age, Family Income, and Family Structure by Sex

	1	2	3	4	5	6	7	8	9
1. Low self-control		.27	.32	.31	.24	.23	*.11*	*.11*	.27
2. Vandalism	.37		.80	.74	.58	.65	.63	.59	.83
3. Alcohol use	.39	.81		.76	.55	.60	.50	.48	.79
4. Drug use	.35	.66	.74		.72	.82	.73	.65	.91
5. School misconduct	.32	.57	.66	.85		.81	.67	.67	.83
6. General deviance	.37	.57	.68	.88	.87		.84	.78	.92
7. Theft	.36	.61	.67	.83	.73	.79		.85	.86
8. Assault	.35	.56	.60	.79	.74	.79	.86		.82
9. Total deviance	.41	.77	.84	.94	.89	.92	.89	.87	

Note: All correlations were significant at $p < .001$; *italicized* correlations were nonsignificant. Correlations for male youth are below the diagonal and those for female youth above it. Because of pairwise deletion, sample sizes varied by analysis.

TABLE 4 Analysis of Variance on Deviance and Low Self-Control for Total Sample and by Sex

	Total Sample				Males				Females			
	n	M	SD	skew	n	M	SD	skew	n	M	SD	skew
Low self-control	440	2.91	.76	−.21	178	3.03	.78	−.20	262	2.84	.74	−.27
Deviance												
Vandalism	511	2.06	1.11	.78	214	2.47	1.11	.31	297	1.75	1.02	1.29
Alcohol use	507	2.16	1.12	.55	213	2.56	1.13	.07	294	1.87	1.03	.99
Drug use	506	1.90	1.10	.98	214	2.30	1.16	.44	292	1.61	.95	1.54
School misconduct	491	2.13	1.12	.77	204	2.46	1.16	.36	287	1.89	1.04	1.15
General deviance	488	1.91	1.09	.99	203	2.34	1.18	.36	285	1.61	.91	1.67
Theft	481	1.78	1.11	1.22	199	2.16	1.24	.62	282	1.50	.92	1.87
Assault	479	1.92	1.12	1.01	197	2.29	1.22	.44	282	1.66	.97	1.59
Total deviance	513	1.97	.98	.80	216	2.36	1.02	.30	297	1.69	.84	1.28

Note: Because of pairwise deletion, sample sizes varied by analysis.

none of the terms were statistically significant. On the other hand, age explained 2.7 percent in total deviance for females, and between .6 percent to 3.4 percent in each deviance subscale. Age effects were statistically significant with the exception of vandalism and theft. Next, family income was also not a statistically significant variable for males; however, it was significant for females and explained 2.9 percent of the variance in total deviance and between 1.9 percent and 5.3 percent in deviance subscales for females with the exception of school misconduct (see Table 5).[4] Finally, low self-control explained 15.2 percent of the variance in total deviance and between 8.4 percent to 13.0 percent in each subscale for males. Low self-control also explained 5.5 percent of the variance in total deviance for females and between .8 percent and 8.4 percent in each deviance subscale. However, as found in previous partial correlations, low self-control did not predict theft or assault for females. Table 5 includes the percent variance explained in each deviance measure by sex, and Table 6 presents unstandardized regression coefficients.

Finally, we examined whether the low self-control-deviance relationship differed by sex (for

African American youth; controls: age, SES) and by race (African American versus Caucasian youth; controls: age, SES). For this purpose, a series of z-tests were completed for total deviance and all deviance subscales. Results from z-tests indicated that the unstandardized regression coefficients of low self-control did not differ between male and female African American youth (see Table 6), with the exceptions of theft and assault. However, this was not unexpected because self-control did not significantly predict theft and assault for African American females.

A series of z-tests was also completed between the African American sample and the Caucasian sample to determine whether the low self-control-deviance relationship was similar or different. For the purpose of these comparisons, and to match the available Caucasian high school sample, the African American sample was reduced to only 9th- through 12th-grade male and female participants ($n = 393$; males = 166, females = 227) ranging in age from 12.9 to 20.7 years (males, $M = 16.7$ years, $SD = 1.3$; females, $M = 16.6$ years, $SD = 1.2$). The Caucasian high school sample also included youth in 9th through

TABLE 5 **Results from Hierarchical Regressions of Background Variables and Low Self-Control on Deviance for Total Sample and by Sex (in percentages)**

	Vandalism	Alcohol Use	Drug Use	School Misconduct	General Deviance	Theft	Assault	Total Deviance
Males								
Age	.0	.1	.0	.0	.1	.0	.0	.0
SES	.1	.0	.0	.8	.0	.1	.4	.0
LSC	13.0***	12.9***	11.3***	8.4***	11.3***	11.7***	10.7***	15.2***
Total R^2	13.1***	13.0***	11.3***	9.2***	11.4***	11.9***	11.2***	15.2***
Females								
Age	.6	2.5*	2.2*	2.2*	3.4**	1.6	2.4*	2.7*
SES	2.1*	2.4*	1.9*	.5	2.5*	5.3**	1.9*	2.9*
LSC	6.0***	8.4***	7.7***	4.5**	4.0**	.8	.9	5.5***
Total R^2	8.6***	13.3***	11.8***	7.2***	10.0***	7.7***	5.1***	11.1***

Note: Variables are shown in order entered. SES is family income. LSC is low self-control. Statistically significant R^2s are noted as follows: *$p < .05$, **$p < .01$, ***$p < .001$, italicized percentages were nonsignificant. Because of pairwise deletion, sample sizes varied slightly by analysis.

TABLE 6 Unstandardized Regression Coefficients for African American Adolescents by Sex

	Males		Females		
	b	SE	b	SE	z-Score
Vandalism	.51**	.12	.34**	.09	*1.16*
Alcohol use	.54**	.12	.40**	.09	*.94*
Drug use	.48**	.12	.38**	.09	*.70*
School misconduct	.42**	.12	.30**	.10	*.80*
General deviance	.50**	.12	.25**	.08	*1.68*
Theft	.55**	.13	*.19*	.09	2.86*
Assault	.51**	.12	*.10*	.09	2.71*
Total deviance	.50**	.11	.28**	.08	*1.71*

Note: Unstandardized regression coefficients and z-scores were statistically significant at *$p < .05$, **$p < .01$, italicized coefficients were nonsignificant; because of pairwise deletion, sample sizes slightly varied by analysis.

12th grade ($n = 626$, 13.7 to 19.7 years, $M = 16.3$, $SD = 1.1$; males, $n = 315$; females, $n = 311$).

For males, results indicated that the unstandardized regression coefficients did not differ by race, with the exception of school misconduct. Table 7 includes the findings from these comparison. Next, in comparisons between African American and Caucasian females, results from z-tests indicated that regression coefficients differed for three of seven deviance measures, namely for school misconduct, alcohol use, drug use, as well as for the total deviance score (see Table 7). Interestingly, whereas self-control did not significantly predict theft and assault in African American females, the comparison of regression coefficients indicated that they did not differ by racial group, despite the fact that self-control significantly predicted the two behaviors for Caucasian females.

Discussion

The current investigation provides important evidence on the validity and dimensionality of low self-control and on the relationship between low self-control and deviance in a sample of rural, low SES African American youth. First, findings indicated that the low self-control measure was a multidimensional construct based on a sample of African American youth as hypothesized by Gottfredson and Hirschi (1990). This was also found in analyses by sex. These findings of construct validity are consistent with previous research conducted on mostly Caucasian youth (Arneklev et al. 1999; Longshore et al. 1996; Vazsonyi et al. 2001); at the same time, these findings supporting a multidimensional construct were also inconsistent with other work that found support for a unidimensional construct of self-control (e.g., Piquero and Rosay 1998). Second, consistent with past research on African Americans (Hay 2001; Longshore and Turner 1998), the evidence suggested that low self-control was consistently predictive of deviance in the current sample. In addition, low self-control was predictive of a variety of deviant behaviors in both male and female adolescents, namely of vandalism, alcohol use, drug use, school misconduct, and general deviance. However, findings also indicated that low self-control did not predict theft or assault for African American females although it did predict these behaviors for males. Thus, with these latter two exceptions of more

TABLE 7 Unstandardized Regression Coefficients for African American and Caucasian Adolescents by Sex

	African American Males		Caucasian Males			African American Females		Caucasian Females		
	b	SE	b	SE	z-Score	b	SE	b	SE	z-Score
Vandalism	.48**	.15	.72**	.07	*1.44*	.37**	.12	.52**	.05	*1.20*
Alcohol use	.52**	.15	.75**	.10	*1.32*	.49**	.12	1.05**	.09	3.69*
Drug use	.44**	.15	.70**	.10	*1.45*	.41**	.12	.79**	.09	2.50*
School misconduct	.32*	.15	.78**	.08	2.65*	.41**	.12	.77**	.07	2.57*
General deviance	.44**	.15	.65**	.07	*1.22*	.32**	.11	.51**	.05	*1.52*
Theft	.47**	.16	.60**	.07	*.72*	*.20*	.11	.39**	.05	*1.57*
Assault	.45**	.15	.54**	.07	*.54*	*.19*	.12	.42**	.05	*1.83*
Total deviance	.45**	.13	.68**	.07	*1.65*	.34**	.10	.63**	.05	2.54*

Note: Unstandardized regression coefficients and z-scores were statistically significant at *$p < .05$, **$p < .01$, italicized coefficients were nonsignificant. Because of pairwise deletion, sample sizes slightly varied by analysis.

serious deviant conduct, it appears that low self-control is an equally important variable in explaining the etiology of deviance in African American males and females.

It is important to further address the implications of one particular finding, namely that low self-control was not predictive of theft or assault in African American females. This finding may in part be due to the lack of variability in these behaviors for females as suggested by Snyder and Sickmund (1999). They found that only 5 percent of females have ever stolen something worth $50 or more and only 12 percent of females have ever committed assault. However, closer inspection of the current data do not support this explanation. In fact, considering individual theft and assault items rated by African American females, the data indicate that a sizeable number of youth engage in both theft and assault behaviors in this population. More specifically, between 21.1 percent and 28.0 percent of African American females indicated having ever tried to or having actually stolen something (average across seven items: 24.3 percent). This was in contrast to Caucasian females in the current study who reported rates much more consistent with the estimates provided by Snyder and Sickmund (1999), namely between 3.9 percent and 30.4 percent (average: 15.9 percent). A similar picture emerged when studying the assault indicators. Whereas 41.3 percent of African American females indicated having hit a student or peer (average of six assault items: 28.5 percent), only 26.8 percent of Caucasian adolescents indicated the same (average: 15.1 percent). Thus, explanations focusing on low frequencies of behaviors among African American youth do not seem to apply. One alternative explanation is that other restraint mechanisms, such as perceived sanctions for these more serious behaviors, could account for variability in deviance. Gottfredson and Hirschi specifically operationalized the self-control construct as a probabilistic one—low self-control is not deterministic, and in fact, other individual or contextual factors might be equally or more potent predictors of who is restrained and who is not restrained to commit these behaviors. It is worth noting that the association between low self-control and both theft and assault were in the right direction. Of course all this is mostly speculation, and further data from African American females might provide some answers to why low self-control did not significantly predict theft or assault in this sample.

The third important finding from the current study provided evidence that the low self-control-deviance relationship was similar based on direct comparisons of African American and Caucasian adolescents, particularly for males. This was so despite the fact that at face value, the associations appeared slightly weaker in the African American sample in comparison to the Caucasian one. However, z-tests of the regression coefficients revealed only one difference between males from the two groups, namely school misconduct. More differences were found for females, namely for alcohol use, drug use, and school misconduct. In addition, coefficients for total deviance were also significantly different for female adolescents, something that was to be expected given that three of seven indicators differed. Interestingly, despite the fact that self-control did not predict theft and assault for African American females, comparative tests by race indicated no differences in the importance of self-control in these two behaviors.

In conclusion, findings from the current study have important implications for the General Theory of Crime. They provide new evidence on the etiology of deviance in African American youth. First, the findings provide support for one of the main propositions of the General Theory, namely that low self-control predicts adolescent deviance in African American youth. Second, the study provided evidence of offender versatility in that self-control explained variability in a variety of deviance measures. Similar findings of versatility (unrelated to self-control) have been made in previous work (Jessor and Jessor 1977; Osgood et al. 1988). Third, the findings provided support for the

proposition that the General Theory appears generalizable for males and females as well as in different racial groups in the United States, although a number of differences were found between female participants in the two racial groups. For example, self-control exerted a more potent predictive effect on measures of alcohol use and drug use as well as school misconduct in Caucasian female youth. This may indicate that consuming alcohol or drugs as well as misbehaving in school are more common in African American youth, and therefore, a much smaller amount of variability can be explained by low self-control. Interestingly, a similar explanation applies for school misconduct in males. Together these findings add to the growing empirical evidence on the low self-control-deviance relationship in different cultural or racial groups; they suggest that especially for males, this relationship might be largely invariant across these groups. They also provide additional support to one of Gottfredson and Hirschi's (1990) central hypotheses, namely that the General Theory and its basic tenets apply to "all crime, at all times, and for that matter, many forms of behavior that are not sanctioned by the state" (p. 117).

Limitations and Future Directions

There are a number of limitations that require some discussion. First, the present investigation set out to test only part of the General Theory of Crime, namely how low self-control predicted deviant behaviors. The study did not investigate the etiology of self-control (socialization processes) or the import of opportunity structures in the self-control-deviance relationship. Thus, it is necessary that future research examine how parents influence the socialization of self-control and, in turn, how this predicts deviance in African American youth. In addition, the moderating effect of opportunity needs to be further examined in the self-control-deviance relationship, especially in different cultural and national populations. A related shortcoming of the paper is that it only compared the total self-control construct between male and female adolescents and between African American and

Caucasian youth; future work could consider the importance of individual subscales as a number of studies have pointed out how the different dimensions of self-control appear to be differentially important for measures of deviance, although we believe that there is limited value to doing this for the reasons outlined in our introductory comments.

Third, the present study was conducted on rural, low-SES African American youth in the south, and thus, findings may not be generalizable to other rural African American youth from other regions of the country, to African American youth with different levels of SES, or to urban African American youth. Future research will need to examine the potential confound between SES, residence (rural), and race. For example, by comparing the present findings to urban, low-SES African American youth or rural, low-SES Caucasian youth, new evidence may be found on whether living in rural/urban areas, or coming from a low versus high SES background may influence the relationship between low self-control and deviance. In addition, future research is necessary in other areas of the country to determine whether the current findings can be replicated and thus generalize across different samples.

Next, the findings in this study are based exclusively on questionnaire data. It is important to consider additional data sources and methods to further validate the current findings. Other potential sources include teacher reports, school-based information, (e.g., number of detentions) as well as criminal records obtained from the local police department. Fifth, because the data were school-based, this may have excluded adolescents who do not attend school and who may be more deviant. In other words, because there is a positive association between juvenile delinquency and dropping out of high school (Tracy, Wolfgang, and Figlio 1990), more serious juvenile delinquents may have dropped out of school and thus were excluded from data collection. Therefore, the current findings need to be considered in light of this potential shortcoming. Finally, the current investigation was

a cross-sectional analysis of the relationship between low self-control and deviance. Future studies should also examine this relationship in similar samples employing longitudinal data (see e.g., Turner and Piquero 2002).

Notes

[1] Although analyses did not compare findings between African American and Caucasian youth, the sample from the United States included African American youth.

[2] Of the 661 participants, only 374 participants completed the entire low self-control measure. Initially, a confirmatory factor analysis for the one-factor model on this sample indicated the following fit: $\chi^2 = 952.71$, $df = 209$, CFI = .78, GFI = .78, and a RMSEA = .10.

[3] Initial regression analyses were completed to examine whether age or sex moderated the relationship between low self-control and deviance; none of the interaction terms reached statistical significance with the exceptions of Sex—Low Self-Control for theft and assault; this contributed to the decision to compute analyses by sex. Subsequently, analyses by sex confirmed some sex differences because no relationships were found for females between low self-control and theft as well as assault, whereas significant relationships were found for males.

[4] Regression analyses on the Caucasian sample that also included the same controls indicated no effect by family income for males or females with the exceptions of male theft and assault, where the variable explained 2 percent and 3 percent respectively. Although the family income measure was simply used as a control variable (a proxy for socioeconomic status [SES]), and therefore, not as a variable of substantive interest in the current study, findings for African American females require some discussion. We have limited confidence in the importance of these observed SES effects, especially because more than 90 percent of the sample is eligible for free and reduced lunches based on official data. In addition, it is customary for the

federal government to adjust the percentage of youth eligible for these meal services if all students are eligible in order to not stigmatize youth. So, it is conceivable that almost all youth were poor, and therefore, we hesitate to interpret these findings as substantive and how they might be important for the General Theory. Finally, in follow-up analyses employing alternative measures of SES (maternal education, paternal education, and the primary wage earner's occupation), we found that SES explained no significant amount of variance across all deviance measures with one exception, namely paternal education had a small effect on female school misconduct.

References

Alabama Department of Education. 2001. *State Board of Education School Report Card for 2000-2001: Bullock Country High School.* Retrieved August 2, 2002, from http://www.alsde.edu

Arneklev, Bruce J., Harold G. Grasmick, and Robert J. Bursik. 1999. "Evaluating the Dimensionality and Invariance of 'Low Self-Control.'" *Journal of Quantitative Criminology* 15: 307-331.

Arneklev, Bruce J., Harold G. Grasmick, Charles R. Tittle, and Robert J. Bursik. 1993. "Low Self-Control and Imprudent Behaviors." *Journal of Quantitative Criminology* 9:225-47.

Browne, Michael W. and Robert Cudeck. 1993. "Alternative Ways of Assessing Model Fit." Pp. 136162 in *Testing Structural Equation Models*, edited by Kenneth A. Bollen and J. Scott Lond. Newbury Park, CA: Sage.

Burton, Velmer S., Francis T. Cullen, T. David Evans, Leanne Fiftal Alarid, and R. Gregory Dunaway. 1998. "Gender, Self-Control, and Crime." *Journal of Research in Crime and Delinquency* 35:123-47.

Burton, Velmer S., T. David Evans, Francis T. Cullen, Kathleen M. Olivares, and R. Gregory Dunaway. 1999. "Age, Self-Control, and Adults' Offending Behaviors: A Research Note Assessing a General Theory of Crime." *Journal of Criminal Justice* 27:45-54.

Crowley, Susan L. and Xitao Fan. 1997. "Structural Equation Modeling: Basic Concepts and Applications in Personality Assessment Research." *Journal of Personality Assessment* 68:508-31.

Enders, Craig. 2001. "The Impact of Nonnormality on Full Information Maximum-Likelihood Estimation for Structural Equation Modeling with Missing Data." *Psychological Methods* 6:352-70.

Gibbs, John J. and Dennis Griever. 1995. "Self-Control and Its Manifestation among University Students: An Empirical Test of Gottfredson and Hirschi's General Theory." *Justice Quarterly* 12:231-55.

Gibbs, John J., Dennis Griever, and Jamie S. Martin. 1998. "Parental Management and Self-Control: An Empirical Test of Gottfredson and Hirschi's General Theory." *Journal of Research in Crime and Delinquency* 35:40-70.

Gottfredson, Michael R. and Travis Hirschi. 1990. *A General Theory of Crime.* Stanford, CA: Stanford University Press.

Grasmick, Harold G., Charles R. Tittle, Robert J. Bursik, and Bruce J. Arneklev. 1993. "Testing the Core Empirical Implications of Gottfredson and

Hirschi's General Theory of Crime." *Journal of Research in Crime and Delinquency* 30:529.

Hay, Carter. 2001. "Parenting, Self-Control, and Delinquency: A Test of Self-Control Theory." *Criminology* 39:707-36.

Hirschi, Travis and Michael R. Gottfredson. 2001. "Self-Control Theory." Pp. 81–96 in *Explaining Criminal and Crime*, edited by Raymond Paternoster and Ronet Bachman. Los Angeles: Roxbury.

Jessor, Richard and Shirely L. Jessor. 1977. *Problem Behavior and Psychosocial Development: A Longitudinal Study of Youth.* New York: Academic Press.

Junger, Marianne and Robert West, and Reinier Timman. 2001. "Crime and Risky Behavior in Traffic: An Example of Cross-Situational

Consistency." *Journal of Research in Crime and Delinquency* 38:439-59.

Junger, Marianne and Richard E. Tremblay. 1999. "Self-Control, Accidents, and Crime." *Criminal Justice and Behavior* 26:485–501.

Keane, Carl, Paul S. Maxim, and James J. Teevan. 1993. "Drinking and Driving, Self-Control, and Gender: Testing a General Theory of Crime." *Journal of Research in Crime and Delinquency* 30:3046.

LaGrange, Teresa C. and Robert A. Silverman. 1999. "Low Self-Control and Opportunity: Testing the General Theory of Crime as an Explanation for Gender Differences in Delinquency." *Criminology* 37:41–72.

LeBlanc, Marc. 1993. "Late Adolescence Deceleration of Criminal Activity and Development of Self- and Social Control." *Studies on Crime and Crime Prevention* 2:51-68.

Longshore, Douglas. 1998. "Self-Control and Criminal Opportunity: A Prospective Test of the General Theory of Crime." *Social Problems* 45:102–13.

Longshore, Douglas and Susan Turner. 1998. "Self-Control and Criminal Opportunity: Cross-Sectional Test of the General Theory of Crime." *Criminal Justice and Behavior* 25:81-98.

Longshore, Douglas, Judith A. Stein, and Susan Turner. 1998. "Reliability and Validity of a Self-Control Measure: Rejoinder." *Criminology* 26:175-82.

Longshore, Douglas, Susan Turner, and Judith A. Stein. 1996. "Self-Control in a Criminal Sample: An Examination of Construct Validity." *Criminology* 34:209–28.

Osgood, D. Wayne, Lloyd D. Johnston, Patrick M. O'Malley, and Jerald G. Bachman. 1988. "The Generality of Deviance in Late Adolescence and Early Adulthood." *American Sociological Review* 53:81-93.

Paternoster, Raymond, Robert Brame, Paul Mazerolle, and Alex R. Piquero. 1998. "Using the Correct Statistical Test for the Equality of Regression Coefficients." *Criminology* 36:859-66.

Piquero, Alex R. and Andre B. Rosay. 1998. "The Reliability and Validity of Grasmick et al.'s Self-Control Scale: A Comment on Longshore et al." *Criminology* 36:157-173.

Pratt, Travis C. and Francis T. Cullen. 2000. "The Empirical Status of Gottfredson and Hirschi's General Theory of Crime: A Meta-Analysis." *Criminology* 38:931-64.

Snyder, Howard N. and Melissa Sickmund. 1999. *Juvenile Offenders and Victims: 1999 National Report.* Retrieved August 10, 2002, from: http://www.ncjrs.org/html/ojjdp/nationalreport99/toc. html

Tabachnik, Barbara G. and Linda S. Fidell. 1996. *Using Multivariate Statistics.* New York: Harper Collins.

Tibbetts, Stephen G. 1997. "Gender Differences in Students'Rational Decision to Cheat." *Deviant Behavior* 18:393-414.

Tracy, Paul E., Marvin E. Wolfgang, and Robert M. Figlio. 1990. *Delinquency Careers in Two Birth Cohorts.* New York: Plenum Press.

Turner, Michael G. and Alex R. Piquero. 2002. "The Stability of Self-Control." *Journal of Criminal Justice* 30:457–71.

Vazsonyi, Alexander T., Lloyd E. Pickering, Lara M. Belliston, Dick Hessing, and Marianne Junger. 2002. "Routine Activities and Deviant Behaviors: American, Dutch, Hungarian and Swiss Youth." *Journal of Quantitative Criminology* 18:397-422.

Vazsonyi, Alexander T., Lloyd E. Pickering, Marianne Junger, and Dick Hessing. 2001. "An Empirical Test of a General Theory of Crime: A Four-Nation Comparative Study of Self-Control and the Prediction of Deviance." *Journal of Research in Crime and Delinquency* 38:91-131.

Wood, Peter B., Betty Pfefferbaum, and Bruce Arneklev. 1993. "Risk-Taking and Self-Control: Social Psychological Correlates of Delinquency." *Journal of Research in Crime and Delinquency* 16:111-30.

Alexander T. Vazsonyi is an associate professor of human development and family studies at Auburn University. His research interests include the etiology of adolescent deviance, criminological theory, and the comparative approach to the study of human development.

Recent publications have appeared in the Journal of Quantitative Criminology, the Journal of Research in Crime and Delinquency, and Criminal Justice and Behavior.
Jennifer M. Crosswhite, MS, is a doctoral student at Auburn University in the Department of Human Development and Family Studies. Her *current research interests include adolescent development, the causes of adolescent delinquency, understanding the mechanisms by which the family influences adolescent delinquency, and translating research into practical application for the lay audience.*

Conclusion

This chapter examined social bonding and self-control theories. These theories maintain that most individuals do not commit crime and focus on why individuals do not commit crime. Social bonding theory maintains that the withering or disconnect of four bonds (i.e., attachment, commitment, involvement, and belief) will result in crime and also implies that minorities have more worn or broken bonds. Self-control theory suggests that crime occurs because of the lack of self-control. It also suggests that minorities have less self-control than whites due to differences in the socialization practices of parents at an early age.

Meta-analyses indicate that social bonding theory has promise in understanding race–crime relations, but that self-control theory is not as successful. First, the studies on social bonding are crime specific, which leaves the question of whether social bonding theory will apply equally when other crimes are examined. Further, in studies on self-control theory, different ways of measuring self-control are used. However, these theories are helpful in understanding race–crime relations to some extent.

Discussion Questions

1. Control theory focuses on why individuals do not commit crime and delinquency. According to Hirschi (1969), how does this focus explain the differences among the races?

2. According to the reading presented in this chapter, some disagreement exists pertaining to the way that self-control explains crime and criminality across the races. Why does this occur?

References

Gottfredson, M. R., & Hirschi, T. (1990). *A general theory of crime.* Stanford, CA: Stanford University Press.

Hirschi, T. (1969). *Causes of delinquency.* Berkeley, CA: University of California Press.

Pratt, T. C., & Cullen, F. T. (2000). The empirical status of Gottfredson and Hirschi's general theory of crime: A meta-analysis. *Criminology, 38,* 931–964.

CHAPTER **8**

Life Course Perspective

The life course perspective strives to better understand the connection between age and crime. For example, an inspection of age and crime reveals that at the age of 7, some individuals begin to commit crime; however, by the age of 17, many individuals stop committing crime. This chapter provides an overview of the life course perspective and two prominent theories (i.e., Sampson & Laub, 1993; Moffitt, 1993) based on this perspective.

Because of the age–crime connection, many criminologists spent a substantial amount of effort studying juveniles in the ages of 7 to 17. These studies have made use of self-report surveys. A self-report survey is a series of questions or statements that have been developed by a researcher and given to a research subject to complete. When the subject completes a self-report survey regarding crime, the researcher is able to determine the things that may or may not have a connection to the individual's criminal behavior. The advent of the self-report survey has resulted in a substantial growth in criminology and criminal justice research and theories, because a researcher could have access to an entire group of students in a community simply at the local junior or high schools, without having to carry out expensive longitudinal studies (i.e., studies over time).

Longitudinal studies were able to document that the events in one stage of life affect the events that take place in another stage of life. In the life course perspective, this view is often expressed as different pathways that are shaped by transitions and turning points that occur at different stages of life. Caspi et al. (1987) argue that the life course is a "sequence of culturally defined age-graded roles and social transitions that are enacted over time" (p. 15). In essence, these age-graded transitions are embedded in different social institutions and can be brought about by different events.

The life course perspective is based on two major components—trajectories and transitions. A trajectory is a pattern or sequence of events. A transition is a specific event that is embedded in a trajectory. Transitions may or may not be reliant on age. Thus, according to this perspective, the life course is based on the normative timing and the sequencing of the changes that take place in an individual's life.

Trajectories and transitions are by definition joined. Because they are joined, they may have important implications for the individual by developing specific turning points or changes in an individual's life course (Elder, 1985). It is clear now that the childhood path of an individual has a connection to the adulthood path of the individual. However, the trajectory may not always be long term. A short-term trajectory can redirect an individual's life course. Further, transitions and trajectories are influenced by social institutions (e.g., schools, marriage, and military experience).

The life course perspective can be applied to several different themes in an individual's life, including crime. For instance, many see the life course perspective as a criminal career perspective on crime and this view has its roots in cohort studies. In cohort studies, the focus is generally on the onset (i.e., the beginning of criminal career), the duration (i.e., how long the career lasts), the frequency (i.e., lambda), and the ending of the criminal career (i.e., desistance). Some have focused on developing specific theories to explain these phenomena.

For instance, Sampson and Laub (1993) utilize a control perspective that is combined with social learning theory. They proposed that individuals who have transitions that come with getting older increase social bonds. For example, individuals who get married or find stable employment develop this sort of bond. From this point of view, those who are younger are more likely to offend but desist when they grow older. However, if these transitions do not occur, the individual is likely to persist in their offending. Thus, the stability of one's behavior is related to the stability of the events that produce them. That is, as long as the individual has stable employment, they are likely to refrain from criminal activity.

According to Terri Moffitt (1993), neuropsychological deficits are instrumental in the development of behavioral problems. That is, when an individual demonstrates behavioral problems as a child and exhibits delinquency and criminality at an early age, they are more likely to be life-course persistent. However, some individuals begin their criminality later in life (i.e., during adolescence). These individuals do not continue their criminal behavior beyond this point in life. Moffitt refers to these individuals as adolescent limited. According to Moffitt, the life-course–persistent individual would have shown signs of problems due to hyperactivity, low verbal ability, and an impulsive personality. These individuals are rather resistant to peer influences. However, the adolescent-limited individual is much more responsive to peer influences, and he or she is less likely to commit crime in adulthood.

These theories have enjoyed some empirical support in the criminological literature, but most of them have not been specifically applied to study racial differences in crime. For instance, Sampson and Laub (1993) would argue that racial minorities have less stable social bonds with society and, therefore, they are likely to have higher rates of criminal activity. Whereas, Moffitt (1993) would argue that racial minorities are more likely to experience higher levels of neuropsychological deficits because they are unable to afford quality prenatal and perinatal care for their child. Piquero, MacDonald, and Parker explore these views in the selection that follows.

Race, Local Life Circumstances, and Criminal Activity

Alex R. Piquero, *University of Florida*
John M. MacDonald, *University of South Carolina*
Karen F. Parker, *University of Florida*

Objective. Life-course researchers suggest that changes in local life circumstances explain changes in criminal activity in adulthood. Although the extent to which local life circumstances propel offenders toward/away from criminal behavior is a subject of considerable debate, the issue *of race has largely been ignored. The objective in this research is to incorporate race into a life-course perspective that examines the influence of changes in life circumstances on changes in criminal activity. Methods. This objective is met by using longitudinal data on 524 parolees released from the California Youth Authority (CYA) who were followed for seven consecutive years after release. Results. The results suggest that changes in local life circumstances are related to changes in criminal activity, but do not eliminate the race/crime relationship for violence. At the same time, the effect of local life circumstances on criminal activity appears more similar than different across race, with the exception that common-law marriages are crime-generating among nonwhites as compared to whites. Conclusions. Because race continues to be associated with criminal activity over life course, future research should increase efforts to better understand how race might condition life circumstances when influencing criminal activity. Implications of these findings for life-course theory are discussed.*

Introduction

In recent years the life-course perspective has increasingly been applied to criminological theory (Piquero and Mazerolle, 2001). This perspective assumes that there are age-graded pathways through which individuals mature that affect their decision making and the course of events that give shape to their lives (Elder, 1985:17). According to the life-course perspective, there is likely to be both continuity and discontinuity in criminal offending over time.

The trajectories or pathways of development over the life span suggest a positive relationship between past and future crime, yet "turning points" may occur that explain transitions away from crime (Sampson and Laub, 1993). Two competing processes have been advanced to account for the positive association between past and future crime. The first contends that repeated offending among crime-prone individuals is simply a series of continuing realizations that is the result of a relatively time-stable latent criminal propensity. Since this perspective assumes that criminal propensities are age invariant, it rules out the possibility of "turning points" as a causal explanation for the change in offending over time (Gottfredson and Hirschi, 1990). The second position argues that the link between past and future crime is due to the impact that the commission of criminal acts has on reducing inhibitions and strengthening motivations to commit crime (Nagin and Paternoster, 1991). This perspective also suggests that entrance into adult institutions of social control (marriage and employment) can foster turning points in the lives of offenders (Sampson and Laub, 1995; Uggen, 2000).

However, neither perspective alone seems to be able to account for the paradox that adult criminality virtually requires juvenile delinquency and yet not all juvenile delinquency become adult offenders (Robins, 1978). To reconcile this paradox, life-course scholars have developed theoretical models that posit that both persistent individual differences (continuity) and turning points (change) are important ingredients for a complete understanding of crime over the life course (Paternoster et al., 1997). Absent from these discussions, however, is the role of race. Although scholars suggest that race is not a central feature of crime over the life course (Sampson and Laub, 1993), research continues to document divergent offending trends between whites and nonwhites (Blumstein et al., 1986; Elliott, 1994a). Hawkins, Laub, and Lauritsen (1998:34) note that race is related to differential rates of offending and that the distribution varies considerably by crime type. In particular, race differences in violent arrests have been "longstanding" with nonwhites in general, and African Americans in particular, evidencing higher rates for violence across official and self-reported measures. For example, Elliott (1994a) found that almost twice as many African Americans as whites continued violent offending into early adulthood.

Still, an examination of the factors that account for race differences remains unexplored. In fact, Horney, Osgood, and Marshall (1995:661) commented that the extent to which local life circumstances vary across groups would be "an appropriate direction for future research." To address this issue, the present study examines two key questions: (1) Do changes in local life circumstances eliminate the race/crime relationship? and (2) Is the relationship between changes in local life circumstances and changes in criminal activity invariant across race?

Local Life Circumstances and Crime

Life-course criminologists argue that crime is inhibited when persons are bonded to conventional institutions of social control (Sampson and Laub, 1993). The specific sources of social control that are believed to inhibit criminal behavior include the family, school, marriage, education, and employment. Moreover, informal social controls are believed to be subject to within-individual variation over time. Thus, while stable individual differences in criminal propensity are important, changes in life events can also lead to changes in criminal activity. Others, however, contend that such events exert no meaningful impact on the course of future crime because the decisions to enter into particular life events are a function of the same latent mechanism that leads to crime initially (Hirschi and Gottfredson, 1995).

Empirical research suggests that both continuity and change are important (Paternoster et al., 1997). For example, a study of institutionalized males indicated that short-term variations in the attachment to adult institutions of social control were associated with changes in offending, controlling for individual differences in criminal propensity (Horney, Osgood, and Marshall, 1995). When offenders held jobs, were off alcohol and drugs, and were living with their spouses, they were less likely to be involved in crime. Laub, Nagin, and Sampson (1998) also found that after controlling for individual differences, satisfying marriages were important in promoting desistance.

Although evidence suggests that adult institutions of social control can promote changes in offending trajectories (Piquero et al., 2002), the extant research on crime over the life course has largely ignored the role of race. Given the disproportionate rate of minority involvement in the criminal justice system (Mauer, 1990) and the importance of race in the public discourse on

social welfare (Smelser, Wilson, and Mitchell, 2001), it would seem prudent for race to be incorporated into the discussion of crime over the life course. This is important since few studies have focused on how age-graded processes vary across race during the transition into early adulthood, a time period that evidences the greatest race differences in violent offending (Elliott, 1994a).

Although researchers have studied the relationship between changes in adult social bonds and changes in criminal activity, research has not examined whether such changes eliminate race differences in the continuity of early adult offending. This is likely due to the fact that most longitudinal data are comprised of predominately white samples. For some, however, this is of little concern because they contend that race should be of little importance. Sampson and Laub (1993:255) argue that race only affects crime indirectly through the "structural disadvantage, weakened informal social bonds to family, school, and work, and the disruption of social relations between individuals and institutions that provide social capital." In other words, "variations by race, ethnicity, and structural context in social capital and its role in promoting successful transitions to young adulthood" may help explain race differences in criminal offending (Laub and Sampson, 1993:312). Whether the influence of changes in adult social bonds on changes in offending is invariant across race remains unexplored.

Race, Local Life Circumstances, and Crime

The contextual and institutional factors that explain differences in the transition to adulthood are likely embedded in issues of race (Ousey, 1999). Employment and marriage represent two distinct indicators of the transition into adulthood that are invariably tied to historical social inequalities in America. The structural and cultural changes that have occurred since the 1960s have invariably changed the influence of employment and family in the transition into adulthood (Shanahan, 2000:671). For example, the transition to full-time adult employment and marriage took longer in 1980 than in 1960 (Morris et al., 1998). Research suggests that this may have to do, in part, with a shift from a largely industrial to a more service-based economy (Morris et al., 1998) and the growth in cohabitation (Bumpass and Sweet, 1989).

These changes appear to have had the most pronounced effect on the African-American community. Historically, nonwhites have been disproportionately affected by unemployment, poverty, single-parent head of households, and other indicators of social inequality. These conditions have worsened in the inner city since the 1960s (Wilson, 1987). In terms of family relations, Wilson (1987) notes that nonwhites in general, and African Americans in particular, are less likely than whites to be married and more likely to experience marital separation. The relationship between joblessness and marital instability appears to have had a disparate impact on the African-American family. The historical growth in unemployment among inner-city African-American men relative to African-American women since the 1960s has had a role in the formation of families, and Wilson (1987:145) notes that although African-American women are confronting a "shrinkage of 'marriageable' (that is economically stable) men, white women are not experiencing this problem." The growth in unemployment for African-American men may make them less attractive marriage partners and increase the prevalence of single female-headed households in African-American communities (Wilson, 1996). Thus, differences across race in adult criminal behavior may reflect a combination of factors that put nonwhites at greater risk. According to Sampson and Wilson (1995), the combination of poverty and family disruption is so concentrated by race that African Americans experience the brunt of these disparate effects, and the differential participation of African Americans in adult institutions of social control places them at greater risk of offending into adulthood. In fact, research shows higher rates of African-American family disruption are associated with higher rates of violent crime (Sampson and Lauritsen, 1994).

Although it appears that race is inextricably linked to differences in participation in both crime and adult institutions of social control, few studies have examined the interrelationships of race and adult social bonds on the transition into adult offending. While the literature indicates that adult social bonds are important ingredients in the cessation from crime among adults in general, less is known about how these factors mediate the relationship between race and offending in early adulthood in particular. One of the few studies that examined this issue found that marriage was an inhibitor of future crime for whites but had little effect on nonwhites (Rand, 1987). In fact, the only inhibitory effect of marriage for nonwhites was for the seriousness of offending. In contrast, other research found no differences in offending continuity for employed or married African Americans and whites, but that continuity differences continued for those who were unemployed or living alone (Elliott, 1994a). In other words, if married or employed, African Americans and whites shared the same continuity rates; if not, then African Americans exhibited a higher offending continuity than whites. Thus, the higher continuation in offending for nonwhites could be explained, in part, by their lower rates of employment and marriage (Elliott, 1994b:198). Other research has found that while adult social bonds were associated with fewer drinking episodes, they did not eliminate race/ethnicity effects (Nielson, 1999). Also, marriage was found to be important for inhibiting drinking for whites but not for African Americans.

Current Focus

Unfortunately, prior research has neither examined issues related to race with the sort of dynamic statistical analyses necessary to study within-individual change nor provided adequate controls for persistent individual differences in criminal propensity. Also, the extent to which the relationship between race and local life circumstances varies across crime types has not been studied. Given that nonwhites are overrepresented in violent crimes and underrepresented in involvement in marriage and employment, this presents an additional area of inquiry. For example, recent data from the Census Bureau (2000:43) shows that, whereas 80.7 percent of whites are married, only 47.1 percent of African Americans are married. Similarly, the percentage of unemployed whites is 2.5 percent, whereas the percentage of unemployed African Americans is 5.3 percent.

Data and Methods

The data for this study are based on 524 parolees from the California Youth Authority (CYA) who were followed for seven consecutive years after release (during the 1970s). The sample was 48.5 percent white (n = 254) and 51.5 percent nonwhite (n = 270). Nonwhites were represented by African Americans (33 percent), Hispanics (16.6 percent), and other (1.9 percent).[1] Data on criminal activity and life events were collected for each parolee over the seven-year period. Crime data were obtained from the California Department of Justice Criminal Identification and Investigation (CII) rap sheets, while data on life events were collected from individual CYA case files.

Three dependent variables are utilized. Violent arrests include murder, rape, aggravated assault, robbery, and other person offenses such as extortion and kidnapping. Nonviolent arrests include burglary, receiving stolen property, grand theft, forgery, and grand theft auto. Total arrests represent the sum of violent and nonviolent arrests.

Our two key independent variables are the adult social bonds of full-time employment and marriage. We also include two measures of substance abuse (heroin and alcohol dependence) because research suggests that during periods of substance abuse there is an increased risk of crime (Chaiken and Chaiken, 1990). Information for marriage and employment came from CYA case files. Heroin and alcohol dependence measures came from prison and probation records, including self-report and collateral information. Since only substance dependence was of interest, minor alcohol and heroin use was not coded. During the course of each of the seven years of post-parole observation, each individual was given a score of 1 if they were involved in each of the four respective local life circumstances noted; otherwise, they were coded 0. For example, when marriage was coded 1, all nonmarried conditions were coded 0. The local life circumstances were coded in terms of change in status. Offenders were assumed to maintain the same status unless a change was noted in the CYA files.

We also control for race and street time. Race was coded 1 for white and 0 for nonwhite. Street-time measures were obtained from rap sheets with parolees being coded as free for the number of months they were not serving time in jail, prison, or in CYA detention; otherwise, they were coded as under some form of CYA supervision. Controlling for street time is important because of its influence on offending (e.g., more street time equates with more opportunity), and because research has shown that conclusions regarding offending continuity are influenced by street-time considerations (Piquero et al., 2001). Descriptive statistics, found in Table 1, show that, compared to whites, nonwhites have a higher mean for heroin and alcohol dependence and violent arrests, and a lower mean for marriage dependence and violent arrests, and a lower mean for marriage and full-time employment.

The Statistical Model

Since the dependent variables represent the frequency of arrests within each year of the panel, we employ a model appropriate for count data. A useful first approximation is the Poisson model, which assumes that the mean and the variance of the outcome variable are equal. Often, this assumption is violated by overdispersion in the data (i.e., mean/variance inequality). To control for overdispersion, we estimate a negative-binomial model that includes a random disturbance term. The negative-binomial model provided a better fit than the Poisson model.

Additionally, since the data contain multiple observations for the same individual and we are interested in within-individual change, we also estimate a random-effects specification. This model is similar to the negative-binomial model

---

[1] Small sample sizes across racial groups forced us to combine all nonwhites into one category.

TABLE 1 Descriptive Statistics

	Full Sample (N = 524) (3,668 obs)		White (N = 254) (1,778 obs)		Nonwhite (N = 270) (1,890 obs)		T-Value Race Comparison
	Mean	SD	Mean	SD	Mean	SD	
Race (1 = white)	0.484	0.499					
Heroin dependence	0.302	0.459	0.289	0.453	0.315	0.464	1.73
Alcohol dependence	0.251	0.434	0.235	0.424	0.266	0.442	2.17*
Street time	7.333	4.727	7.626	4.648	7.057	4.785	3.65*
Married	0.231	0.421	0.264	0.441	0.199	0.399	4.70*
FT employment	0.157	0.364	0.180	0.384	0.136	0.343	3.60*
Total arrests	2.143	2.881	2.082	2.835	2.200	2.787	1.28
Violent arrests	0.300	0.770	0.194	0.547	0.400	0.922	8.26*
Nonviolent arrests	1.842	2.600	1.887	2.711	1.800	2.491	1.01

$*p < 0.05.$

except that a different probability is entered into the likelihood function.[2] Although random-effects models with time-varying covariates can be estimated, some adjustments must be made because there is a time-stable component and a time-varying component to the covariate (see Horney, Osgood, and Marshall, 1995). To accomplish this, we first create a time-stable component that is the average score on the time-varying covariate across the time periods (for each individual). These average scores, for each of the time-varying local life circumstances variables, are included in the random-effects model specification as time-stable covariates (i.e., overall individual differences). Second, for each of the time-varying local life circumstances variables at each period (for $t = 1...7$), we also calculate the difference between that average and that period's score. This difference becomes the time-varying covariate (i.e., deviations from each individual's mean calculated across the entire period of observations).

This formulation satisfies our need for an estimator that reflects the effects of within-person change (found among the time-varying components) with controls for individual differences, i.e., persistent unmeasured differences that exist above and beyond the observable persistent individual differences that affect the likelihood of criminal behavior (λ) (Greene, 1995).[3]

Results

The first question we address is the extent to which local life circumstances mediate the effect of race and crime. Table 2 presents the results for the full sample for the number of total, nonviolent, and violent arrests. Examining the race effect from Model 1 indicates that race does not exert a significant effect on the total number of arrests. The key results from Model 2 are found under the within-individual effects. Changes in heroin dependence are positively associated with changes

---

[2] The ratio $v/(1 + v)$ is distributed as a beta random variable, $B(a,b)$, with parameters a and b estimated from the data.

[3] For all specifications, the negative-binomial model with controls for individual differences fit the data better than a negative-binomial model without controls for individual differences.

TABLE 2 Regression Analyses for Full Sample

| | Total Arrests | | | | Nonviolent Arrests | | | | Violent Arrests | | | |
| | Model 1 | | Model 2 | | Model 3 | | Model 4 | | Model 5 | | Model 6 | |
	Est	Se	Est	Se	Est	Se	Est	Se	Est	Se	Est	Se
Between-Person Effects												
Alcohol dependence			0.205	0.056*			0.234	0.061*			0.119	0.111
Heroin dependence			0.500	0.058*			0.573	0.063*			−0.016	0.114
Street time			0.046	0.007*			0.061	0.008*			−0.027	0.016
Marriage			−0.080	0.071			−0.051	0.076			−0.123	0.151
FT employment			0.025	0.097			0.015	0.107			0.234	0.210
Within-Person Effects												
Alcohol dependence			0.047	0.083			0.041	0.085			0.175	0.186
Heroin dependence			0.660	0.065*			0.611	0.068*			0.845	0.140*
Street time			0.076	0.004*			0.075	0.005*			0.081	0.010*
Marriage			−0.113	0.054*			−0.150	0.057*			0.145	0.115
FT employment			−0.047	0.054			−0.044	0.056			−0.145	0.120
Race	−0.063	0.041	−0.071	0.044	0.010	0.046	0.006	0.048	−0.601	0.086*	−0.593	0.088*
Constant	−0.000	0.045	−0.458	0.080*	−0.055	0.048	−0.700	0.086*	−0.617	0.111*	−0.420	0.175*
a	6.941	0.876*	8.162	1.059*	5.147	0.604*	6.531	0.810*	9.839	2.357*	10.274	2.447*
b	13.22	1.813*	13.626	1.950*	8.173	1.006*	9.571	1.307*	6.284	1.758*	5.804	1.584*
Log-likelihood	−7119.628		−6866.665		−6623.373		−6393.188		−2460.969		−2396.624	

*$p < 0.05$.

in total number of arrests, holding stable individual differences constant. And while parolees with greater street time incurred a higher number of total arrests, changes in marriage were negatively related to changes in total arrests over and above stable individual differences. Neither changes in alcohol dependence nor full-time employment were related to changes in total arrests. In addition, race was not significantly related to total arrests.

The results from the nonviolent arrests model are displayed as Models 3 and 4. Model 3 shows that race fails to exhibit a significant effect on nonviolent arrests. The estimates in Model 4 are consistent with the predictors of total arrests and indicate that changes in marriage are negatively related to changes in nonviolent arrests, while changes in heroin dependence and street time are positively related to changes in nonviolent arrests. Race, changes in full-time employment, and changes in alcohol dependence were unrelated to changes in nonviolent arrests.

The results for violent arrests are presented as Models 5 and 6. The results from Model 5 indicate that nonwhites are significantly more likely to accumulate violent arrests. When the other covariates are introduced in Model 6, the results for the violent arrests model are similar to those for the total arrests model; however, marriage is no longer statistically significant. Although this finding is inconsistent with the perspective that changes in adult social bonds eliminate the race/crime relationship, it is consistent with prior research indicating that nonwhites are more likely to incur violent arrests throughout their 20s (Elliott, 1994a, 1994b).[4]

Do local life circumstances operate differently across race? Table 3 shows that, for total arrests, while changes in heroin dependence and street time are positively related to changes in total arrests for both whites and nonwhites, changes in marriage are negatively (and significantly) related

to changes in total arrests for nonwhites but not whites. For violent arrests, changes in heroin dependence and street time are positively related to changes in violent arrests for both whites and nonwhites, but among whites, changes in alcohol dependence and marriage are also positively related to changes in violent arrests, while changes in full-time employment are negatively related to changes in violent arrests.[5] For nonviolent arrests, changes in heroin dependence and street time are positively related to changes in nonviolent arrests for both whites and nonwhites, while changes in marriage are related to changes in nonviolent arrests for both whites and nonwhites.

To provide an additional examination of the inhibitory effect of marriage on early adult offending, we substituted common-law marriage (coded 1 for common-law marriage only, all other conditions coded 0) in lieu of a conventional marriage to determine if the marriage effect was contingent on the legal level of commitment. To the extent that "formalizing a relationship through marriage indicates attachment" (Horney, Osgood, and Marshall, 1995:667), we would expect that marriage would inhibit arrests while relationships not formalized would fail to do so. In the full sample, the common-law marriage effect was positive for both total and violent arrests, indicating that changes in common-law marriages were positively associated with changes in arrests during the follow-up period. When the sample was stratified by race, the common-law marriage effect was insignificant for whites, but for nonwhites the effect was positive and significant for total, nonviolent, and violent arrests. Thus, for nonwhites, common-law marriages were positively associated with all three types of arrests, while conventional marriages were negatively associated with postparole

---

[4] The significance of race in the violent arrests analysis is not surprising in light of national arrest statistics. Hawkins et al. (1998) find that a larger racial gap exists in arrests for violent—as opposed to property—crime (where nonwhites make up a larger proportion of arrests).

[5] Initially, the positive effect for marriage on violent arrests among whites is counterintuitive. We note here, however, that a similar finding was observed by Laub et al. (1998) among 500 white men. It may be that the married white men are weakly tied to their spouses, to whom they direct their violent proclivities and engage in domestic assaults (Sampson and Laub, 1993:212).

TABLE 3 Regression Analyses Stratified by Race

| | Total Arrests | | | | Violent Arrests | | | | Nonviolent Arrests | | | |
| | Whites | | Nonwhites | | Whites | | Nonwhites | | Whites | | Nonwhites | |
	Est	Se	Est	Se	Est	Se	Est	Se	Est	Se	Est	Se
Between-Person Effects												
Alcohol dependence	0.180	0.086*	0.233	0.074*	0.086	0.177	0.145	0.146	0.211	0.093*	0.263	0.082*
Heroin dependence	0.521	0.089*	0.457	0.079*	−0.039	0.198	−0.031	0.145	0.583	0.095*	0.540	0.086*
Street time	0.030	0.011*	0.060	0.010*	−0.061	0.027*	−0.006	0.020	0.043	0.011*	0.078	0.011*
Marriage	−1.104	0.103	−0.054	0.103	−0.272	0.214	−0.009	0.211	−0.052	0.109	−0.056	0.113
FT employment	0.059	0.133	−0.030	0.148	0.660	0.314*	−0.175	0.326	0.005	0.142	0.020	0.171
Within-Person Effects												
Alcohol dependence	0.137	0.131	−0.032	0.113	0.624	0.285*	−0.031	0.252	0.114	0.131	−0.028	0.114
Heroin dependence	0.662	0.095*	0.664	0.092*	1.167	0.235*	0.698	0.178*	0.575	0.098*	0.654	0.098*
Street time	0.067	0.006*	0.084	0.006*	0.054	0.020*	0.093	0.012*	0.068	0.007*	0.081	0.007*
Marriage	−0.087	0.076	−0.132	0.079+	0.611	0.187*	−0.133	0.154	−0.135	0.079+	−0.161	0.080*
FT employment	−0.072	0.075	−0.018	0.079	−0.346	0.170*	−0.006	0.170	−0.055	0.077	−0.029	0.084
Constant	−0.410	0.116*	−0.551	0.108	−0.434	0.369	−0.708	0.206*	−0.583	0.123*	−0.785	0.117*
a	7.309	1.444*	9.236	1.647*	16.782	9.559*	8.833	2.721*	5.931	1.111*	7.339	1.266*
b	12.300	2.663*	15.302	2.984*	6.217	4.026*	6.054	2.090*	9.199	1.885*	10.185	1.902*
Log-likelihood	−3306.523		−3555.684		−888.685		−1493.566		−3155.135		−3233.822	

$*p < 0.05$; $+p < 0.10$.

TABLE 4   One-Way ANOVA

Variable	Nonwhite Married (Group 1)	Nonwhite Unmarried (Group 2)	White Married (Group 3)	White Unmarried (Group 4)	F	Tukey's B
Alcohol dependence	0.212	0.280	0.193	0.251	6.099	(3/2,4) (1/2)
Heroin dependence	0.389	0.296	0.273	0.294	5.386	(1/2,3,4)
FT employment	0.228	0.113	0.227	0.163	18.100	(2/1,3,4) (4/1,3)
Street time	8.748	6.635	8.955	7.147	42.800	(2/1,3,4) (4/1,3)
Violent arrests	0.382	0.404	0.222	0.184	22.439	(4/1,2) (3/1,2)

Note: Under Tukey's B, (4/1,2) indicates that Group 4 is significantly different from Groups 1 and 2.

arrests.[6] Importantly, this estimation did not substantively alter any of the other coefficients. The preventive effects of marriage and the deleterious effects of common-law marriages is similar to those obtained by Horney, Osgood, and Marshall, who found that while marriage was negatively (though not significantly) related to property crime, it was negatively and significantly related to assault. Having a girlfriend was positively related to both any crime and property offending, but negatively related to assault. Thus, the results suggest that there is an added level of attachment or commitment in conventional marriages that is missing in common-law marriages, and it is this particular type of bond that seems to inhibit continuity in criminal activity.

Given the significant and inhibitory marriage effects observed, we created four groups to further examine the interaction between race and marriage: (1) married nonwhites, (2) unmarried nonwhites, (3) married whites, and (4) unmarried whites. A series of one-way ANOVAs (Table 4) compared these four groups across the independent and dependent variables. (Note: The ANOVA results represent combined between- and within-person effects.)

In only two of seven comparisons (nonviolent and total arrests) did we fail to uncover a statistically significant difference across groups. For example, marriage was a significant inhibitor of alcohol dependency across whites and nonwhites. In terms of heroin dependence, nonwhite married men incurred the highest value. Married whites and nonwhites were most gainfully employed, with both white and nonwhite unmarried men having the lowest full-time employment. This finding highlights the "marriage premium," or the earnings advantage that married men enjoy over unmarried men (Cohen, 1999). Both married nonwhites and whites also had more street time compared to their unmarried counterparts. Marriage, however, does not appear to be a significant inhibitor of violent arrests among nonwhites: married nonwhites still had a higher frequency of violent arrests than unmarried whites. These findings are largely driven by the fact that violent arrests were both more prevalent and frequent among nonwhites.[7]

---

[6] Whites were significantly more likely than nonwhites to be involved in conventional marriages (white mean = 0.264, nonwhite mean = 0.199), whereas nonwhites were significantly more likely than whites to be involved in common-law marriages (nonwhite mean = 0.264, white mean = 0.144).

[7] Approximately 24 percent of nonwhites were rearrested for a violent offense versus only 14 percent of whites. Nonwhites incurred a total of 756 violent arrests versus 346 violent arrests for whites.

Discussion

The results of this study indicate that, even after controlling for stable individual differences, marriage is negatively associated with nonviolent, but not violent, arrests for whites and nonwhites alike. In addition, our results also show that "traditional" as opposed to "common-law" marriages have differential effects on criminal activity, thereby suggesting that turning points need to be measured through more finely tuned variables such as "type of marriage" rather than general variables such as "marriage." By finding that both persistent individual differences and significant life events are important determinants of criminal activity, the results also contradict the view that once controls for persistent individual differences are introduced, life events do not influence criminal activity. The findings also suggest that race remains an important predictor of violence, even after controlling for changes in local life circumstances.

Several plausible explanations exist for this race effect. First, although research shows that racial patterns are more pronounced in violent crimes than in property crimes, Hindelang (1978) found that individuals victimized by nonwhites, and African Americans in particular, were more likely to report the crime to the police than individuals victimized by whites. When he controlled for victimizations not reported to the police, the racial discrepancies in the proportion of offenders disappeared. This finding indicates some evidence for "differential selection for criminal justice processing." A second explanation posits that race may not represent a persistent characteristic or trait, but a "social construct." Specifically, it could be argued that race, as a social construct, can change over the life course and/or serve as a proxy for social events or negative "turning points." For example, among nonwhites (and African Americans in particular), social capital may have less salience in areas where there are concentrations of high-rate offenders or areas where there are heightened levels of concentrated disadvantage. Under such conditions, race will have greater importance when explaining the propensity of individuals to engage in criminal activity, particularly violence (Sullivan, 1996). Thus, perhaps another way to incorporate race into the life-course perspective would be to build on the life-course ideas and language by arguing that race, and the differential levels of disadvantage faced by racial groups, serves as a "breaking point" in life events. A third and final explanation for the persistent race effect concerns the type of crime examined. For example, Harris and Meidlinger (1995) argue that there are significant race differences in street crime, especially serious street crime, that are independent of class and police discrimination that lead nonwhites to be overrepresented in crimes of violence. In particular, these scholars argue that a type of "caste segregation" leads to the commission of street crimes among nonwhites and suite crime among whites. In sum, race relations may have strong implications for the ability of individuals to build social capital and thus race may be the point where life events diverge.

The data used in the present study are limited in that they only address the issue of criminal activity among a group of high-risk males in California. Therefore, it is unclear whether the results are generalizable to populations in different areas. The data on life events are also limited since they do not measure the strength or quality of social bond attachment. For example, our inability to detect significant effects for employment (albeit with one exception, among whites for violent arrests), may be due to measurement. Since job opportunities are largely structured by the ecological characteristics of where people live and their access to employment (Wilson, 1996), it is reasonable to suspect that these factors are not invariant across race.[8] Future research with more sensitive

---

[8] Given the dated nature of the data employed, it is worth pointing out that the CYA parolees were being released into a less than favorable economy in the 1970s. It may be the case that if the parolees were released during the more favorable economic climate of the 1990s, especially given the record low (official) levels of African-American unemployment, the effects of full-time employment might have had a depressing effect on African-American arrest rates.

employment measures that include indices of job stability is warranted. Also, the data do not contain any information on the neighborhood conditions to which the parolees returned. Given that crime is in part a function of opportunity (Cohen and Felson, 1979) and that whites and nonwhites generally live in different ecological contexts (Sampson and Wilson, 1995), the race differences in violent arrests could be explained by the different opportunity structures that exist in residential areas (Parker and McCall, 1999). Given the different ecological contexts evident across races, future research should incorporate both the life-course and ecological perspective and prospectively examine the influence of both individual and neighborhood effects on crime over the life course (Lynam et al., 2000; Piquero and Lawton, 2002; Sullivan, 1996). Finally, future efforts should present breakdowns within violent arrests to determine if local life circumstances have different effects as a result of the nature of the incident.

This study suggests that the relationship between local life circumstances and criminal activity in early adulthood may be only partially invariant across racial groups. It is possible that adult institutions of social control may have different meanings across racial groups. Cohabitation and marriage, for example, may have a different role in the lives of nonwhite versus white offenders, which in turn may be a reflection of the different historical and ecological contexts that shape the role of marriage in inner-city communities (Staples, 1997; Wilson, 1996). Since we observed a crime-exacerbating effect of common-law marriages but a crime-inhibiting effect of marriage among nonwhites, finding ways to help nonwhites transition from common-law to "legal" marriages may be beneficial. This is no small task, however, because the decrease in marriage rates among nonwhites in general, and inner-city African Americans in particular, is a function of increased economic marginality, changing attitudes toward sex and marriage, and the interaction between material and cultural constraints (Wilson, 1996:97). Early childhood socialization into the idea that marriage is a positive institution

that one should run toward rather than from would present one avenue by which attitudes toward marriage could be changed, although it remains a long-term strategy. As race becomes more salient in the transition from adolescence to adulthood (Arnett, in press), helping nonwhites access more economic opportunities, which likely open avenues for "legal" marriages, may provide pathways out of the illicit economy that flourishes in inner-city neighborhoods (Anderson, 1999; Elliott, 1994a).

References

Anderson, E. 1999. *Code of the Streets*. Chicago, Ill.: University of Chicago Press.

Arnett, J. J. In press. "Conceptions of the Transitions to Adulthood Among Emerging Adults in American Ethnic Groups." In J. J. Arnett and N. Galambos, eds., *New Directions in Child and Adolescent Development*. San Francisco, Cal.: Jossey-Bass.

Blumstein, A., J. Cohen, J. Roth, and C. Visher. 1986. *Criminal Careers and "Career Criminals."* Washington, D.C.: National Academy Press.

Bumpass, L. L., and J. A. Sweet. 1989. "National Estimates of Cohabitation." *Demography* 26:615–25.

Chaiken, J., and M. Chaiken. 1990. "Drugs and Predatory Crime." Vol. 13 in M. Tonry and J. Q. Wilson, eds., *Drugs and Crime*. Chicago, Ill.: University of Chicago Press.

Cohen, L., and M. Felson. 1979. "Social Change and Crime Rate Trends: A Routine Activity Approach." *American Sociological Review* 44:588–608.

Cohen, P. N. 1999. "Racial-Ethnic and Gender Differences in Returns to Cohabitation and Marriage: Evidence from the Current Population Survey." Population Division Working Paper No. 35. Washington, D.C.: U.S. Census Bureau.

Elder, G. H., Jr. 1985. "Perspectives on the Life Course." In G. H. Elder, Jr., ed., *Life-Course Dynamics*. Ithaca, N.Y.: Cornell University Press.

Elliott, D. S. 1994a. "1993 Presidential Address: Serious, Violent Offenders: Onset, Developmental Course, and Termination." *Criminology* 32:1–22.

———. 1994b. "Longitudinal Research in Criminology: Promise and Practice." In E. G. M. Weitekamp and H.-J. Kerner, eds., *Cross-National Longitudinal Research on Human Development and Criminal Behavior.* Netherlands: Kluwer Academic Publishers.

Gottfredson, M. R., and T. Hirschi. 1990. *A General Theory of Crime.* Stanford, Cal.: Stanford University Press.

Greene, W. 1995. *Econometric Analysis.* New York: Prentice Hall.

Harris, A. R., and L. R. Meidlinger. 1995. "Criminal Behavior: Race and Class." In J. F. Sheley, ed., *Criminology,* 2nd ed. Belmont, Cal.: Wadsworth.

Hawkins, D. F., J. H. Laub, and J. L. Lauritsen. 1998. "Race, Ethnicity, and Serious Juvenile Offending." In R. Loeber and D. P. Farrington, eds., *Serious and Violent Juvenile Offenders.* Thousand Oaks, Cal.: Sage.

Hindelang, M. J. 1978. "Race and Involvement in Common Law Personal Crimes." *American Sociological Review* 43:93–109.

Hirschi, T., and M. R. Gottfredson. 1995. "Control Theory and Life-Course Perspective." *Studies on Crime and Crime Prevention* 4:131–42.

Horney, J., D. W. Osgood, and I. H. Marshall. 1995. "Criminal Careers in the Short-Term: Intra-Individual Variability in Crime and its Relation to Local Life Circumstances." *American Sociological Review* 60:655–73.

Laub, J. H., D. S. Nagin, and R. J. Sampson. 1998. "Trajectories of Change in Criminal Offending: Good Marriages and the Desistance Process." *American Sociological Review* 63:225–38.

Laub, J. H., and R. J. Sampson. 1993. "Turning Points in the Life Course: Why Change Matters to the Study of Crime." *Criminology* 31:301–26.

Lynam, D., A. Caspi, T. E. Moffitt, P. O. Wikstrom, R. Loeber, and S. Novak. 2000. "The Interaction Between Impulsivity and Neighborhood Context on Offending: The Effects of Impulsivity Are Stronger in Poorer Neighborhoods." *Journal of Abnormal Psychology* 109:563–74.

Mauer, M. 1990. *Younger Black Men and the Criminal Justice System: A Growing National Problem.* Washington, D.C.: Sentencing Project.

Morris, M., A. Beernhardt, M. Handcock, and M. Cot. 1998. "The Transition to Work in the Post Industrial Labor Market." Presented at the meetings of the American Sociological Association. San Francisco, Cal.

Nagin, D. S., and R. Paternoster. 1991. "On the Relationship of Past and Future Participation in Delinquency." *Criminology* 29:163–90.

Nielson, A. L. 1999. "Testing Sampson and Laub's Life Course Theory: Age, Race/ Ethnicity, and Drunkenness." *Deviant Behavior* 20:129–51.

Ousey, G. C. 1999. "Homicide, Structural Factors, and the Racial Invariance Assumption." *Criminology* 37:405–26.

Parker, K., and P. McCall. 1999. "Structural Conditions and Racial Homicide Patterns: A Look at the Multiple Disadvantages in Urban Areas." *Criminology* 37:447–77.

Paternoster, R., C. W. Dean, A. Piquero, P. Mazerolle, and R. Brame. 1997. "Generality, Continuity and Change in Offending." *Journal of Quantitative Criminology* 13:231–66.

Piquero, A. R., R. Blaine, P. Mazerolle, and R. Haapanen. 2002. "Crime in Emerging Adulthood." *Criminology* 40:137–69.

Piquero, A. R., A. Blumstein, R. Brame, R. Haapanen, E. P. Mulvey, and D. S. Nagin. 2001. "Assessing the Impact of Exposure Time and Incapacitation on Longitudinal Trajectories of Criminal Offending." *Journal of Adolescent Research* 16:54–74.

Piquero, A. R., and B. Lawton. 2002. "Individual Risk for Crime is Exacerbated in Poor Familial and Neighborhood Contexts: The Contribution of Low Birth Weight, Family Adversity, and Neighborhood Disadvantage to Life-Course-Persistent Offending." In R. A. Settersten, Jr. and T. J. Owens, eds., *Advances in Life-Course Research: New Frontiers in Socialization.* London: Elsevier.

Piquero, A. R., and P. Mazerolle. 2001. *Life-Course Criminology.* Belmont, Cal.: Wadsworth.

Rand, A. 1987. "Transitional Life Events and Desistance from Delinquency and Crime." In M. E. Wolfgang, T. P. Thornberry, and R. M. Figlio, eds., *From Boy to Man, From Delinquency to Crime*. Chicago, Ill.: University of Chicago Press.

Robins, L. 1978. "Sturdy Childhood Predictors of Adult Antisocial Behavior: Replication from Longitudinal Studies." *Psychological Medicine* 8:611–22.

Sampson, R. J., and J. H. Laub. 1993. *Crime in the Making*. Cambridge, Mass.: Harvard University Press.

——. 1995. "Understanding Variability in Lives Through Time: Contributions of Life-Course Criminology." *Studies on Crime and Crime Prevention* 4:143–58.

Sampson, R. J., and J. L. Lauritsen. 1994. "Violent Victimization and Offending: Individual-, Situational-, and Community-Level Risk Factors." In A. J. Reiss, Jr. and J. A. Roth, eds., *Understanding and Preventing Violence: Volume 3, Social Influences*. Washington, D.C.: National Academy Press.

Sampson, R. J., and W. J. Wilson. 1995. "Toward a Theroy of Race, Crime, and Urban Inequality." In J. Hagan and R. D. Peterson, eds., *Crime and Inequality*. Stanford, Cal.: Stanford University Press.

Shanahan, M. J. 2000. "Pathways to Adulthood in Changing Societies: Variability and Mechanisms in Life Course Perspective." *Annual Review of Sociology* 26:667–92.

Smelser, N. J., W. J. Wilson, and F. Mitchell (eds.). 2001. *America Becoming: Racial Trends and Their Consequences*, Vols. I and II. Washington, D.C.: National Academy Press.

Staples, R. 1997. "An Overview of Race and Marital Status." In H. P. McAdoo, ed., *Black Families*, 3rd ed. Thousand Oaks, Cal.: Sage.

Sullivan, M. L. 1996. "Developmental Transitions in Poor Youth: Delinquency and Crime." In J. A. Graber, J. Brooks-Gunn, and A. C. Petersen, eds., *Transitions Through Adolescence: Interpersonal Domains and Context*. Mahwah, N.J.: Lawrence Erlbaum Associates.

Uggen, C. 2000. "Work as a Turning Point in the Life Course of Criminals: A Duration Model of Age, Employment, and Recidivism." *American Sociological Review* 67:529–46.

Wilson, W. J. 1987. *The Truly Disadvantaged*. Chicago, Ill.: University of Chicago Press.

——. 1996. *When Work Disappears: The World of the New Urban Poor*. New York: Knopf.

Conclusion

This chapter examined the key themes in the life course perspective. According to this perspective, some individuals may commit crime at different points in their lives and some may maintain rather consistent and long-term criminal careers. Their behavior can be understood by determining the key turning points in their life trajectories.

While the reading in this chapter does contribute to uncovering some evidence on race and life course, it is unable to provide definitive information pertaining to the ability of the life course perspective to explain crime rates and criminality. Moreover, it does not use uniform points in an individual's life trajectory. Another limitation is that only one theoretical perspective is actually tested using this study.

Discussion Questions

1. What is the difference between a transition and a trajectory? How are trajectories and transitions used to predict crime rates and criminality? What are some of the transitions that are prominent in reducing crime rates and criminality across the races?

2. From Sampson and Laub's (1993) perspective, what are the implications of social control issues that change an individual's life course from career criminality to desistance? How does this work across the races?

3. Moffitt's (1993) theory emphasizes the role of neuropsychological deficits in developing two types of offending trajectories. What are these, and how do they differ across the races?

4. What do Piquero, MacDonald, and Parker suggest for reducing instances of career criminality?

References

Caspi, A., Elder, G. H., & Bem, D. J. (1987). Moving against the world: Life-course patterns of explosive children. *Developmental Psychology, 23,* 308–313.

Elder, G. (1985). Perspectives on the life course. In H. Glen Elder Jr. (Ed.), *Life course dynamics* (pp. 23–49). Ithaca, NY: Cornell University Press.

Moffitt, T. (1993). Adolescence-limited and life-course persistent antisocial behavior: A developmental taxonomy. *Psychological Review, 100,* 674–701.

Sampson, R., & Laub, J. (1993). *Crime in the making: Pathways and turning points through life.* Cambridge, MA: Harvard University Press.

Future Research in Race, Crime, and Delinquency: A Criminological Theory Approach

In addition to the theories presented in the preceding chapters, other theories have also been developed in criminology. Researchers seem to be rather slow in examining these theories. However, these theories have hypotheses and research questions that are specific to race and crime. In this chapter we will discuss three such theories—control balance theory, shaming, and Krohn's network analysis.

CONTROL BALANCE THEORY

Tittle's (1995) version of control balance theory (CBT) suggests that individuals commit crime when their perception of control is out of balance. Specifically, the amount of control that an individual experiences relative to the amount of control the individual can assert may determine the probability of committing crime (Tittle, 1995). This allows for three ways in which an individual may perceive control. First, the individual may feel that he or she is experiencing more control than one is able to exert, creating the perception of a control deficit. Second, the individual may feel that he or she is exerting more control than he or she is experiencing, creating the perception of a control surplus. Third, the individual may perceive that he or she is exerting and experiencing the same amount of control, creating the perception of a control balance.

For Tittle (1995), because the control ratio is the barometer for the different perceptions of control, there is a likelihood for deviance when the control ratio is out of balance. An individual who is experiencing a control deficit is likely to commit deviance that is repressive, predatory (e.g., theft, rape, homicide, assault, and fraud), and in defiance (e.g., contempt or hostility for social norms, groups, or an individual) (Tittle, 1995). However, an individual who is experiencing a control surplus is likely to commit deviance that is exploitative (e.g., manipulative or coercive), plunderous (e.g., acts that are self-serving), and decadent (e.g., impulsive and thriving for excess).

According to Tittle (1995), race has specific implications for the control ratio and the likelihood of deviance. In particular, Tittle (1995) posits that individuals with similar features—either in personality or physically—end up informally organizing to solve problems or satisfy needs. This creates a subculture. Within these subcultures, individuals begin to adopt similar points of view, language, status, and norms. Tittle (1995) argued that these subcultures can have important effects on control ratios. Because of collective or implied group action, individuals may have more opportunity to exercise control or escape the control that is being thrust on them. This sort of effect on the control ratio would not be possible without the subculture. Tittle (1995) wrote:

> Until fairly recently, blacks in the South were exceptionally repressed by a united white majority. They were subject to controls by white employers, merchants, police, landlords, and random whites, and as individuals they had few ways of exercising control back over whites. However, because blacks usually lived in designated parts of towns and cities, they were able to interact around their common needs and problems, the most important one being their oppression at the hands of whites. Out of this grew a black subculture with distinctive norms, language, customs, and ideas. From time to time this subculture could be stirred into collective action to protect individuals from suffering the full force of white oppression. When white creditors or the police came looking for specific individuals, the black community usually united in silence as to their whereabouts, often even denying any knowledge of their existence. When some blacks refused to work for whites under intolerable conditions, the black subcultural community often shared scarce resources. When the demands of white employers were extreme, black workers often collectively dragged their feet, knowing that all of them would not be fired. In a number of ways, then, an informal black, or African-American, subculture helped change and improve the control ratios of individuals (p. 158).

However, CBT has not faired very well in empirical testing (see Piquero & Piquero, 2006, and Tittle, 2004, for reviews of the empirical literature on the theory). This has led Tittle (2004) to revise CBT so that the concept of deviance is streamlined.

In particular, instead of considering deviance as a series of discreet categories he considers it as a continuum, known as the control balance desirability. As Tittle (2004) puts it:

> deviance with points on the continuum differentiated with respect to what will be called their control balance desirability. By definition, control balance desirability will refer to the quality possessed in different degrees by various potential deviant acts. In empirical terms, it is a composite variable of two indicators: (1) the likely long-range effectiveness of the deviant act in question for altering a control imbalance; and (2) the extent to which a given form of misbehavior requires a perpetrator to be directly and personally involved with a victim or an object that is affected by the deviance (p. 405).

This view suggests that the control ratio will have a connection not with any specific form of deviance but with the acts that are on the continuum. Therefore, different control ratios (either a deficit or a surplus) may result in the same form of behaviors. However, no study to date has examined the ability of the revised CBT to explain racial differences in crime.

SHAMING

Braithwaite's (1989) theory of shaming integrates opportunity, subcultural, control, learning, and labeling theories. Braithwaite discusses issues pertaining to the opportunity for legitimate and illegitimate means. Crime and delinquency occur when legitimate means are blocked; illegitimate means are then learned and transmission of law-breaking values occurs. However, social control can balance this process by providing cues for conforming behavior, and the individual may also learn conforming values. Therefore, crime and delinquency are central when there is a "tipping point."

For Braithwaite, the tipping point is shaming. In criminology, several forms of shaming exist. However, in Braithwaite's theory, two are central. The first is disintegrative shaming. Disintegrative shaming does not provide an environment that is conducive for the offender's return to society. That is, there are no attempts to welcome the offender back into society, and therefore the offender is branded as an outcast. The second area of shaming is integrative and involves reconciliatory acts that help separate the offender from the action. Integrative shaming allows the offender to be welcomed back into society and the offender is provided an opportunity to be forgiven for his or her transgressions.

KROHN'S NETWORK ANALYSIS

Krohn (1986) devised a series of arguments that explain delinquency through social learning and social control theories. This theory suggests that social networks are important for engaging in criminal behavior; a social network is defined as a set of actors, individuals, or groups that are linked by some type of relationship (e.g.., friendship, kinship, school, or church). Krohn (1986) is consistent with control theory in the view that social networks constrain an individual's behavior. However, he then diverges from control theory by arguing that the constraints do not have to be for conforming behavior—as postulated in social learning theory. Whether an individual will be constrained to engage in crime or delinquent behavior depends on two aspects of the social network—multiplexity and density.

Multiplexity is the number of different relationships or contexts that a social network maintains. For example, friends may attend the same school, live in the same neighborhood, and attend the same church. Krohn (1986) argued that the higher the multiplexity, the greater the constraints on behavior. In general, the constraint would lower multiplexity, but this is generally because the family, church, and schools are the sources of multiplexity. These activities are important because they are the keepers of conventional activities. Under this view, the key is that multiplexity is able to account for who the individual is in contact with and how the individual is in contact with them.

Density is the ratio of the number of connections an individual has in a social network to the total possible number of connections that an individual could have in the network. According to Krohn's analysis, when density is high, the delinquency rate is lower, and vice versa.

These are promising theories in criminology that have undergone very little empirical testing. They may be able to provide answers to important questions about criminality and crime rates, but they have not been examined in the context of race and delinquency. This will be left for future researchers to take up.

Conclusion

This chapter examined the key components and efficacy of three promising theories in criminology. Tittle's (1995, 2004) control balance theory suggests that deviance can be explained using an individual's perception of the amount of control that he or she can exert and the amount of control that is being exerted over him or her (i.e., the control ratio). When the control ratio is out of balance, the individual is likely to commit some form of deviance along the control desirability continuum. Braithwaite's (1989) shaming focus introduces a "tipping point" that influences criminality and crime rates. When an individual is disintegratively shamed, he or she is likely to commit crime because he or she does not have ties to the community that constrain his or her behavior. However, when an individual is integratively shamed, he or she is less likely to commit crime. Combining social control and social learning theories, Krohn (1986) argued that social networks that are not very large and do not have multiple connections are likely to produce individuals who contribute to crime rates.

Overall, these studies assist in understanding crime rates and criminality but they have not been used to specifically study race–crime connections. If this is done, these theories can be used to develop sound policy implications that can help reduce crime rates and criminality.

Discussion Questions

1. What is meant by an individual's control imbalance? How does the control ratio play a role in this process? Why would this be different across the races?
2. According to Braithwaite, what factors influence individuals to refrain from committing crime? What are the racial implications of this view?
3. How does Krohn's theory relate to social control and social learning theories? What is the difference between multiplexity and density? How could multiplexity and density be used to develop interventions to reduce criminal behavior? How do you think multiplexity and density differ racially in the commission of crime?

References

Braithwaite, J. (1989). *Crime, shame, and reintegration*. Cambridge, UK: Cambridge University Press.

Krohn, M. (1986). The web of conformity: A network approach to the explanation of delinquent behavior. *Social Problems, 33*, 81–93.

Tittle, C. R. (1995). *Control balance: Toward a general theory of deviance*. Boulder, CO: Westview.

Tittle, C. R. (2004). Refining control balance theory. *Theoretical Criminology, 8*, 395–428.

CHAPTER 10

Conclusion

Throughout this book, I have presented the contributions of several scholars who have specifically examined the relationships between race, criminality, and crime rates. While the works of these scholars have made some contribution toward understanding race–crime connections, their actual influence is difficult to judge without additional research.

Greene and Gabbidon (2000) argued that a theory's influence was based on the proponent's impact on the discipline. However, the works that are presented in this book have not been judged as influential based on this standard. They can be considered as influential because they take up a potentially controversial issue. This conclusion will assess the works presented in this book by examining the influence that they have had in three ways. First, I examine the completeness with which they present the theory. Second, I examine each work for its use of proper scientific methodology in examining racial implications for crime rates and criminality. Finally, I review directions for future research that result from that work.

Chapter 2 presents the deterrence and rational choice perspectives, which suggest that individuals of different races will have different perceptions of the consequences and the motivations to commit crime. The article presented in this chapter provides a proper overview of the theories. However, it does not provide sound methodologies for the examination of race. That is, it treats race as a control variable rather than as the central focus of the article. This leaves a gap in our understanding of how deterrence and rational choice can help understand race, crime rates, and criminality.

Chapter 3 presents the social disorganization perspective, which suggests that individuals are influenced by their locations. That is, where an individual resides and land usage have implications for race–crime relations. The work in this chapter provides a solid representation of the social disorganization theory. However, it is not able to explain race–crime relations across different demographics, and therefore has a limited effect on criminology.

Chapter 4 examines the roles of differential association and social learning theories in explaining the interactions between race, crime rates, and criminality These perspectives suggest that different races are likely to reside to varying degrees in areas where there are more opportunities for individuals to come into contact with other individuals who are criminals.

Thus, they are likely to pass along their criminal definitions. The work in this chapter is restricted to differential association theory. It provides a very good review and study of differential association theory in the context of criminality. The study has been carried out using sound methodology; however, it is deficient in that it does not examine the efficacy of Akers's (1998) version of social learning theory to explain criminality.

Chapter 5 presents social strain theory, which assumes that minorities are more likely to endure fewer opportunities to fulfill their American Dream (i.e., aspirations). Further, racial minorities are likely to encounter economic inequality, which hinders their ability to achieve their aspirations through legitimate means. In addition, this perspective suggests that there are subcultures where the "code of the streets" may be influential. Finally, Agnew's perspective on personal strains also provides important insights. The article presented in this chapter is methodologically sound because it specifically addresses the theories at hand, but its influence is diminished because it has not used longitudinal methodologies or different measures of emotions (i.e., static versus fluid) to study race–crime relations.

Chapter 6 presents conflict theory, according to which there will be power differences among individuals that influence criminality and perceptions of criminals. This chapter also presents racial threat theory, which suggests that as the racial minority groups grow, the majority groups will attempt to reduce their growth and influence by applying greater social controls. The selection presented in this chapter supports the views that conflict and racial threat theories can explain the relationships between race, crime rates, and criminality. However, it primarily focuses on crime rates and less on criminality, thereby reducing its potential influence in criminology.

Chapter 7 presents social bonding and self-control theories. These perspectives seek to understand why individuals do not commit crime. However, they pursue different paths to achieve this understanding. That is, social bonding focuses on the insulation from criminality that social bonds (i.e., attachment, commitment, involvement, and belief) offer. Self-control theory suggests that individuals with lower levels of self-control are more likely to contribute to criminality and crime rates. However, the selection presented in this chapter addresses criminality with respect to only one age group, and is therefore limited in explaining social-control theory's ability to explain race–crime connections.

Chapter 8 presents the perspective that some individuals may commit crime at different points in their lives or maintain rather consistent and long-term criminal careers. The pattern of their criminality can be determined by examining the key turning points in an individual's life trajectories. The work in this chapter suggests that race is an issue in career criminality but does not use uniform points in an individual's life trajectory in its study

The articles presented in this book provide us an understanding of race–crime relations, but the understanding is limited. They point to areas of future research. For instance, specific studies that are designed to understand racial differences in deterrence and rational choice should be performed. This is one example of the additional work that is necessary. While the works presented in this book have limitations, they do provide important information and frameworks for conducting high-quality studies that address the interactions between race, crime rates, and criminality.